Wellbeing from Birth

This book is due for return on or before the last date shown below.

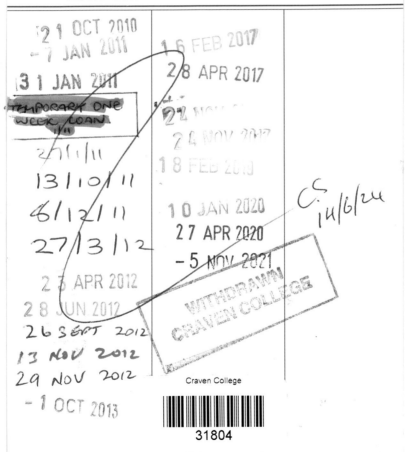

Education at SAGE

SAGE is a leading international publisher of journals, books, and electronic media for academic, educational, and professional markets.

Our education publishing includes:

- accessible and comprehensive texts for aspiring education professionals and practitioners looking to further their careers through continuing professional development

- inspirational advice and guidance for the classroom

- authoritative state of the art reference from the leading authors in the field

Find out more at: **www.sagepub.co.uk/education**

Wellbeing from Birth

Rosemary Roberts

SAGE

Los Angeles | London | New Delhi
Singapore | Washington DC

First published 2010

SAGE Publications Ltd
1 Oliver's Yard
55 City Road
London EC1Y 1SP

SAGE Publications Inc
2455 Teller Road
Thousand Oaks, California 91320

SAGE Publications India Pvt Ltd
B 1/I 1 Mohan Cooperative Industrial Area
Mathura Road
New Delhi 110 044

SAGE Publications Asia-Pacific Pte Ltd
33 Pekin Street #02–01
Far East Square
Singapore 048763

Library of Congress Control Number: 2009930843

British Library Cataloguing in Publication data
A catalogue record for this book is available from the British Library

ISBN 978-1-84860-720-0
ISBN 978-1-84860-721-7 (pbk)

Typeset by Dorwyn, Wells, Somerset
Printed in Great Britain by TJ International, Padstow, Cornwall
Printed on paper from sustainable resources

Mixed Sources
Product group from well-managed
forests and other controlled sources
www.fsc.org Cert no. SGS-COC-2482
© 1996 Forest Stewardship Council
FSC

For Sadie, Fraser and Esme's generation – and their companions

"Read, trust and be sceptical at the same time"
Seamus Heaney

Contents

second level of play: achieving competence; The third level of play: imagination and creativity. **Thinking patterns in play:** The idea of thinking patterns; Making the most of thinking patterns. **What children need for wellbeing play:** Anchoring; Authority (their own); Apprenticeship materials; Allowed time and space. **Companions supporting wellbeing play. All to play for:** Anchored play for wellbeing; Authority in play for wellbeing; Apprenticeship play for wellbeing; Time and space to play for wellbeing

List of Figures

Acknowledgements

I would like to thank everyone who helped me to write this book. Some people have been especially significant companions on the journey. First and foremost are the children and families who so unreservedly shared their experiences with me. I am indebted to Professor Christine Pascal and Professor Philip Gammage for their support, wisdom and friendship. The generosity of the Hamilton Trust, and support from Oxfordshire County Council Early Years and Childcare Services, enabled me to carry out the research and practical work that underpins the book.

I am grateful to the Bernard van Leer Foundation, Rich Learning Opportunities and Britain Yearly Meeting of the Religious Society of Friends (Quakers) for kind permission to use their published material.

My warm thanks go to friends and colleagues for their interest and support, particularly to Chris Athey, Tricia David, Annie Davy, Mary Jane Drummond, Hannah Hill, Elizabeth Jones, David Jones, Caron Lubin and Helen Ruff; to the practitioners who gave their time so generously in the three Oxfordshire projects; to Carolynn Gold for her line drawings of 'the main players'; and to Ann Robinson at the National Children's Bureau for providing the material in the Appendix.

Thank you, too, to Zillah Scott and David Ashton, who in their special ways effected my last-minute rescue; and most of all to my family for their love and support.

About the Author

Rosemary Roberts has taught in nursery, primary and higher education, and trains early years professionals. She holds a post-graduate Diploma in Psycho-analytic Observational Studies from the Tavistock Clinic, and a PhD in early years research. She was a founder director of Peers Early Education Partnership (PEEP), working with Sure Start programmes in disadvantaged areas to raise educational attainment by supporting parents, carers and other service providers. In 1999 she was awarded the OBE for services to early childhood. She is author of *Self Esteem and Early Learning* (3rd edn, 2006, also published by SAGE).

Foreword

In producing the review of the literature[1] for the *Birth to Three Matters* materials[2], we drew heavily on Rosemary Roberts's work concerning young children's self-esteem. The importance of self-esteem and resilience fed into the *Birth to Three Matters* framework developed by Professor Lesley Abbott and the team, highlighting the essential foundations for all areas of development and learning provided by emotional strength. With this study Rosemary has illuminated the field with fresh insights into wellbeing and the processes leading to the achievement of such a state, with concomitant resilience and agency. In many ways, one might argue that this passion to explore and explain wellbeing, in order that this be achieved by every child through supportive relationships and contexts, has been her life's work and we are all the richer for her quest.

Wellbeing from Birth, written in Rosemary's wise, clear style is highly informative, drawing on relevant theoretical and research information, skilfully interwoven with her own very practical explorations with children, parents and practitioners. The book is a mine of examples demonstrating how young children in supportive relationships and contexts are enabled to feel they belong and are secure, have agency, and trust those with whom they communicate and who share their lives.

Early childhood practitioners will, especially, welcome this text, because it includes a whole section on *Investing in wellbeing*, dedicated to explaining the purposes, principles and recording methods appropriate for observing wellbeing, assessing those observations and using wellbeing codes, before moving on to planning. Further, *Wellbeing from Birth* provides rich descriptions of other helpful texts and a wealth of references.

This book suggests that children need first-hand experience of goodness – pointing out sadly how we, as a society, have a long way to go to address the feeling of having lost (or never having acquired) a sense of wellbeing in many of our citizens, whatever their age or stage in life. In the Epilogue she proposes five practical 'advices' as a call to action. They entail each of us:

- taking time to learn about children's and other people's experiences

- working adventurously

- standing up for the humanity of all people

- sometimes taking unpopular stands

- helping children show loving consideration to all creatures and seeking to maintain the beauty and variety of the world.[3]

With this book, Rosemary's aim is to foster wellbeing not only in young children, but in families and whole communities – *collective wellbeing*. To this end she cites Jane Lane's[4] discussion of Archbishop Desmond Tutu relating the southern African concept of *Ubuntu*, which means largeness of spirit and humanity to others, a person with *Ubuntu* being someone who rejoices in others being able and good but who feels diminished when others are humiliated. By taking the information and advice offered in *Wellbeing from Birth* to heart, and putting it all into practice, maybe we can create a climate in which children, families and we ourselves achieve wellbeing, becoming people with *Ubuntu*.

Tricia David

Emeritus Professor of Education, Canterbury Christ Church University and Honorary Emeritus Professor of Early Childhood Education, University of Sheffield.

1   David et al., *Birth to Three Matters: Literature Review Research Report 444*. London: DfES, 2003.
2   DfES (2003) *Birth to Three Matters*. Nottingham: DfES, 2003.
3   Adapted from the Epilogue of this book.
4   Lane, J. (2008) *Young Children and Social Justice*. London: NCB.

Introduction

Although some people read books from the beginning to the end, many readers begin somewhere in the middle, dipping in and out of what interests them. In this book, Part 1, which contains the general background to the rest of the book, is not necessarily the place to start. Parts 2 and 3 are the heart of the book, describing the theory of wellbeing and what it looks like in real life. Part 4 is about various areas of professional development, while the Epilogue links back to the Prologue to come full circle.

'Families' are changing. This is evident in early years settings, many of which are located in areas of disadvantage, both urban and rural. Families in towns and cities – especially in inner cities – and increasingly also in less populated areas, are richly diverse in terms of ethnicity, culture and social class. The structure of families varies hugely, from a single mother with one child, to families where newly born babies may join children from both partners' previous partnerships. Family structures are becoming increasingly complex, the needs of families are changing too, and there are, importantly, the very particular needs of looked-after children to be met, in foster homes and institutions.

The Wellbeing Framework in this book offers a way of thinking about the wellbeing needs of children and of their companions; and how they might be met in such diverse circumstances. It is derived partly from three PhD studies entitled 'Companionable Learning', one in which 100 mothers of young children in different parts of the UK were interviewed; one where a series of focus group seminars were held with practitioners, researchers, service managers and policy makers; and the main study involving extended case studies of nine very diverse families. These families included a Pakistani family, an Indian Sikh family and a mixed race family. Family backgrounds and structures in this study were very varied, as were the extended families and the needs of the children, and the numbers of children in the families ranged from one to seven. Material for the professional development chapters in Part 4 was drawn from three subsequent projects with childminders, local authority managers and advisers, and practitioners working in children's centres. All names have been changed.

Starting in Part 2, the chapters contain real life, illustrative anecdotes, all of which are taken from interviews, or written or video observations. Much of this material was collected in homes and communities, and some in settings. This introduction to the book concludes by introducing the main players – the children who, with their companions, have featured again and again in my wellbeing explorations, and who will become familiar in the anecdotal examples throughout the book.

Figure I.i   The 'main players'

Prologue

Every morning they would come pouring through the nursery school door, bringing in the life of the streets outside, the arguments and the laughter; for adults the daily round of tasks, burdens and concerns, and for children the excitement of a new day. Mostly they were mothers with a three- or four-year-old, but sometimes there would be a dad, a granny or – more often – younger siblings who had to be dragged away after half an hour because 'you're not old enough yet … one day!' One morning a four-year-old girl proudly brought her little brother to say hello. They were having a hard time – their father was terminally ill, there was no money, and the mother was frantic with distress and worry; and even at first glance there was something about this very young child that concerned me. I could not make eye contact with him, and after a while he crawled away under a table and would not come out. However, children could not start at nursery until they were three, and his older sister was getting on reasonably well, so there was nothing to be done but wait until he was old enough to come.

About a year later he started at the nursery. By now his father had died, and not much else had changed. He never spoke. At home he had taken to climbing out of the window and running away down the street, and once had managed to set fire to his bed. For the next two years we did our very best to contain his difficulties and to help him, working with him and his mother in an effort to support them both. It seemed that we made a great difference to his mother, and so perhaps to him too. But his progress was agonizingly slow, and we were left with a conviction that by now it was all too late – that what his mother had most needed was support with him in his first three years, during her husband's long illness.

From then on we looked carefully at the toddlers who came in the mornings in the wake of their older siblings, and often wished we could offer support from birth. Although this conviction is now solidly supported by research findings and government policy, barely a couple of decades have passed since those days. Extraordinary progress has been made, with an ever-increasing awareness of the great complexities of child development at this vital stage, the challenges involved in supporting it, and the gaps in our knowledge.

Not least among the challenges is that, even after the recent expansion of day care, most children between birth and three years spend most of their time at home. Very many early childhood practitioners maintain that this is wholly appropriate, especially for the majority of children aged from birth to 12 months; and the needs of the very youngest children constitute a major argument for expanding and supporting family day care, or child-minders. Yet the home context of early childhood is the one on which there is least research, and about which the state is most uncertain as to its role. This is why the main focus of the initial background research for this book has been the developing wellbeing of babies and young children in the home context.

Increased awareness of the likely long-term impact of situations and experiences in early childhood and a growing conviction about the importance of the period from birth lead to pressing questions about the lives of adolescents and young adults, for whom life tends to be a roller-coaster. They are subject to extremely unsettling pressures and transitions, physically, emotionally and socially; and there are likely to be plenty of bad times mixed in with the good. While most young people manage to survive the challenges of this period, wellbeing comes and goes at this time, sliding around on the roller-coaster continuum ranging from peaks of high hope to troughs of total despair. Although this period is so challenging, most keep roughly on track and succeed in steering around the obvious pitfalls, hanging on in there while grappling for the balance they need. But for some, things can go differently. School lives may become a catalogue of failure, sometimes leading to mental or physical illness. There may be dependence on alcohol or drugs, and related criminal activity. Subsequent unemployment, long-term addiction, imprisonment, family problems and homelessness are spectres at the bottom of this slippery slope.

Strategies are urgently needed to reduce the significantly increasing numbers of adolescents and young people (and their families) who suffer in these ways, at such a cost to themselves and to society. Increasingly, the term 'wellbeing' is used as a target for a wide range of programmes and interventions aimed at reducing child poverty, improving support for families, strengthening communities, building social inclusion, improving health, raising education standards, and improving access to work. The accumulating body of evidence showing the impact of early childhood on later outcomes brings the relevance of wellbeing in early childhood sharply into focus.

But what exactly does being in 'a state of wellbeing' mean? And what situations and experiences are needed in early childhood, that might help – not only at the time, but also during the challenging times ahead? This book is an attempt to address these complex questions.

Part 1

INTRODUCING WELLBEING

1

Early Childhood Matters

Messages from Research

Research reviews

'Research' is about finding things out, another word for enquiry. In the field of early childhood, practitioners are all – consciously or uncon-sciously – researchers. We need to find out about the needs of the individual children with whom we work, and how best to meet those needs; and so our daily enquiries are centred on their lives and on their development, and on our own professionalism. In a more academic and general sense, other people's research, when it has been done well, can also tell us useful things about those children and about our work. Research designs range from small-scale studies about a particular child or children, to large-scale reviews of statistical studies of hundreds or even thousands of children and families. But bigger does not always mean better, and the crucial issue is about the questions an enquiry sets out to answer. Some questions can only be answered reliably by big statistical studies, while smaller qualitative studies may be more appropriate and revealing for others. The best kind of design will be the one that is most appropriate, the most fit for the purpose of finding answers to the questions being asked.

We know from research reviews that wellbeing in early childhood really matters. Health and happiness are needed to underpin the kind of childhood that is *every* child's right; and a strong sense of wellbeing is likely to be protective in relation to the challenging situations that may be experienced in adolescence and young adulthood.[1] A very great deal has been written about the scientific study of the nervous system to explain behaviour in terms of brain activity – neuroscience. Within this preliminary Part 1 which provides a research context for a study of wellbeing, it will only be possible to reflect this and other evidence selectively. Texts have been chosen that appear most relevant to early childhood practitioners, particularly in relation to the development of resilient wellbeing.

Three research reviews, drawing on a range of research approaches including neuroscience, have been particularly relevant in relation to studying the development of resilient wellbeing in early childhood. In 2000, Schonkoff and Phillips edited *From Neurons to Neighborhoods*, a wide-ranging report for the Committee on Integrating the Science of Early Childhood Development, for the National Research Council and the Institute of Medicine in Washington DC.[2] Three years later David, heading a team of early years researchers in the UK, edited the comprehensive literature review underpinning *Birth to Three Matters* in England.[3]

Also in 2003 Hannon, a professor in early childhood at the University of Sheffield, wrote a succinct journal paper addressing the implications of developmental neuroscience for early childhood intervention and education.[4] Hannon made the important point that 'Findings from developmental neuroscience are fascinating for anyone concerned with early childhood interventions and education, but "fascinating" is not the same as having implications' (Hannon, 2003: 58–63). However, he concluded that 'developmental neuroscience findings are generally confirmatory of current thinking in early childhood intervention and education'. They do not so much provide implications for changing existing practices, as reassurance for maintaining them.

But in spite of over a decade of major investment in the early childhood sector in the UK, in 2007 a UNICEF comparative study of 21 OECD countries generated gloomy findings about the wellbeing of children and adolescents in the UK. These findings related to poverty and inequality, to disorder, crime and insecurity; and above all to the lamentable quality of relationships with parents and peers that these children and adolescents experience.[5]

There have been vigorous debates about the significance of the research findings, for policy makers and for those living and working with young children. There now appears to be some general agreement as to the key messages, which resonate with the policies now driving early childhood education and care.

Mother–baby interaction

We know that babies' and young children's 'important people' make a decisive impact on the way their brains develop; as do all their early situations and experiences. The important work of Trevarthen, an eminent researcher in developmental psychology and psychobiology, has given us much to think about, especially in relation to the concept of 'interplay' between mother and baby. His focus on intersubjectivity – the development of active 'self-and-other' awareness in infancy – is particularly relevant here. He shows that the natural sociability of infants serves to motivate 'companionship', eliciting the intuitive parenting that is evident in so very many observations of mothers and infants.[6] Stern, an American psychoanalytic theorist specializing in infant development, also uses this idea of 'intersubjectivity' as a key concept in his work, as do others.[7]

The concept of intersubjectivity originally owed much to Bowlby, the psychiatrist whose theory of attachment was published in 1969.[8] Attachment has been described more recently by Howe as a theory of personality development in the context of close relationship.[9] This has been the cornerstone of the key person approach.[10] It was described in *Birth to Three Matters* by Abbott and Langston as 'essential to young children's wellbeing'.[11] However Trevarthen takes issue with attachment theory, suggesting that it 'fails to grasp the importance of motives for relationships between offspring and their parents that serve shared discovery of new ways of behaving'. He says:

> A good human mother is more than a protector of the human infant from fear, and more than a known and secure 'base' from which the infant may explore and gain experience. She, like others whom the infant may know and like, is a friend and playmate.[12]

Although focusing mainly on the findings of neuroscience, Meade described *a convergence* of these findings with cognitive science, developmental psychology and early childhood education research.[13] Many recent writers have taken these findings as their starting point, incorporating them into findings from behavioural and social sciences.[14]

Children's needs

Waldfogel's book *What Children Need* looked at the latest research very largely although not entirely from the day care perspective. Drawing on evidence from the US, Waldfogel wrote about the wellbeing of children of working parents. In her careful analysis of social science research, the author concluded that there are key messages, for instance that:

> children would tend to do better if they had a parent at home at least part-time in the first year of life ... the quality of parental care and the type and quality of child care that the child receives are also very important ... maternal sensitivity is the most important predictor of child social and emotional development ... [15]

The author stated that a majority of parents in the US now work, and we need to bear in mind the impact of part-time working on children: they do not necessarily spend the majority of their time in day care. The tip of the iceberg that we see represents children's hours in day care, while the invisible critical mass represents their hours at home. Waldfogel asks what should be done to meet better the needs of infants and toddlers in day care? An additional question could be 'and what should be done to meet better the needs of infants and toddlers at home?'

In *The Learning Brain: Lessons for Education*, authors Blakemore and Frith examined implications for the wider sweep of education policy and practice, taking in a range of relevant issues for both primary and secondary schools, for instance: the resilience of the brain beyond the age of three; the teaching and learning of numeracy and literacy; the brain in adolescence; and learning and remembering.[16] In addition to the view that birth to three is indeed the most influential period of the developing brain, this book also emphasises the brain's plasticity. It is thought-provoking that in relation both to a stimulating environment in the first three years and to nutrition, the authors point out that 'in both cases ... too little is damaging, but we know very little about the effects of too much' (p.186). In summary they argue that 'learning is not limited to childhood ... learning can be lifelong'.

The 2003 literature review for *Birth to Three Matters* tells us a great deal about what children need, its 'people under three' perspective moving us away from the limiting 'born at three' implication of previous early childhood education provision in England. Two conclusions relating to parents and the children themselves are of particular importance here, and can be taken as key elements of the research evidence about wellbeing: 'Parents need time to be with their babies and young children, to help them learn and develop, and sufficient finances to enjoy them', and 'Children need loving, responsible key persons around them ... to live in a society which is informed about their development and learning, and which is involved in their amazing abilities.'[17]

How do these findings translate into policy and practice for wellbeing?

Policy and Practice for Wellbeing

From birth to three at home

The period from birth to three is like an iceberg – we see only the tip, i.e. the minority of a child's time spent in day care; whereas most children spend the majority of their time – the invisible underwater bulk of the iceberg – in the privacy of the home. Policy, however, focuses mainly on children's minority time outside the home – in day care and other early childhood settings. There is still a long way to go in promoting the over-riding importance of the home and the family in the earliest years, and in developing commensurately appropriate services to support families at this time.

Much, however, has been done. Since the research findings of the last decades of the twentieth century, awareness of the importance of the first three years of life has made a profound impact on policy and practice. Various factors have fed this awareness. These include the on-going debate about the policy and practice implications of studies on the early development of the brain, and the UK government's commitment to families with the youngest children, as evidenced by investment in the Sure Start programmes.

A new framework was developed to support all service providers of children's learning and care from birth to three years in England, called Birth to Three Matters.[18] This framework was subsequently subsumed into the single framework of the Early Years Foundation Stage.[19] In the development of these frameworks there was increasingly a focus on the related factors of 'relationships' and 'wellbeing' in the thinking about children's long-term development.

A contributing factor to an often confused and contradictory picture of information and support for parents and carers may have been a high degree of uncertainty about *what* information and support could or should be offered to *all* parents and carers, especially in view of the rich cultural diversity of families in the UK. Many issues relating to young children and racial justice have been comprehensively addressed by Lane.[20]

UK Labour's decade of reform

The UK Labour Party swept to power in 1997 and embarked on a decade of reform which transformed policy and practice in the UK for children and families. Sure Start programmes, Neighbourhood Nurseries and

Children's Centres represent an investment of resources at an unprecedented level, aiming to achieve reform involving fundamental change.[21]

Behind these developments have been some fundamental driving forces which it is important to acknowledge. The relationship between education and social policy has become both increasingly uncertain yet increasingly relevant because of the economic, cultural and social transformation of post-industrial societies. Issues of poverty and its impact on child health are dismayingly evident. As Spencer, author of *Poverty and Child Health*, argued:

> Social policy decisions have a major impact on poverty and child health ... there is a strong case for child-centred policies which aim to give all children an equal start in life – the long-term benefits of such policies are likely to far outweigh the short-term costs.[22]

Clearly concerns about citizenship, benefit dependency and social exclusion are matters for on-going debate. In relation to parenting, Halsey et al., active in the fields of social policy and educational reform, pointed out that 'what governments can do is to foster the social conditions that maximize the chances of committed parenting'.[23] These wider considerations need to be taken into account, in order to develop holistic models, policies and provision that are appropriate for a holistic view of the world, the children and families who inhabit it, and the services that they need.

It may be instructive to consider the rationale for the development of UK day care policy in this light. The drivers for twenty-first-century policies for day care have been twofold, and both financial. Firstly, awareness of the importance of early intervention for later development had been gathering momentum, fed in the 1990s by *Starting With Quality*, the report of the Rumbold Committee,[24] by the *Start Right* Report,[25] and subsequently by a growing number of syntheses of research focusing on child development in the early years.[26] The economic benefits of early intervention shown by the High/Scope Perry Pre-School Study made a powerful impact,[27] and in 2000 the Neighbourhood Nursery Initiative was launched, with the purpose of expanding childcare provision in the most disadvantaged areas in England.[28]

In the same year Feinstein, a London University Research Director and a government adviser, wrote a paper entitled 'The Relative Economic Importance of Academic, Psychological and Behavioural Attributes Developed in Childhood'.[29] This was extremely influential in the policy context that was soon to generate the most far-reaching UK policy of all: Sure Start.

The second driver for affordable childcare was the Labour government's social inclusion and social investment policy, with its determination to lift families out of poverty. This became linked not only with the need to raise family incomes through employment, but also with a strong national economy in which more women were employed in the workforce. Consequently, the availability of quality childcare (or rather the lack of it) became a key issue.

While these reasons for early day care were clearly very important, it was concerning that early childhood education and care policy was driven by economic considerations, rather than the needs and the wellbeing of children. Hence there is ongoing tension both within families and in services for children and families, between the workforce perspective, and the developmental needs of the youngest children. Many parents and early childhood professionals say that the needs of the youngest children, especially from birth to 12 months, have been ruthlessly over-ridden by financial perspectives.

The drive to end poverty, with the consequent need to increase the availability of day care, are among the factors that led to Labour's hectic decade of reform, a truly astonishing investment in the nation's future.

Figure 1.1 shows the main reforms in early childhood services in the UK since 1997. It is a picture not only of radical change, but of a quite extraordinary pace of legislation and guidance to which the sector has struggled to accommodate itself. The government's commitment to a Children's Centre in every community by 2010 has been a transforming agenda, representing the universal provision of fully integrated education, health and welfare services. Centres are expected to play a central role in improving outcomes for all children; and in reducing inequalities in outcomes between the most disadvantaged and the most advantaged. While this vision took only around a decade to materialise in terms of legislation, several decades and on-going government commitment to the youngest children will be needed to embed this agenda into reality for families and communities.

1997	• Launch of Early Excellence Centre programme: aiming to develop models of good practice.
	• Effective Provision of Pre-school Education (EPPE) research started: 1997–2003.
1998	• National Childcare Strategy: aiming to provide good quality, affordable childcare for age 0–14s, but little reference to 0–3s.
	• Launch of Sure Start.
1999	• Working Families Tax Credit and Childcare Tax Credit began.
2000	• Care Standards Act 2000: re-registration, regulation and training of child-minders and day care providers.
	• Foundation Stage curriculum began.
2001	• Launch of Neighbourhood Nurseries Initiative: aiming to create 900 nurseries in deprived areas by 2004.
	• National Standards for under 8s day care and child-minding in force.
	• OFSTED responsible for registration and inspection of day care 0–8.
	• Early Years Sector-Endorsed Foundation Degree.
2002	• Foundation Stage Profile replaced baseline assessment.
	• Special Educational Needs Code of Practice in place.
	• Birth to Three Matters framework introduced.
2003	• Working Tax Credit replaced Working Families Tax Credit.
	• Government forbade 'smoking and smacking' by child-minders.
	• First Minister for Children appointed.
	• EPPE '97–'03 report published, and research continued 2003–2008.
2004	• *Every Child Matters: Change for Children* green paper – five central outcomes for children: be healthy; stay safe; enjoy and achieve; make a positive contribution; achieve economic wellbeing.
	• Children Act: taking forward proposals in Every Child Matters.
	• Ten-year childcare strategy Choice for Parents, the Best Start for Children: Making it Happen unveiled: goals included 3,500 children's centres and an out-of-school childcare place for 3–14 year-olds from 8am–6pm each weekday, by 2010, and 20 hours a week for 38 weeks for all three- and four-year-olds.

Figure 1.1 Labour's decade of reform

2005	• First Children's Commissioner for England appointed.
	• Education Act aligns early years inspections with school inspections.
	• New 'no notice' inspections for early years settings.
	• Children's Workforce Strategy launched, including Children, Young People and Families Workforce Development Council (CWDC).
	• National Professional Qualification in Integrated Centre Leadership (NPQICL) set up.
	• Children's Centres faced cash shortfall.
2006	• Childcare Act placed duties on local authorities.
	• Parents, Early Years and Learning (PEAL) project: a national approach to training in parental support for early learning.
	• Qualifications and Credit Framework: unit-based qualification framework underpinned by system of credit accumulation and transfer.
	• Early Years Professional (EYP) Status: Children's Workforce Strategy.
	• *Choice for Parents. The Best Start for Children. Making it Happen. Action Plan for the Ten-Year Strategy.*
	• 13 other 'guidance' documents, including the *Rose Report*, and *Extended Services in Primary Schools*.
	• Early Years Foundation Stage (EYFS) consultation launched amid much criticism.
2007	• £152 per week: average nursery day care cost for a child under 2.
	• Paid maternity leave extended to nine months, with long-term goal of 12 months.
	• OFSTED undergoes massive expansion.
	• 19 legislation and policy documents; 24 practice reports, guidance and standards; and eight workforce development documents published.
	• Final (partially amended) EYFS pack launched: to be statutory from September 2008.

Figure 1.1 *(continued)*

The need for integration

In the circular process of policy, practice and research, these findings have instructed the on-going formation of policy and practice. A review of government policy for children and families in 2008 by the UK Conservative Party's Social Justice Policy Group in the Centre for Social Justice reported, echoing the rationale for Sure Start, that 'a key thread is a call for greater integration throughout service provision'. However, while recent early years policy had focused on the wider provision of affordable, quality childcare, on standards for this childcare and on the development of a public health strategy for children aged 0–5, the report stressed that:

> despite current policy's far-reaching positive implications, a 'golden thread' is missing: a recognition, in the underpinning framework, of the importance of relationships in every young child's development ...

> Economic and academic concerns trump relational ones, despite the latter's crucial role in child, and later adult's, well-being. Children's policy misses the importance of relationships, and political thinking in general misses the relevance of high levels of relational stress and relational poverty in the early years as key underlying factors for a whole host of social problems we face today.[30]

The wellbeing of the youngest children is liable to be affected, directly or indirectly, by the whole range of local and national UK government policies and priorities for expenditure. Babies and young children are not just *potential* citizens, but are citizens *now*. Policies in general do not impact only on adults, they affect these youngest citizens too. A prime example is the need to balance work and family life, which is especially pressing for working mothers of young children, and fathers working long hours.

Other policies need to be integrated into the picture too. There are permeating issues of racial and ethnic diversity, taxation, law and order, transport, and planning and housing policies – in addition to the more obviously relevant areas of maternity and paternity leave, and the quality and availability of day care. Many UK children's experiences of growing up, especially in disadvantaged areas, would be radically more positive if all policies and legislation were screened in relation to generating opportunities for wellbeing for the youngest children – or at the very least, for not damaging their wellbeing.

One of the policy documents published in the UK in 2008 was *The Children's Plan: Building Brighter Futures*.[31] This 10-year strategy to improve schools and bring about radical changes in the way parents and families are supported points the way to the integration that is needed. The Plan was underpinned by the following five principles:

- Governments do not bring up children – parents do – so the government needs to do more to back parents and families.

- All children have the potential to succeed and should go as far as their talents can take them.

- Children and young people need to enjoy their childhood as well as grow up prepared for adult life.

- Services need to be shaped by and responsive to children, young people and families, not designed around professional boundaries.

- It is always better to prevent failure than tackle a crisis later.

As the early childhood sector continues to work towards these principles in the coming years, the wellbeing of young children and their families can be transformed.

Key messages

- Key messages from brain research highlight the importance of babies' and young children's experiences, especially with their 'important' people.
- Intersubjectivity – especially between mother and child – is a key concept.
- In the decade from 1997 to 2007, government guidance and legislation aimed to transform policies and services for young children and their families in the UK.
- Transformation in the early years needs to be underpinned by an integrated approach to policy and service provision.

Questions to think about and discuss

1. What matters in the earliest years of a child's life? Can you think of 'real life' examples?
2. Research tells us that everything babies and young children see, hear, touch and smell influences the way their brains develop. What daily situations and experiences do you think are especially important for them?
3. If you were asked to advise the government, what policies would you recommend for the youngest children and their families; and why?

Further reading

CALLAN, S. (ed.) *Breakdown Britain: The Next Generation.* London: Centre for Social Justice, 2008.

This report of the Conservative Party's Social Justice Policy Group in 2008 examines the reasons for Britain's social malaise and describes five multi-causal drivers of poverty, all of which impact directly on the wellbeing of the youngest children. Both its analyses and recommendations make thought-provoking reading in relation to early childhood services.

GROARK, C. & McCALL, R. 'Community-Based Interventions and Services', in M. Rutter et al. (eds) *Rutter's Child and Adolescent Psychiatry*, 5th edn. Oxford: Blackwell Publishing, 2008, pp 971–988.

Just one chapter in an enormous and enormously interesting reference book, that you can expect to find in a university library. The chapter contains clear explanations of attachment theory and social learning theory as different approaches to parenting that are thought to be associated with child outcomes. It brings a hard-edged and perhaps controversial perspective to a review of the characteristics, possible outcomes and limitations of parenting programmes. Plenty of food for thought and debate about approaches to policy and research.

PUGH, G. 'Policies in the UK to Promote the Well-Being of Children', in J. Scott & H. Ward (eds) *Safeguarding and Promoting the Well-Being of Vulnerable Children*. London: Jessica Kingsley, 2005.

This is another reference book chapter that you can expect to find on the library shelf. Adopting an ecological approach, it sets out very clearly the risk and resilience factors of which we need to be aware. The very helpful framework provides a strong foundation for thinking about policy in relation to the early development of wellbeing.

References

1 PUGH, G. 'Policies in the UK to Promote the Well-Being of Children', in J. Scott & H. Ward (eds) *Safeguarding and Promoting the Well-Being of Vulnerable Children*. London: Jessica Kingsley, 2005.
2 SHONKOFF, J. & PHILLIPS, D. (eds) *From Neurons to Neighborhoods: The Science of Early Childhood Development*. Washington DC: National Academy Press, 2000.
3 DAVID, T., GOOUCH, K., POWELL, S. & ABBOTT, L. *Birth to Three Matters: Literature Review Research Report 444*. London: DfES, 2003.
4 HANNON, P. 'Developmental Neuroscience: Implications for Early Childhood Intervention and Education', *Current Paediatrics*, 2003 (13): 58–63.
5 INNOCENTI REPORT CARD 7 *Child Poverty in Perspective: An Overview of Child Well-Being in Rich Countries*. Florence: UNICEF, 2007.
6 TREVARTHEN, C. & AITKEN, K. 'Infant Intersubjectivity: Research, Theory, and Clinical Applications', *Journal of Child Psychology and Psychiatry*, 2001, 42(1): 3–48.
7 STERN, D. *The Interpersonal World of the Infant*. New York: Basic Books, 1985; CROCKENBERG, S. & LEERKES, E. 'Infant Social and Emotional Development in the Family Context', in C.H. Zeanah (ed.) *Handbook of Infant Mental Health*. London: Guilford Press, 2000.
8 BOWLBY, J. *Attachment*. London: Penguin Books, 1969.
9 HOWE, D. *Attachment Theory for Child and Family Social Work*. London: Macmillan Press, 1999.
10 ELFER, P., GOLDSCHMIED, E. & SELLECK, D. *Key Persons in the Nursery*. London: David Fulton, 2003.
11 ABBOTT, L. & LANGSTON, A. (eds) *Birth to Three Matters: Supporting the Framework of Effective Practice*. Maidenhead: Open University Press, 2005: 5.
12 TREVARTHEN, C. 'Stepping Away from the Mirror: Pride and Shame in Adventures of Companionship: Reflections on the Nature and Emotional Needs of Infant Subjectivity', in C.S. Carter, L. Ahnert, K.E. Grossman, S.B. Hardy, M.E. Lamb, S.W. Porges & N. Sachser (eds) *Attachment and Bonding: A New Synthesis*, Vol. 92, Dahlem Workshop Report. Cambridge, MA: The MIT Press, 2005: 56.
13 MEADE, A. *The Brain Debate*. Washington: Fulbright Lecture, 2000.
14 MURRAY, L. & ANDREWS, L. *The Social Baby*. Richmond, UK: CP Publishing, 2000; HOBSON, P. *The Cradle of Thought: Exploring the Origins of Thinking*. London: Pan Books, 2002; GERHARDT, S. *Why Love Matters: How Affection Shapes a Baby's Brain*. Hove: Routledge, 2004.
15 WALDFOGEL, J. *What Children Need*. London: Harvard University Press, 2006: 62, 20.
16 BLAKEMORE, S-J. & FRITH, U. *The Learning Brain: Lessons for Education*. Oxford: Blackwell Publishing, 2005.
17 DAVID, T., GOOUCH, K., POWELL, S. & ABBOTT, L. *Birth to Three Matters: Literature Review Research Report 444*. London: DfES, 2003: 140, 142.
18 DEPARTMENT for EDUCATION AND SKILLS (DfES) *Birth to Three Matters: A Framework to Support Children in Their Earliest Years*. London: DfES, 2003.
19 DEPARTMENT for EDUCATION and SKILLS (DfES) *The Early Years Foundation Stage: Setting the Standards for Learning, Development and Care for Children from Birth to Five*. London: DfES, 2007.
20 LANE, J. *Young Children and Social Justice: Taking Action for Racial Equality in the Early Years — Understanding the Past, Thinking about the Present, Planning for the Future*. London: National Children's Bureau, 2008.
21 SURE START www.surestart.gov.uk ; SMITH, T. *National Evaluation of Neighbourhood Nurseries Initiative: Integrated Report SSU/FR/2007/024*. London: DfES, 2007; NATIONAL AUDIT OFFICE *Sure Start Children's Centres: Report by the Comptroller and Auditor General/HC 104 Session 2006–2007 19 December 2006*. London: The Stationery Office, 2006; DEPARTMENT FOR EDUCATION AND SKILLS (DfES) *Every Child Matters*. London: The Stationery Office, 2003.
22 SPENCER, N. *Poverty and Child Health*. Oxford: Radcliffe Medical Press, 2000: 302–303.
23 HALSEY, A.H., LAUDER, H., BROWN, P. & STUART WELLS, A. (eds) *Education: Culture, Economy, and Society*. Oxford: Oxford University Press, 1997: 786.
24 DEPARTMENT for EDUCATION and SKILLS (DfES) *Starting with Quality*. London: HMSO, 1990.
25 BALL, C. *Start Right: The Importance of Early Learning*. London: RSA, 1994.
26 BLAKEMORE, S-J. *Early Years Learning*, Parliamentary Office of Science and Technology (POST) Report, 2000: 140; GOPNIK, A., MELTZOFF, A. & KUHL, P. *How Babies Think*. London: Phoenix, 1999; OECD *Starting Strong: Early Childhood Education and Care*. Paris: OECD, 2001; SHONKOFF, J. & PHILLIPS, D. *From Neurons to Neighborhoods: The Science of Early Childhood Development*. Washington DC: National Academy Press, 2000.
27 SCHWEINHART, L. & WEIKART, D. A. 'Summary of Significant Benefits: The High/Scope Perry Pre-School Study Through Age 27', in C. Ball (ed.) *Start Right: The Importance of Early Learning*. London: RSA, 1994.
28 SMITH, T. *National Evaluation of Neighbourhood Nurseries Initiative: Integrated Report SSU/FR/2007/024*. London: DfES, 2007.
29 FEINSTEIN, L. *The Relative Importance of Academic, Psychological and Behavioural Attributes Developed in Childhood*. London: Centre for Economic Performance, LSE, 2000.
30 CALLAN, S. (ed.) *Breakdown Britain: The Next Generation*. London: Centre for Social Justice, 2008: 16–20.
31 DEPARTMENT for CHILDREN, SCHOOLS AND FAMILIES (DCSF) *The Children's Plan: Building Brighter Futures*. Norwich: The Stationery Office, 2008.

2

Wellbeing Themes

This chapter contains:

FOUR RECURRING THEMES

- Early relationships
- The ecology of early childhood
- Being resilient
- Wellbeing

Four Recurring Themes

Research now leaves us in no doubt of the importance of the earliest years from birth in terms of child development and wellbeing.[1] The literature relating to early childhood wellbeing is essentially about child development and about the many factors that impact on that development. Such factors include our comparatively recent knowledge of how the human brain develops in the early years, early environments, the nature of society, and policy and practice in services for children and families. In this sweep of perspectives, certain early childhood themes frequently recur, and these are the focus of this chapter.

The first theme is early relationships. We know from many sources ranging from Bowlby to Buchanan and Gopnik to Gerhardt that early relationships are fundamental to children's wellbeing.[2] This idea is certainly not new. Between her pioneering work at the Malting House School from 1924 to 1927 and taking up her 10-year post as Head of the Department of Child Development at the University of London Institute of Education in 1933, Susan Isaacs wrote three seminal books on young children, their intellectual growth and social development.[3] Six years after Isaacs' death in 1948 these words of hers were published by The British Association of Early Childhood Education. 'Above

14

everything else, a child needs warm human relationships, and spontaneous feelings of friendship'.[4] So many copies of the booklet were circulated that it is still easily available today.

John Bowlby, born in 1907, was a psychiatrist who was commissioned by the World Health Organisation after the Second World War to study the mental health needs of homeless and orphaned children. His theory of attachment, which has developed and evolved since Bowlby published his ideas in the 1960s, laid the foundations of our understanding about the importance of children's relationships in the earliest years.[5] Michael Rutter, a developmental psychopathologist and consultant psychiatrist based at King's College, London, extensively reviewed Bowlby's concept of attachment to the mother, consequently arguing that babies can enjoy multiple attachments, and suggesting the term 'multiple mothering'.[6] The Early Years Foundation Stage principle of Positive Relationships has its roots in the work of Bowlby, Rutter and others. The principle states that 'children learn to be strong and independent from a base of loving and secure relationships with parents and/or a key person'.[7]

Urie Bronfenbrenner, who lived from 1917 to 2005, was a well-known American psychologist and Professor in Human Development, Family Studies and Psychology at Cornell University. Building on the theme of early relationships, his ecological perspective plays an increasingly central role in policy and research. Bronfenbrenner argued that:

> the understanding of human development demands more than the direct observation of behavior on the part of one or two persons in the same place; it requires examination of multiperson systems of interaction not limited to a single setting and must take into account aspects of the environment beyond the immediate situation containing the subject.[8]

In other words, we need to think about children's development within the context of the family, in the community, in society – a series of ever-widening circles. This ecological perspective is the second wellbeing theme.

'Being resilient' is the third central wellbeing theme. Here, the focus is on resilience as a descriptor (for instance, 'a resilient child') rather than as a theoretical concept (as in 'the concept of resilience'). Although not explicit in the policy literature, this concept is a main driver of policy in Every Child Matters.[9] Resilience from birth may sound like a contradiction in terms, yet in the context of laying the foundations of wellbeing, the idea that resilience only becomes relevant as children grow up seems less and less tenable. The concept of 'resilient wellbeing' invites further investigation about the kinds of early experiences that may lead to better later outcomes, for all children.

These three themes lead to the fourth: perceptions of wellbeing itself. Wellbeing is often represented as the part of child development that is not about health – as in 'health and wellbeing'. On examination this frequently appears to be about social and emotional wellbeing, begging the question of whether cognition is not, therefore, appropriately perceived as part of wellbeing.[10] What is certain is that there is a measure of confusion about what is meant by wellbeing. If we are to make the most of new opportunities to work with children and families, especially in the earliest years, we need to be clearer about this.

These central themes, of early relationships, the ecology of childhood, resilient responses to challenges, and the nature of wellbeing itself constitute starting points towards a better understanding of wellbeing.

Early relationships

When young children and their caregivers are tuned in to each other, and when caregivers can read children's emotional cues and respond appropriately, their relationships blossom. These warm, responsive early relationships are likely to support healthy development in multiple domains, including communication, cognition, social–emotional competence, and moral understanding. As the *Birth to Three Matters: Literature Review* concluded: 'The research points to the centrality of positive relationships with parents and other key people in young children's lives'.[11]

The same message has been central in Reggio Emilia, a small municipality in northern Italy where the services for young children are uniquely and famously superb.[12] In a radical and inspiring approach to the needs of the youngest children, learning is seen as a process of social construction – the child learns in relationship with others.

Neurobiology has provided evidence that caring relationships are key to emotional, social and cognitive development.[13] However, this perspective is by no means new. In the 1960s, Winnicott, resonating with Bowlby's work on attachment, wrote about the bond between mother and child in which he held firmly to the idea of the baby as a person.[14] Bowlby's theory of attachment – an enduring affective bond between the child and the caregiver who becomes a source of safety in times of stress – is still central to the concept of caring relationships.[15]

Peter Fonagy and his colleagues reviewed longitudinal studies examining the results of the quality of attachment in infancy.[16] They showed that security during the first two years *predicts* many of the attributes in preschool, and of subsequent stages of development, which have been shown to be the characteristics of the resilient child. Parent–child attachment has been extensively confirmed as a central contributing factor to children's positive developmental outcomes.[17] Gerhardt explained why early interactions have lasting consequences, and promoted the importance of sensitive, caring responses to a baby's needs.[18] Gammage described consistency of attachment as 'the seed-bed of wellbeing'.[19]

So, relationships are absolutely central to babies' and young children's development – which is largely why the ability to communicate in a range of ways and gradually to acquire spoken language is so central to their early development.[20] Encouraging and supporting these early communications are very direct ways to enrich their lives. We need to discover as much as we can about the kinds of situations and experiences in which these early relationships can thrive.

The ecology of early childhood

A vital theme in early childhood, especially in the policy context, is the importance of an ecological approach, acknowledging the interdependence of child, family, community and society. In a chapter entitled 'Policies in the UK to Promote the Wellbeing of Children' Pugh wrote that: 'children and young people saw their family and friends as the most important influence on achieving good outcomes' and that

> ... wellness or wellbeing is both an individual and a collective concept, something that is measured in terms of individual lives, but is very often delivered through families and communities. This ecological approach, which grounds work with children and young people in their families, and within the community and the culture in which they are growing up has been central in informing the policies ... .[21]

Bronfenbrenner, who argued that human abilities and their realisation depend to a significant degree on the larger social and institutional context of individual activity, broke down some of the barriers between the social sciences of psychology, sociology and anthropology. He suggested that human development could be analysed in terms of systems. Writing of the dyad, or two person system, he suggested that:

> it appears that if one member of the pair undergoes a process of development, the other does also. Recognition of this relationship provides a key to understanding developmental changes not only in children but also in adults who serve as primary caregivers – mothers, fathers, grandparents, teachers, and so on.[22]

In addition to the 'microsystem' of the family, Bronfenbrenner described a series of systems. Exo- and macrosystems of work, neighbourhood, wider social networks, and the structure of socio-economic systems, policies and cultural values go to make up the child's wider context of society.

Between 1979 and 1992 Bronfenbrenner elaborated his original theory to develop a 'bioecological theory' as a paradigm for the future. He identified 10 wise and thought-provoking propositions, four of which are of particular relevance to understanding the development of resilient wellbeing. The first of these propositions concerns the importance of experience, in relation to the realm of subjective feelings. Bronfenbrenner wrote:

> Experience pertains to the realm of subjective feelings: for example, anticipations, forebodings, hopes, doubts, or personal beliefs. These ... emerge in early childhood, continue through life, and are characterized by both stability and change.

In another of his propositions Bronfenbrenner referred to interactions over extended periods of time as 'proximal processes'.

> Examples of such processes include feeding or comforting a baby; playing with a young child; child–child activities; group or solitary play; reading; learning new skills; athletic activities; problem solving; caring for others; making plans; performing complex tasks; and acquiring new knowledge and know-how.

Bronfenbrenner also proposed that:

> In order to develop – intellectually, emotionally, socially, and morally – a child requires, for all of these, the same thing: participation in *progressively more complex activities*, on a regular basis over an extended period of time in the child's life, with one or more persons with whom the child develops *a strong, mutual, emotional attachment, and who are committed to the child's well-being and development, preferably for life*. (original emphases)

Bronfenbrenner's sixth proposition is a deeply interesting one. It proposes something that, once identified, seems so obvious that it is a wonder the idea is not more familiar to us. It concerns the support that main carers of young children need, describing the way that progressively more complex interactions and emotional attachment between parent and child depend to a substantial degree on the availability and involvement of another (second) adult. In other words, main carers need someone else 'to back them up'. Bronfenbrenner wrote: 'What mattered most was not only the attention given to the child – important as this was – but also the assistance provided to the single parent or by others serving in the supportive roles ....'.[23]

Many of Bronfenbrenner's perspectives were echoed by researchers Prilleltensky and Nelson, who argued that:

> child wellness is predicated on the satisfaction of material, physical, affective, and psychological needs. Wellness is an ecological concept; a child's wellbeing is determined by the level of parental, familial, communal, and social wellness ... Family wellness is more than the absence of discord; it is the presence of supportive, affectionate and gratifying relationships that serve to promote the personal development of family members and the collective well-being of the family as a whole.[24]

Rogoff, an America psychologist, also emphasised the vital role of family and community in children's development, describing 'an apprenticeship – it occurs through guided participation in social activity with companions who support and stretch children's understanding of and skills in using the tools of culture'.[25]

These ecological perspectives of wellness (or wellbeing) show a child's wellbeing as determined by the level of parental, familial, communal and social wellness. Not only is wellbeing seen to be about the importance of the context of the child's developing wellbeing; it extends to the idea of collective wellbeing which is at the heart of 'community'.

Historically, the roots of community in early childhood are very deep. But through most of the twentieth century, early education was guided by the developmental psychology of learning which focused on the *individual* child as an active learner. Towards the end of the twentieth century there was a rise in the influence of ideas relating to the social nature of learning, with the Russian psychologist Vygotsky's *Mind in Society* making a significant impact.[26] By the beginning of the twenty-first century 'community' – with its implications of belonging and responsibility – was firmly back on the agenda of early childhood policy in the UK.[27]

Being resilient

The word 'resilience' comes from the Latin 'resilire', to recoil or leap back. This Latin derivation is reminiscent of the analogy often used for attachment, as if the child were on the end of an invisible piece of elastic with the other end attached to the primary care-giver. The child moves away – but only a secure distance – and back again at will, in a psychological sense remaining attached.

Should what we think of as 'positive adjustment' be reserved for such exceptional attainments as, for instance, a positive outcome despite the experience of adversity, continued positive or effective functioning in adverse circumstances, or recovery after significant trauma? Or perhaps for more ordinary achievements? According to Masten and Gewirtz:

> In the majority of cases, resilience arises from ordinary adaptive processes rather than rare or extraordinary ones. ... This view offers a far more optimistic outlook for action aiming to promote competence and human capital in individuals and society than the assumption of outstanding capabilities.[28]

In relation to the concept of 'resilient wellbeing' it can be argued that exposure to the 'normal' adversities of childhood is something that happens to a certain degree to *all* children. While acknowledging the gravity of traumas experienced by many children through such experiences as poverty, war and child abuse, this perspective of 'normal' adversities takes the wider focus of the difficult conditions that most, if not all, children and young people are likely to experience from time to time in the life course. So here is a more universal perspective:

> How many times have you wondered why some kids seem to do OK even when awful things happen around them? Their families break up, someone dies, their parents lose their jobs, money becomes very tight, but they still manage to come to school, keep their friends, and participate positively in the life of the school. How come? Aren't they supposed to succumb to these stresses and tumble in an ever downward spiral to school failure, unemployment, drug-taking, delinquency and teen pregnancy? Well some do, but some don't and it is these kids who are attracting more and more interest. They are the ones who are being described as 'resilient' because they seem to have an ability to hang on in there when the going gets tough.[29]

What do we know about how 'resilient wellbeing' develops? A straightforward and helpful definition of the kind of resilience that relates directly to wellbeing is provided by Fonagy and colleagues as: 'Resilience is *normal* development under difficult conditions'.[30] They also identified protective features of a child's immediate circumstances, i.e. the family. These features included:

• competent parenting

• a good (warm) relationship with at least one primary caregiver

• networks of informal relationships.

Grotberg, working in 1995 as part of The International Resilience Project funded by the Bernard Van Leer Foundation, pointed out that resilience is important because it is the human capacity to face, overcome and be strengthened or even transformed by the adversities of life. 'Everyone faces adversities; no one is exempt'. She described three sources of resilience as, 'I have', I am' and 'I can'. The content of these three sources was drawn from the conclusions of a series of international meetings to discuss the construct of resilience, and from the literature (see Figure 2.1).

A crucial task in relation to wellbeing is to identify the key risk factors that are likely to have an adverse effect on children's development, together with the corresponding protective factors that can help to develop resilience. Also adopting an ecological approach in her work on risk and resilience in early childhood, Pugh provided important pointers to key issues. By examining risk and protective factors in the child, in the family, and in the community, Pugh specified four characteristics that have been found to be particularly important in creating resilience in children, as follows:

- an adequate standard of living

- a temperament/disposition that encourages care-giving, leading to high self-esteem, sociability and autonomy, the ability to solve problems, and an internal locus of control

- dependable care-givers, where children can grow up in a family with one or two caring adults, who have positive and appropriate child-rearing practices

- networks of community support, including a pro-social peer group, high quality early education and schools where children are valued and learning is encouraged.[32]

There is repeated evidence from research about resilient children that, firstly, if a parent is incapacitated or unavailable, other significant people in a young child's life can play an enabling role, whether they are grand-parents, older siblings, child-care providers, or nursery school teachers; and secondly that a young child needs enough consistent nurturance to trust in its availability.[33] Children need an organised and predictable environment that combines warmth and caring with a clearly defined structure and established explicit limits that are consistently enforced.

I HAVE	People around me I trust and who love me, no matter what. People who set limits for me so I know when to stop before there is danger or trouble. People who show me how to do things right by the way they do things. People who want me to learn to do things on my own. People who help me when I am sick, in danger or need to learn.
I AM	A person people can like and love. Glad to do nice things for others and show my concern. Respectful of myself and others. Willing to be responsible for what I do. Sure things will be alright.
I CAN	Talk to others about things that frighten me or bother me. Find ways to solve problems that I face. Control myself when I feel like doing something not right or dangerous. Figure out when it is a good time to talk to someone or to take action. Find someone to help me when I need it.

Figure 2.1 Grotberg's three sources of resilience[31]

Wellbeing

How are the foundations of wellbeing laid in the earliest years? This is an important question. We need ways of thinking about wellbeing that are not only appropriate in early childhood, but that can remain applicable throughout life. Although this book is primarily about early childhood, it is useful to explore the idea of wellbeing and what it means, both from the point of view of the youngest children, and of the people who live and work with them.

The idea of 'subjective' wellbeing in the context of the youngest children and their families is the approach to wellbeing that is taken in this book. In subjective wellbeing the focus is on how individuals perceive their own wellbeing; as distinct from using a process of measurement in which one person attempts objectively to assess the wellbeing of another.

Another aspect to consider is the way in which child development is conceived in categories. For early childhood practitioners over at least half a century these categories have most often been described in broad areas of physical, emotional, social and cognitive development. However, as Hobson pointed out, the division of activity – 'rents in the mind' is how he described it – does not help our understanding of the ways that children think and develop.[34] Many people deeply involved with child development have searched for a model that brings together affect and cognition – how we feel and what we know – in a way that genuinely combines rather than separates them. The study of wellbeing offers an opportunity to achieve this.

The term 'wellbeing' has been described as 'a compendium term' indicating a travel bag or case containing many things.[35] For more experienced travellers this might imply an impeccably packed bag, but in the context of children and young people it raises a different image, of tangled garments hastily stuffed in, some even bursting out. With the central place that the term 'wellbeing' now occupies in policy documents, it is important that the concept of wellbeing becomes clearer – metaphorically sorting out and tidying up the bag, folding the jerseys, putting pairs of socks together, and stray items in a pocket. Hypothetically then, this metaphorical process of tidying the wellbeing travel bag is – as far as is possible – the focus of this section.

Laevers defined wellbeing outcomes in terms of enjoyment, relaxing and inner peace, vitality, openness, self-confidence, and being in touch with oneself.[36] His six areas for achieving those outcomes were physical needs, the need for affection, warmth and tenderness, the need for safety, clarity and continuity, the need for recognition and affirmation, the need to experience oneself as capable, and the need for meaning and (moral) values. In relation to quality indicators Laevers argued that while previously attention has been paid to context variables and outcomes variables, his development of process variables enabled important progress to be made, in particular in relation to the two factors of emotional wellbeing and involvement. His wellbeing and involvement indicators are widely valued and used by many practitioners.[37]

In his organisation of these indicators, Laevers framed 'wellbeing' in terms of mental health, and 'involvement' in terms of learning, upholding the long-held division between affect and cognition. For children, these elements are tangled strands in the situations and experiences of their lives. Thinking about the overall wellbeing of babies and young children certainly requires the use of categories to make it accessible. Perhaps a new way of doing so that brings together affect and cognition can build further on Laevers' illuminating work.

A debate has been gathering strength in relation to the concept of happiness, and whether happiness and wellbeing are related concepts, or even essentially the same concept. Mihaly Csikszentmihalyi, Professor of Psychology at the University of Chicago, proposed the idea of 'flow', meaning that happiness is based on the complete absorption and engagement in an activity which produces an exhilarating sense of progress; and that this over-rides emotional problems.[38] Nel Noddings, emeritus Professor of Education at Stanford University, argued that happiness and education are inextricably linked.[39] These writers are proposing more integrated ways of thinking about subjective wellbeing.

The UK's *Children's Plan: Building Brighter Futures* frames wellbeing like this:

> Emotional wellbeing and good mental health are crucial for every aspect of a child's life, now and in the future. These capabilities are derived from a loving and supportive family and a breadth of positive experiences in childhood. Strong social and emotional skills are essential to success in life and work … they build resilience …[40]

Similarly, the idea emerges from Buchanan and Hudson's work that wellbeing is 'something different from the absence of problems, something more than a lack of depression, something more than happiness. Into the model comes confidence, empathy, prosocial behaviour, creativity and a sense of achievement'.[41] The authors point out that this 'global' sense of wellbeing incorporates many of the existing measures used to assess different components of wellbeing in children; for example, scales to measure strengths/difficulties, self-esteem, self efficacy, locus of control, empathy. But they say that none of these scales appears to capture the essence of a person's global emotional wellbeing.

A term for such universal wellbeing emerged from a report on discussions with Afghan families called *The Children of Kabul*.[42] This report explored three main topics: wellbeing goals for Afghan children; the threats children face in achieving wellbeing; and the coping resources children already have for dealing with their difficulties. In spite of the extraordinarily different political and cultural context, considerable overlap with the themes explored in this chapter was evident. Children and their parents in Kabul agreed that they wanted more than mere physical survival; that emotional and social development were important; and that children require both positive and supportive *contexts* as well as positive and supportive relationships, to achieve wellbeing. The concept in Afghanistan for global wellbeing is termed '*tarbia*'; and in a women's group discussion tarbia was explained thus:

> The difference between a child with good tarbia and a child with bad tarbia is like the difference between a complete house and a destroyed house. If a mother and father pay attention to a child's tarbia, the child will grow and develop into a useful person. If not, they will grow up useless and will be a disadvantage for their family and country – just like a destroyed and ravaged home.

This powerful analogy makes a most persuasive argument for the crucial importance of supporting wellbeing in the family. As the grandmothers said: 'Tarbia is everything – the people who get on well with their life have good tarbia and the people who don't get on well with their life have bad tarbia, and all this comes from the family'; while the fathers confirmed: 'If you give children good tarbia they will keep that until the end of their lives'.

In this review of recurring early childhood themes, many threads have emerged – threads that in real life are generally embedded in the web of children's and families' lives, at home and in their communities. In order to explore and attempt to make sense of the foundations of resilient wellbeing, a theoretical framework is needed for people who live and work with the youngest children – parents and families, practitioners, managers and policy-makers. This framework is the subject of Part 2.

Key messages 🔑

- Relationships are fundamental to the early development of babies' and young children's wellbeing.
- The collective wellbeing of a child's parents and family, community and society makes a profound impact on that child's individual wellbeing.
- All children need resilient wellbeing, to manage the normal adversities of their lives as they grow and develop.
- Holistic wellbeing in childhood is about every aspect of a child's development.

Questions to think about and discuss

1. What do babies and young children need on a daily basis for their relationships to flourish? How can practitioners help to meet those needs?

2. Can you think of examples from your own professional experience of Bronfenbrenner's sixth proposition, about the need for the availability and involvement of another (second) adult? What do you think about its importance – do you agree with him?

3. What are the attributes of a resilient child? Can you describe a resilient child that you know? (Remember the need for confidentiality.)

Further reading

BRONFENBRENNER, U. (ed.) *Making Human Beings Human: Biological Perspectives on Human Development.* Thousand Oaks, CA: SAGE Publications, 2005.

Bronfenbrenner radically re-visited his own well-established theory to edit this inspirational collection of writing. Focusing on how individuals develop in ever-changing, multi-level contexts, it contains many pearls of wisdom; not least a set of defining properties of his bio-ecological model, in the form of propositions. That sounds very theoretical, and so it is ... and yet the theory is absolutely rooted in real life, and makes a wonderful read. We know we are standing on the shoulders of giants, and Bronfenbrenner surely is one of them.

GERHARDT, S. *Why Love Matters: How Affection Shapes a Baby's Brain.* Hove: Routledge, 2004.

This is an accessible exposition of neuroscience findings and their relevance to early childhood. It explains why love is essential to brain development in the early years of life, and about the long-term importance of early relationships. Bringing a psychotherapeutic perspective to the subject, Gerhardt's writing is humane, lively and illuminating.

HOBSON, P. *The Cradle of Thought: Exploring the Origins of Thinking.* London: Pan Books, 2002.

The central contention of this book is that humans need nurture in order to think. As for language, thinking may be hard-wired in new-born infants, but they need nurturing for the thinking ability to develop. Hobson says that the quality of babies' interactions with nurturing adults in the first 18 months lays the foundations for their later emotional, social and intellectual lives. It is a fascinating book, full of ancient wisdom and new insights – 'providing a theory of human development that has social contact at its core'.

References

[1] UNDERDOWN, A. *Young Children's Health and Wellbeing.* Maidenhead: Open University Press, 2007.
[2] BOWLBY, J. *Attachment.* London: Penguin Books, 1969; BUCHANAN, A. & HUDSON, B. *Promoting Children's Emotional Wellbeing.* Oxford: Oxford University Press, 2000; GOPNIK, A., MELTZOFF, A. & KUHL, P. *How Babies Think.* London: Phoenix, 1999; GERHARDT, S. *Why Love Matters: How Affection Shapes a Baby's Brain.* Hove: Routledge, 2004.
[3] ISAACS, S. *Intellectual Growth in Young Children.* London: Routledge, 1930; ISAACS, S. *The Children We Teach.* London: University of London Press, 1932; ISAACS, S. *Social Development of Young Children.* London: Routledge, 1933.
[4] ISAACS, S. *The Educational Value of the Nursery School.* London: The British Association for Early Childhood Education, 1954: 20.
[5] BOWLBY, J. *Attachment.* London: Penguin Books, 1969.
[6] RUTTER, M. *Maternal Deprivation Re-Assessed.* Harmondsworth: Penguin, 1972: 25.
[7] DEPARTMENT for EDUCATION AND SKILLS (DfES), *The Early Years Foundation Stage: Setting the Standards for Learning, Development and Care for Children from Birth to Five.* London: DfES, 2008: 5.

8 BRONFENBRENNER, U. *The Ecology of Human Development: Experiments by Nature and Design*. London: Harvard University Press, 1979: 21.

9 DfES *Every Child Matters*. London: The Stationery Office, 2003.

10 BUCHANAN, A. & HUDSON, B. *Promoting Children's Emotional Wellbeing*. Oxford: Oxford University Press, 2000.

11 DAVID, T., GOOUCH, K., POWELL, S. AND ABBOTT, L. *Birth to Three Matters: Literature Review Research Report 444*. London: Department for Education and Skills (DfES) 2003: 102.

12 RINALDI, C. *In Dialogue with Reggio Emilia: Listening, Researching and Learning*. Hove: Routledge, 2006.

13 SHONKOFF, J. & PHILLIPS, D. *From Neurons to Neighborhoods: The Science of Early Childhood Development*. Washington, DC: National Academy Press, 2000.

14 WINNICOTT, D.W. *The Child, the Family, and the Outside World*. London: Penguin Books, 1964.

15 BOWLBY, J. *Attachment*. London: Penguin Books, 1969; AINSWORTH, M. *Patterns of Attachment: A Psychological Study of the Strange Situation*. Hillsdale, NJ: Erlbaum, 1978; BRETHERTON, I. 'The Origins of Attachment Theory', *Developmental Psychology*, 1992, 28: 759–775.

16 FONAGY, P., STEELE, M., STEELE, H., HIGGIT, A. & TARGET, M. The Emanuel Miller Memorial Lecture 1992: The Theory and Practice of Resilience, *Journal of Child Psychology and Psychiatry*, 1992, 35(2): 231–257.

17 MARTY, A., READDICK, C. & WALTERS, C. 'Supporting Secure Parent–Child Attachments: The Role of the Non-Parental Caregiver', *Early Child Development and Care*, 2005, 175(3): 271–283.

18 GERHARDT, S. *Why Love Matters: How Affection Shapes a Baby's Brain*. Hove: Routledge, 2004.

19 GAMMAGE, P. *Well-Being: The Generic Perspective; Power and Protection*. Adelaide: Department for Early Childhood Services, 2004: 12.

20 TREVARTHEN, C. & AITKEN, K. 'Infant Intersubjectivity: Research, Theory, and Clinical Applications', *Journal of Child Psychology and Psychiatry*, 2001, 42(1): 3–48.

21 PUGH, G. 'Policies in the UK to Promote the Well-Being of Children', in J. Scott & H. Ward (eds) *Safeguarding and Promoting the Well-Being of Vulnerable Children*. London: Jessica Kingsley, 2005: 45.

22 BRONFENBRENNER, U. *The Ecology of Human Development: Experiments by Nature and Design*. London: Harvard University Press, 1979: 5.

23 BRONFENBRENNER, U. (ed.) *Making Human Beings Human: Bioecological Perspectives on Human Development*. Thousand Oaks, CA: SAGE Publications, 2005: 5, 6, 9, 11.

24 PRILLELTENSKY, I. & NELSON, G. 'Promoting Child and Family Wellness: Priorities for Psychological and Social Interventions', *Journal of Community and Applied Social Psychology*, 2000, 10: 85–105, 87.

25 ROGOFF, B. *Apprenticeship in Thinking: Cognitive Development in Social Context*. Oxford: Oxford University Press, 1990: vii.

26 VYGOTSKY, L.S. *Mind in Society: The Development of Higher Psychological Processes*. Cambridge, MA: Harvard University Press, 1978.

27 DEPARTMENT for EDUCATION AND SKILLS (DfES) *Every Child Matters*. London: The Stationery Office, 2003; DEPARTMENT for EDUCATION AND SKILLS (DfES) *A Sure Start Children's Centre for Every Community: Phase 2 Planning Guidance (2006–08)*. London: Sure Start, 2005.

28 MASTEN, A.S. & GEWIRTZ, A. 'Resilience in Development: The Importance of Early Childhood', *Encyclopedia on Early Childhood Development*, www.child-encyclodedia.com/documents/Masten-GewirtzANGxp.pdf, March 15, 2006: 12.

29 JOHNSON, B. & HOWARD, S. 'Resilience – a Slippery Concept', *AEU (SA Branch) Journal*, May 26 1999: 8.

30 FONAGY, P., STEELE, M., STEELE, H., HIGGIT, A. & TARGET, M. 'The Emanuel Miller Memorial Lecture 1992: The Theory and Practice of Resilience', *Journal of Child Psychology and Psychiatry*, 1992, 35(2): 231–257.

31 GROTBERG, E. 'A Guide to Promoting Resilience in Children: Strengthening the Human Spirit', *Early Childhood Development: Practice and Reflections 8*, Bernard van Leer Foundation, 1995: 5.

32 PUGH, G. 'Policies in the UK to Promote the Well-Being of Children', in J. Scott & H. Ward (eds) *Safeguarding and Promoting the Well-Being of Vulnerable Children*. London: Jessica Kingsley, 2005: 46.

33 WERNER, E. 'Protective Factors and Individual Resilience', in J. Shonkoff & S. Meisels (eds) *Handbook of Early Childhood Intervention*. Cambridge: Cambridge University Press, 2000: 129.

34 HOBSON, P. *The Cradle of Thought: Exploring the Origins of Thinking*. London: Pan Books, 2002.

35 GAMMAGE, P. *Well-Being: the Generic Perspective; Power and Protection*. Adelaide: Department for Early Childhood Services, 2004.

36 LAEVERS, F. *Wellbeing and Involvement in Care: A Process-Oriented Self-Evaluation Instrument for Care Settings*. Leuven, Kind & Gezin and Leuven University Research Centre for Experiential Education, 2005.

37 LAEVERS, F., DEBRUYCKERE, G., SILKENS, K., SNOECK, G. *Observation of Wellbeing and Involvement in Babies and Toddlers*. Leuven, Belgium: CEGO Publishers, 2005: 6.

38 CSIKSZENTMIHALYI, M. *Flow: The Psychology of Happiness*. London: Rider, 1992.

39 NODDINGS, N. *Happiness and Education*. Cambridge: Cambridge University Press, 2003.

40 DEPARTMENT for CHILDREN, SCHOOLS AND FAMILIES (DCSF) *Children's Plan: Building Brighter Futures*. Norwich: HMSO, 2007: 33.

41 BUCHANAN, A. & HUDSON, B. *Promoting Children's Emotional Wellbeing*. Oxford: Oxford University Press, 2000: 232.

42 BERRY, D., FAZILI, A., FARHAD, S., NASIRY, F., HASHEMI, S. & HAKIMI, M. *The Children of Kabul: Discussions with Afghan Families*. Kabul, Save the Children UNICEF, 2003: 8.

Part 2

THE THEORY OF WELLBEING

3

The ABC of Wellbeing

A New Model

Wellbeing is a 'big' word, and it means different things to different people. Although government policy and guidance increasingly refers to the importance of wellbeing, its meaning is not usually explained, beyond a general state of 'doing well'. It is often used as a catch-all term loosely associated with good outcomes. Most early years practitioners would say they are convinced that wellbeing matters; so it is important to understand it – and to find ways of thinking about it that are helpful in our work.

Defining, determining and ascertaining wellbeing

What *is* wellbeing? What determines its development? And how do we know when we are seeing it? In trying to answer these big questions we are faced with the difficulty of thinking about an enormous and diffuse concept in realistic and useable ways. Distinguishing between what determines wellbeing, and what is the result of it, is also an issue. Consequences, as distinct from a model of wellbeing and how it develops, might include such things as energy, confidence, openness, enjoyment, happiness and calm.[1] And what about fundamental emotions such as love – and conversely, fear, hate, loss, jealousy, resentment, anger, and so on? These are beyond the model too. They are about the consequences of being in a state of wellbeing – or of not being in one. We need to break wellbeing down into separate categories in order to make sense of it; and yet, those categories must not be completely separated from each other because they are all interdependent.

This model of wellbeing is the result of six years of research – both my own and others' with whom I worked.[2] The model has three characteristics:

- It is simple, constructed around the familiar sequence of ABC.

- It is valid, having been tested in various ways with many adults and children over several years.

- It is holistic, addressing the wellbeing of the *whole* child or adult (rather than the more usual concept of wellbeing as referring to emotional development).

So this model of wellbeing is a straightforward, reliable way of thinking about the whole child. Although it encompasses the familiar aspects of child development – emotional, social, cognitive and physical – these are embedded in a new integrating set of four constructs that bring together how we feel – affect – with how we learn – cognition. The model offers a practical new way of thinking about holistic child development.

Chapter 2 reflected various approaches to describing wellbeing. Much of the confusion around the term 'wellbeing' seems to stem from the need to distinguish between three aspects of clarifying the concept.

1. Definition – what it is.

2. Determination – how it develops.

3. Ascertainment – how we know when we see it.

These are separate but related issues. This chapter addresses the first – what wellbeing is – while subsequent chapters are about how wellbeing develops, and how we know it when we see it. Here, a new model for wellbeing is introduced and described, consisting of four essential constructs. These are: firstly, agency; secondly, belonging-and-boundaries; thirdly, communication; and fourthly, physical wellbeing.

These four constructs are explained in some detail below. Agency and belonging-and-boundaries are 'states' of wellbeing; while 'communication' is at least partly about how wellbeing develops; and 'physical wellbeing' is different again, being at least partly contextual. The con-

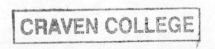

struct of agency will need more explanation than the other more familiar constructs. The model has its roots in Chapters 1 and 2, and has been tested with many children, families and practitioners in homes and in settings over several years. It is not, of course, the only way to think about wellbeing – simply one way.

A new wellbeing model

The 'what' of wellbeing is about the two *states* that define it: 'agency', and 'belonging-and-boundaries'. Having a sense of agency, and a sense of belonging-and-boundaries, are what a sense of wellbeing is about. These two constructs enable people to feel alright in themselves, and with other people, and to feel that they are reasonably 'coping'.

The 'C' construct of this ABC model stands for Communication. It refers not so much to a state, as to a *process*. The process of communication is a crucial determinant of wellbeing. Because of the social context of children's development and their need for reciprocal relationships, the many ways in which babies and young children learn to communicate do much to determine their wellbeing.

The bedrock on which these three ABC constructs of wellbeing rest is the underpinning construct of physical wellbeing. This is multi-faceted, encompassing both health and development, and the physical environment. Although often a powerful *determinant* of wellbeing (for instance, consider the effect on wellbeing of chronic lack of sleep, or conversely of a sound night's sleep) it can also be simply contextual – something to be aware of, but which does not make a profound impact on wellbeing. Examples might be a short-term gastric bug, or a bout of toothache.

Although these four constructs might be seen as theoretically distinct from each other, in real life they operate interdependently; and even theoretically they are interdependent. In using the model to make sense of our observations and experiences (see Chapter 7) we cannot treat each construct as entirely separate. A process of foregrounding and backgrounding the constructs is essential, such as that used by Carr in her explanation of learning dispositions.[3] We need to think about the wellbeing constructs not singly, but *in the context* of the others; perceiving the four constructs as quarters of one whole, rather than as four separate parts. It is like a cake with four main ingredients – leave out any one ingredient (or more) and the cake will not work. As the four constructs of wellbeing are, in real life, operationally dependent on each other, a genuinely integrating model is needed, in which one construct can be the focus of attention while at the same time retaining awareness of the others.

These four interdependent constructs – part states and part determinants – make up this definition of wellbeing. This is only half the story though. The other half of the story is about the mechanisms of wellbeing – how it develops, and how we can use, observe and assess it. The wellbeing constructs are explained here in a triangular 'hierarchy of wellbeing', reminiscent of American psychologist Maslow's well-known 'hierarchy of need'.[4] The four constructs in the wellbeing triangle are described, starting at the bottom of the model with 'physical wellbeing', and ending at the apex with the 'influencing' aspect of 'agency'.

The Four Constructs

The construct of 'physical wellbeing'

The physical wellbeing construct lies along the bottom of this model – the bottom line, so to speak. Physical development is a well documented aspect of child development,[5] and the relationship between child health and poverty is well established.[6] Physical development, always included in basic training to work with babies and young children, is comparatively straightforward to assess. There is, therefore, no need here to elaborate at length on this already familiar aspect of children's wellbeing. Most parents say that their bottom line for their children's wellbeing is that they should be healthy and happy, which sounds quite straightforward, especially in relation to health.

But there are, nonetheless, some complexities to explore. In this model, physical wellbeing is about the impact of the external, physical world on our internal sense of wellbeing, including our health. As well as being a determinant it is essentially a context of wellbeing development – the body's development, and the processes that impact on that development, such as sleeping and eating. The physical wellbeing construct also includes the external context: the environment dictated by a family's income, housing and neighbourhood.

However, the construct is also about determining *processes* of wellbeing development, sometimes going beyond context to make a more active impact. This is why it can also be seen as a determinant. We know that physical activity can lead to a sense of wellbeing; and so can some kinds of environment. Movement involving motor control of various kinds is an important aspect of this construct of wellbeing, making it both a context and a process.

It is important to bear in mind that the states of wellbeing – agency and belonging-and-boundaries – are not necessarily dependent on physical health. A person might be severely disabled, but nonetheless enjoy a strong sense of belonging-and-boundaries and agency.

In the wellbeing model, the physical construct literally forms the basis for the rest (see Figure 3.1).

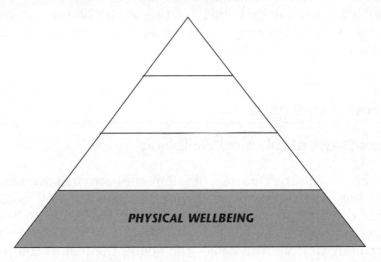

Figure 3.1   'Physical wellbeing' in the wellbeing model

Physical wellbeing here falls into two very distinct components, the individual and the environmental. On the one hand is the individual physical health and development component, incorporating familiar elements such as eating and sleeping, motor control, health routines, and managing illness and pain. Parents and carers sometimes struggle to manage these smoothly, with sleep and food being a frequent source of conflict; but when these things are going well, other aspects of wellbeing are getting an optimal chance to develop. On the other hand, the component that contains environmental elements may, for good or ill, make a profound impact on children's health and wellbeing: family income, housing, and the local environment.

Sometimes an illustrative example of a theoretical concept – or an element of one – can be helpful. Here is a real-life glimpse of Brianna, aged 16 months, with her mother Shauna, placed here with this explanatory purpose in mind. Similar glimpses of certain children are included throughout the rest of the book, drawn from various kinds of recorded observations. (The children's portraits can be seen in the Introduction).

> During the game of hiding the ball, Brianna has had her back to me. Now Shauna says to her 'Is your nose dirty?' and reaches for a paper handkerchief. Instead of wiping Brianna's nose as I had expected, she passes the hanky to Brianna, who wipes her nose herself and then hands the hanky back ... solemnly grown-up. She has managed really well but there is still a bit to do – Shauna says 'Shall I help you'? and Brianna says 'Yeh'.

Aspects of physical health feature regularly in parents' perceptions of their own wellbeing, too. How tired a person feels, and whether they feel fit and healthy, is often mentioned by mothers as they reflect on their own wellbeing. Eating and sleeping patterns for everyone, as well as the relentless pace of life with babies and young children, make a profound impact on wellbeing in families. These are big issues not only in relation to babies and young children, but also for adults.

Here is an extract from an interview with Kathleen, when her baby, Ivan, was nine months old.

> Interviewer: What do you remember about the first few weeks?
>
> Kathleen: (laughs) That it was living hell (lots of laughter).
>
> And it was just relentless, absolutely relentless.
>
> It was like, it was like, suddenly having no time for yourself. Three months of on-going jet lag. I mean it was hell.

In summary then, this construct is about the external and physical contexts and processes that contribute to a sense of wellbeing, including physical health. For children, their mothers and their families, the construct of physical wellbeing (as defined here with two distinct components) is both a determinant of wellbeing, and an essential *context* for the other constructs of wellbeing described below.

The construct of 'communication'

Communication is the central *process* that, in the cultural contexts of family, community and society underpins all emotional, social and cognitive development. This construct of communication is also made up of two elements: received communication, and expressed communication. It is about *processes* of active interaction, and is a key determinant of wellbeing. Communication is the driving process of 'companionable learning', the central mechanism whereby wellbeing develops (see

Chapter 4). While some perspectives of communication focus on the one-way transmission of information, in this wellbeing model the construct is essentially about processes of *connection* – the spoken and unspoken two-way conversations involving what is received, and what is expressed. Dewey's view was that communication leads to community: 'There is more than a verbal tie between the words common, community, and communication', using the word 'common' to mean shared, as in 'common sense'.[7]

The first language we learn to speak is the one that we generally refer to as our first language – for instance Urdu, English, Chinese, French, Swedish. But in reality our first language, for all of us, is body language.[8] Babies and young children use body language with their companions from birth, and we all continue to use it long after we know how to understand and use spoken language. The quality of our touch is an important aspect of our body language with children. There is a world of difference for a baby between the experience of a nappy change done briskly and impersonally, compared with one where the touch is carefully gentle, affectionate and respectful.

These kinds of interactions with people and things on a sensory level – using touch, smell and taste as well as seeing and hearing – are richly important aspects of communication, especially for children. This idea is exemplified by Reggio Emilia's 'One Hundred Languages of Children' exhibition,[9] in which children are shown to communicate in so many rich and diverse ways.

Here is Sasha, aged 10 months. Her mother Lara is talking to me, and her brother Zeb is with us too. Still mostly crawling at this stage, Sasha has been exploring the room looking for something interesting to play with. Now, without saying a word, she asks me to play with her.

> Lara, Zeb and I are all sitting on the sofa, and Lara begins to read one of the books from my bag to Zeb. Sasha crawls over to us but does not seem interested in the book-sharing. She holds on to my knee and pulls herself up, smiling deliberately at me in a lovely friendly way that makes me want to play with her.

The term for this tool of relationship, 'communication', is used here in the very widest sense. Not just about aspects of language acquisition and our relationship with each other, it is also about our interactions with the world around us, in ways that rely on all the senses. It is about how we find out what things are and how they work, by internally and externally questioning and interacting with the environment (including people). We do this exploration by using all our senses – they are our means of discovery.

It is also in these two-way communications, both with companions and with the natural world, that the seeds of moral development and spiritual growth are sown, in children's first-hand experiences of goodness. The seeds are sown in interactions with their special people, and in a growing awareness of the awe and wonder of our natural world.[10] Awareness of goodness and of right and wrong thus develop essentially through interactive processes of communication.

Representation is an important aspect of expressive communication, in which experiences of story-telling, of relaying and inventing stories, of making pictures and music, of moving and pretending are all active elements. In this observation Edward (age two years one month) and his mother Sophie are engaged in one of their favourite activities, playing with playdough together. Edward has an older brother of four years who is at Nursery this morning. Over a period of 15 minutes the subjects of their conversation – each one initiated by Edward – include wanting to get things right, not feeling happy, sharing a joke and fixing things.

Edward is choosing a plastic shape from the box, while Sophie sits at the table between them, drinking her tea. Edward chooses a lorry shape he calls Dizzy. 'Dizzy – eyes', he says, handing her the shape. Sophie says she doesn't think there is enough white playdough, they might have to use the red. 'Not red – white' says Edward. So they roll out the dough together and push down the cutter. 'Shall we see how this is doing?' says Sophie, picking it up and handing it to Edward. Edward looks at it critically. 'Not right – not big bit', he says, pulling off the dough from around the outside of the cutter. 'Get it out, mum'. 'OK, you push it out – nice and gentle', she says. 'Look, that's super!' But 'eyes', says Edward a little uncertainly, examining their handiwork. 'You've got eyes, you've got great eyes', she says, pointing to the dough. 'Great eyes' he echoes with satisfaction ... but then, looking at the dough lorry and shaking his head vigorously, 'Not happy, Mum'. 'Oh, I think she's happy' Sophie replies with cheerful assurance. 'No' says Edward determinedly. '*I* think she's happy' repeats Sophie, although with much less certainty.

As well as a fascinating use of language by Edward, this is interesting on another level. Sophie had told me that Edward worries about her not being happy (she carries a very considerable care role for their paralysed father, as well as for the boys), and that he often asks her 'Are you happy, Mum?' Perhaps this perspective makes sense of his sudden impulse to make her laugh.

Edward now breaks off a piece of the dough and squeezes it. Then, reaching over towards her mug that she is drinking from, he says mischievously, 'Mum, squashed it – in tea?' She replies 'No', pausing her drinking and shaking her head; and then, grinning at him, 'Not in Mummy's tea!' at which they both smile broadly at each other.

Now Edward reaches for an old pen lying on the table, and he and Sophie have a discussion about using it to make more eyes in a bit of dough, a nose – 'oooh, big nose' he says, and she laughs and says '*is* it a big nose?' – but after adding a mouth and some feet the pen comes apart. 'Oops!' he says, laughing, and she echoes 'Oops', and asks 'How are we going to fix that? How *are* we going to fix it?' Edward carefully slides the pen back together again, and says proudly 'Fixed it – fixed it, Mum'. He hands it to her, and she says 'Pretty much there, aren't we?' Then, handing it back to him, she says 'There, you've done it, you've mended it'. Whereupon he pulls it apart again, and they both say 'Oops!' and laugh.

So there are two components of the construct of communication in this model. There are those ways in which children and their companions receive communication – framed around the senses of listening, looking, touching, smelling and tasting. And there are the ways in which they express communication, for instance by body language, talking, visual representing, stories, music and moving. In the model this communication construct appears above the 'physical' construct as the second level (see Figure 3.2).

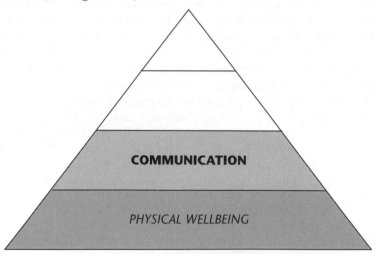

Figure 3.2   'Communication' in the wellbeing model

Babies tell us so much about how they feel, what they need and want, their contentment and discontent, their affections and fears. We have a great deal to learn from them about these things, and we learn by

watching and listening. This is why observing babies is so very important. Here is Ivan, aged nearly 14 months, with his mother. We see him
communicating his own feelings vividly.

> Kathleen sits Ivan up when the bottle is finished, and he climbs down and looks
> with a great deal of interest at the toys in the room. But Kathleen stands up with
> him saying 'We must just quickly do your nappy' which results in a shriek of
> protest and frustration. She carries him upstairs, and the protest continues in
> various more and less conversational ways until the nappy is done. Sometimes
> he sounds as if he is trying to reason with her, sometimes shouting at her, and
> sometimes gently bemoaning to himself.

We know that children are communicators, and that communication
works both ways with them, too. They both receive and make communications. And we know that even without language they absorb an
amazing amount about our feelings, needs and wants, our contentment
and discontent, our affections and fears.

Here is another glimpse of infant conversation, this time with Thomas,
who with his twin Jack is aged seven months. He seems to be telling me
about his toys; and is being remarkably communicative considering
that it is three months since he last saw me.

> Bianca puts Thomas into one of the little bouncy chairs, making sure that the
> suspended toys are within his reach. Thomas now spends quite a long time
> reaching for the toys, looking at them carefully and seeming to 'chat' to them.
> Then he looks at me and keeps up eye contact for several minutes. He is chat-
> ting to me now, apparently about the toys. I can only smile back at him, and
> after a while he turns back to the toys.

Communication, in the widest sense, is how babies and young children
explore their world. Communication is about the processes that determine the higher-order states of wellbeing.

The construct of 'belonging-and-boundaries'

'Belonging-and-boundaries' is a *state* of wellbeing. It is about having a
sense of belonging – with its accompanying boundaries. A sense of
belonging-and-boundaries is rooted in a sense of self, but here it is
about identity in relation to others – a sense of where you fit in. This
vital component of wellbeing is not only about bonding with the primary carer, but crucially rests upon attachment to another – or others.
As Underdown explains:

Bonding and attachment are different. Bonding is the binding love that a parent may feel for their infant, sometimes strongly even before he or she is born. 'Attachment' refers to the enduring 'tie' of affection directed towards a small number of close individuals, leading to pleasure in interactions and comfort by being close at times of stress. Babies become attached to familiar carers who respond to their physical and emotional needs ...[11]

The 'double' concept of belonging-and-boundaries in this wellbeing model emphasises the essential inter-relatedness of its two halves. Here we see Sasha's brother Zeb (now three years eight months) with Sasha (10 months) and their mother Lara. In Lara and Zeb's rough and tumble game in which Sasha is allowed to join, and in Sasha's subsequent need for her mother's attention, we can see how the two halves of the construct, belonging and boundaries, are operating together for Zeb. We also see Lara skilfully handling the needs of the two children.

Soon Lara and Zeb begin quietly to play a little tickling game. At first Sasha stays where she is (the other side of the room) but she is watching this carefully, and smiling broadly. The game has really caught her attention. After a few minutes she crawls over to where they are on the sofa, clearly wanting to join in. Lara skilfully includes her without taking the game from Zeb, and they all play a fairly gentle rough and tumble game for a little while. Both children are clearly loving every minute.

Now Sasha finds herself in her mother's arms (part of the game) and immediately relaxes, putting her thumb in her mouth and suddenly looking tired. Lara immediately comments on this, responding sensitively and letting her stay there quietly. Zeb is able to let her do this: although his game is now at an end, he is able to relinquish his mother without a fuss.

In this construct, the two halves go together, as if they were two sides of the same coin. Belonging – whether with a friend, in a family, or to a community such as a school or college – inevitably brings with it a set of expectations, rules and responsibilities. These, whether explicit or implicit, will be a very real aspect of the lives of all young children. Clearly, belonging in a family does not guarantee compliance with the expectations of others in the family; and yet, when children grow up with the clear understanding that boundaries and rules are the natural consequences of belonging, how much more their world makes sense. This is a similar concept to that of 'rights and responsibilities', with the difference that rights are externally granted, whereas a sense of belonging is an emotional experience. The boundaries that inevitably accompany a sense of belonging – whether to friend, family or community – can be promoted in terms of respect, awareness, familiarity with routines and rules, understanding the reasons for boundaries, and self regulation; right from the start.

We can see this balancing act in the close relationship between Kathleen and Ivan. Here (he is 14 months) he is just learning to walk, but still needs to hold on to things. He is intent on making his way around the room by holding on to one thing after another as he goes. Kathleen has arranged the room accordingly, and now is discreetly behind him to catch if necessary. She is being quietly encouraging, but giving him space to work out his problems himself. On his way he has encountered something he would like to touch, but suspects he is not allowed.

> Ivan reaches out for the circular metal aerial on top of the TV, touching it cautiously with his fingers and immediately looking at Kathleen to see her response. She smiles and shows absolutely no sign of reservation about him touching it. He does this checking process three times, always with the same result. Finally (but looking unconvinced) he moves past the TV table, heading for the edge of the fire guard ...
>
> ... (about 10 minutes later) back at the near corner of the fireguard, he approaches the TV table with caution, eyeing it thoughtfully, touching the little plastic guard on the corner of the table and checking out the aerial again with Kathleen. So far so good. Just behind the little TV table, in the corner, is an arrangement of dried leaves. Ivan's hand brushes the leaves, making a slight noise. This makes him look carefully at them, and he reaches out deliberately to touch them. But then Kathleen's voice behind him says 'Let's leave those'. He turns round to look at her, and she is saying again, seriously, 'Let's leave those'. With barely a glance at the leaves he immediately drops his hand and moves away from the table towards the middle of the room. There is almost a sense of relief and confirmation in the way he does this, as if he is thinking 'I *thought* so!'

In ordinary life at home, the connection between belonging and boundaries is frequently evident. Yet it may be worth reflecting that the way in which service delivery is usually constructed for young children and their families does nothing to support this inter-relatedness. On the one hand we have programmes and strategies to address people's need for a sense of belonging; while on the other, behaviour management strategies are usually seen as a completely different set of issues. While the fundamental importance of belonging – with its elements of attachment, security and trust – is deeply familiar to us in the early years, we are generally less fluent with ways of sharing with the youngest children – or indeed with older ones – a basic *reason* for the boundaries we propose. 'Because you belong' works a great deal better – provided attachment, security and trust *are* in place – than 'because I say so'; especially for vulnerable and challenging children. And if attachment, security and trust are not in place, our first task is surely to work to establish a genuine sense of belonging, as a first step towards putting in place the boundaries that are needed.

Over and over again a sense of belonging, acknowledged as vital in very early development, emerges in policy and guidance.[12] Much less evident is any association with the idea of 'boundaries' in relation to belonging – the expectations, routines and responsibilities that are an inevitable part of belonging. Boundaries are an inevitable consequence of belonging – an inescapable aspect of a close friendship, of family membership, of becoming part of a community. Sometimes these boundaries are made explicit between people, and sometimes they are simply an unspoken set of expectations. On an individual level they are usually negotiated between friend and friend or partner and partner – or indeed child and family. Belonging to a community such as a children's centre or school brings with it expectations that members will abide by the rules (whatever they are), while as members of society we are obliged to obey the law or face the consequences. This kind of belonging does, of course, necessitate shared understandings, collective agreement and commitment.

Here is a picture of a family in which books are very precious; and the youngest child, Rebecca, has grown up in the knowledge that this is the case. Here is Rebecca, now 16 months, with her mother Julie.

Rebecca has been watching me writing notes, and wants to do the same. She experiments with her crayons, on my pieces of paper. Next she finds a book and wants to write on that, but Julie says 'no' gently but firmly. She tries again, but Julie still says 'no'. Rebecca makes a very brief protest, but the 'no' is evidently what she expects. She lies on the floor sucking her thumb, evidently feeling weary. After a moment she is up again, wandering briefly around the room. Then she kneels down in front of Julie and lays her head in Julie's lap – a very appealing gesture. In this position she has a moment or two of what seems like totally secure relaxation.

Perceiving boundaries as a consequence of belonging strongly reinforces the idea of democratic collaboration between all who belong, in the formation of those boundaries. This has far-reaching consequences for consultation within the social structures to which children and families belong. What might be the impact on 'behaviour', in families, schools and other communities, if children were brought up to associate boundaries with belonging? What if they understood that boundaries are, in general, not random and persecuting – that the very reason for them is because you belong?

Returning to the 'belonging' side of the coin, the three elements of belonging are about a sense of identity (in relation to others), attachment to 'companions', including other children, and a sense of belonging to place. The first element of belonging, a sense of identity in relation to other people, is about the questions: 'How do I fit in with these people?' and 'How am I the same as them, and how am I different?' This is one of the most fascinating and important aspects of early childhood development, relating to individual attributes and encompassing issues of additional needs, race and culture.[13]

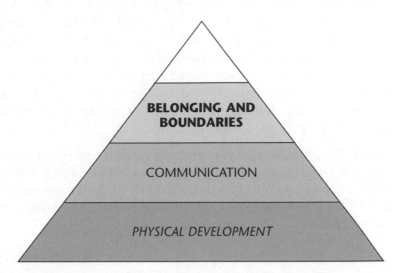

Figure 3.3 'Belonging-and-boundaries' in the wellbeing model

The second element is about the sense of attachment, not only to a primary carer or key person, but also to other important companions such as siblings, extended family members, and same-age friends.[14] Security and trust in others are also part of this picture. Finally, for many people belonging relates to places as well as people. Attachment to a place is often bound up with a sense of identity and overall belonging. When adults talk about their sense of belonging to a place, very often they refer back to a place in their childhood where they had felt secure.

One vital aspect of the other half of the construct – boundaries – is self regulation. The growth of self regulation has been described as a cornerstone of early childhood development that cuts across all domains of behaviour. Here is how Schonkoff and Phillips introduce the concept of self regulation:

> Human infants start life as remarkably helpless individuals who elicit powerful protective responses from their caregivers. On their own, they would die. In relationships with protective nurturing adults, they thrive. Supporting their development, however, requires sustained patience and adaption as infants move gradually and unevenly from needing help in order to do anything, to doing – and even insisting on doing – many things for themselves. Scientists have found it useful to capture this transition from helplessness to competence in terms of the child's growing regulatory capacity. What does this mean? Initially, it refers to the mastery of tasks that were accomplished by the mother's body when the child was

in the womb, but now must be accomplished by the child's body and through signaling needs to responsive adults. These tasks include everything from maintaining a normal body temperature to orchestrating physiology and behavior to conform to the day–night rhythm of human existence, to learning to soothe and settle once basic needs are met. Later, it means developing the capacity to manage powerful emotions constructively and keep one's attention focused.[15]

Much of this extract does of course refer to a child's physical development; this is one example of the way in which the constructs of wellbeing inevitably overlap. And yet it is also clear that self regulation, which is about adaption, relies essentially on a huge range of interactions between the child, other people and the environment. A sense of belonging with those others, and of the boundaries that are an inevitable part of that belonging, can be seen here as an important foundation for the process of self regulation.

Here is a real-life glimpse of this foundation, taking place on a Saturday morning with Dylan (age 21 months) and his father Peter. Dylan, the only child in the family at this point, is in full-time day care during the week. Now that it's the weekend they have made some toast, and are eating it together.

Peter and Dylan sit down to share their toast on the settee in the lounge. Dylan is looking very comfortable sitting on Peter's knee and cuddled up against his shoulder. The toast is on a plate on the cushion beside them. Peter hands a piece to Dylan and says 'Might be a bit hot though'. He eats some himself, blowing on the toast a couple of times first. Dylan looks doubtful, cautiously puts his piece not quite in his mouth, and says 'ah, ah, ah' in the same rhythm as Peter's blowing. Soon they are both munching companionably, keeping an eye on each other and the fair division of the toast.

After a while Dylan looks rather critically at the soggy, chewed fragment still clutched in his left hand, and reaches out with his other hand for the larger remaining piece. But Peter sees this coming and, pointing, says 'No, you've got a bit there still' – and they look at each other. Then Dylan puts the soggy fragment carefully back on the plate; so Peter says 'Have you had enough? No more?' But Dylan, looking hopefully at Peter, points to the bigger bit. And Peter picks up the rejected piece and says 'How about this one?' But Dylan shakes his head, and pointing at the bigger bit, 'chatters' urgently. Now Peter, watched anxiously by a round-eyed Dylan, bites off exactly half of the big bit and hands Dylan the rest. Dylan looks pleased – and finally picks up his rejected piece as well, so now he has toast in both hands.

The elements of 'belonging-and-boundaries' go a long way towards laying the foundations for inclusion. Early relationships are the vital context for the development of identity, attachment, security, trust, acceptance and respect. Within these relationships children learn about respect for their companions, becoming aware of their expectations. These are the elements of 'boundaries' that are hugely important for the development of wellbeing on all levels: between individuals, in families, in communities and in society. They are especially important in relation to the needs and rights of others. Lane explains what is needed: 'Lots of positive support for all children – about who they are, how precious they are, how much their culture, faith, language and skin colour are valued – promotes positive identity and gives positive messages to everyone that they belong'. Lane understands about really belonging in a multicultural society. She writes:

> Understanding what it is like …. means more than meeting and knowing people at work from a variety of cultural backgrounds or seeing them on the street. It includes friendships across ethnic and cultural boundaries, accepting differences between backgrounds as positive opportunities to learn more about our wider world and learning that such differences can be sources of enlightenment as well as things about which we can agree to disagree. It is about re-orientating our thinking and learning to care about and understand each other across cultural backgrounds and boundaries, listening to people's experiences and perspectives and building up trust.[16]

This celebration of rich diversity within families, communities and cultures involving acceptance and friendship leads to a genuine sense of belonging with others. Where – and when – better to put this approach into practice than in early years settings?

A vivid example, linking straight into the 'communication' construct, of how these essentials may be achieved with young children, is offered to us by Paley: '"When my babies do their stories," she (Lillian) had told me, "they really see each other. That's what we need to go after in school, the seeing and the listening to each other"'.[17]

Familiarity with routines and rules, and understanding reasons for boundaries, are essential for a child's emotional and physical security. Yet a child can only be familiar with routines and rules where they exist; and can only understand reasons for boundaries if they have been explained. This element of wellbeing is about understanding reasons, rather than obeying them. The subtle but crucial difference, about an emphasis on understanding rather than obeying, links back to the earlier proposition: that when children are able to perceive rules as a consequence of belonging – rather than as random edicts – they are likely to feel a great deal more comfortable and willing about accepting them.

This wellbeing construct works for adults too. Policies that call for genuine family and community involvement in early childhood services acknowledge that the wellbeing of a community is bound up with the active involvement of its members. Active involvement generates a sense of belonging, the ability and the disposition to make positive and responsible contributions, and a stronger sense of individual and collective wellbeing. Children living in such communities have the benefit of experiencing this positive model of belonging-and-boundaries all around them.

The construct of 'agency'

Agency is, like belonging-and-boundaries, a state of wellbeing. Our sense of agency relates to our internal sense of self, the inner world that drives our conscious and unconscious thoughts and actions, and how we learn. Our sense of agency makes a fundamental impact on our wellbeing. Having a sense of agency is about feeling that we can make a difference, for ourselves and for others.

In this model, agency is about three components. These are: a positive sense of self, generated by the familiar elements of realistic self esteem and confidence; our learning dispositions, coupled with an appropriate sense of pride and achievement; and our positive feelings about our ability to influence what happens, for ourselves and for other people. This final definitive influencing component involves internal decision-making, a sense of being able to make things happen, and a caring disposition that operates in relation to the self, and to others. The caring disposition involves a degree of self-knowledge, and the capacity to empathise with other people. So having a sense of agency – knowing we have the ability to make things happen – is about these three components: a positive sense of self; learning; and influencing. These components of agency make a significant impact on individual wellbeing, and, when experienced collectively, on wellbeing in communities.

Both the wellbeing states, 'belonging-and-boundaries' and 'agency', are about possessing certain attributes: dispositions, attitudes, states of mind. This is why they are classified as 'states' – as distinct from the determinants of communication and physical elements. A robust sense of belonging-and-boundaries makes a firm basis for the development of agency. Here again is the wellbeing triangle, with agency at the apex of the model – Figure 3.4.

A very informal explanation which sometimes helps to introduce the concept of 'agency' to parents and practitioners, is 'you (as "agent"), making a difference to your own life'. This works well in relation to all three components of agency: sense of self; learning; and influencing. An extended version of this informal explanation for having a sense of agency is 'feeling you can make a difference, to your own life and to other people's'; which is better, incorporating as it does the vital wellbeing element of caring for others.

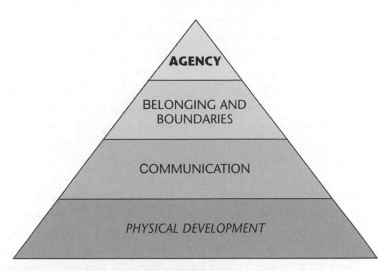

Figure 3.4 'Agency' in the wellbeing model

In relation to wellbeing the term 'agency' is an unfamiliar one, and some reservation has been felt in relation to its use in this model. For many parents and others, the meaning of agency has had more to do with institutions than personal attributes. However, the term 'agency' as defined above captures accurately and comprehensively the concept it describes, and both parents and practitioners have said that in the end they came to like the term, and to appreciate opportunities to think and talk about its various elements, gaining perspectives on their children that they felt they had not had before.

Here is Ivan, now aged 18 months, with his mother Kathleen on a hot and thirsty day in the back yard. I observed all the components of agency that afternoon, most of them in this episode.

Kathleen has the good idea of using the watering can to pour some water into a washing-up bowl with plastic toys for Ivan to play with. Ivan stands watching and holding a bucket. He leans forward to try and catch some of the water from the spout of the can in his fingers. While Kathleen goes to put the watering can down, Ivan peers into the bucket which has caught some water, and tips it up for a drink. Kathleen comes back, laughing, and asks: 'D'you want a bit of a drink? I think you're thirsty, what about a drink? I could have a cup of tea, and you could have a bit of juice'. She goes away towards the kitchen.

Now Ivan looks into the bucket again, and deliberately tips the last remaining drops of water onto the ground at his feet. He has rather a lot of clothes on, and

(Continued)

maybe is rather hot – in any case he would like a bit more water, maybe to play with and maybe to drink, so he sits down near the bowl. But although he can-walk, he is not yet easily getting up and down to the floor without something to hold on to. He has moved a step or two to hang on to the little tractor nearby in order to sit down, and as a consequence finds himself sitting not quite near enough to the bowl. It proves too heavy for him to pull towards himself, even with both hands. He looks around him, clearly wondering how to solve the problem.

A second go at sliding the bowl nearer to him is equally unsuccessful. He seems to figure out that he will need to stand up again, so that he can walk over to the bowl. So using the tractor again, he hauls himself up and then toddles over to the bowl. There, he crouches down rather than sitting, and fishes around in the water for a plastic cup. He dips it under the water to fill it, and then straightens up triumphantly for his drink. I feel like cheering, and am probably grinning from ear to ear. After he has had a drink, he holds the cup out to me; and just then Kathleen returns with juice in a proper mug. He politely has a drink from it too – though looking rather puzzled.

'Agency' is not, as we have seen, a straightforward term. Figure 3.5 shows further definitions of agency, this time derived from discussions with practitioners working with the youngest children and their families. The table further elaborates the three components of agency: 'positive sense of self'; 'learning'; and 'influencing'. Here, the elements build from the bottom up, so that influencing can be understood as the apex of agency, which is in turn the apex of the wellbeing model itself.

The definitions in Figure 3.5 go some way to highlighting the benefits of a strong sense of agency. Perhaps it is the diversity of the three components – positive sense of self, learning, and influencing – that make this such a powerful construct. Affect and cognition are brought together; and, like a chemical reaction, the combination generates the energy of the third component – influencing.

It is easy to see how these three components can lead to a strong sense of individual agency. The 'caring for others' element of influencing, with its associations with belonging-and-boundaries, indicates that influencing is where the seeds of active and effective citizenship are sown. Many of the elements in the construct of agency link in some way with other constructs and their elements, especially between agency and belonging.

An early experience of agency for almost all children, is that of learning how to get around to the things they want to investigate – initially by crawling or 'bum-shuffling'. Here is Sasha at 10 months and her mother Lara, who is commenting on Sasha's enormous satisfaction at being able to get around. Although included here as an example of agency, it could equally well serve as an example of developing physical wellbeing; and for coding (see Chapter 7) would appropriately be coded to both constructs.

WHAT IS AGENCY?		
AGENCY COMPONENTS	**AGENCY ELEMENTS**	**DEFINITIONS**
INFLUENCING ACTING ON THE WORLD	CARING DISPOSITION (FOR SELF AND OTHERS)	'Acting out of concern to make a difference' 'Appreciating wellbeing needs of self or others, and being motivated to act on that appreciation positively' 'Having the capacity to empathise with others' 'Understanding own needs'
	SENSE OF EMPOWERMENT: PURPOSE IN ACTION	'A sense of purpose in action' 'Having the vision and tools to achieve a goal' 'Having awareness and access to the tools to achieve a goal' 'Intentionally doing something for a desired outcome'
	INTERNAL LOCUS OF CONTROL/ DECISION-MAKING	'About making your own inner choices and decisions, not those of others' 'Positive attitudes to taking control' 'A settled and planned, intentional, attentive self-control'
LEARNING EXPLORING AND UNDERSTANDING THE WORLD	POSITIVE LEARNING DISPOSITIONS	'Habitual positive approaches to learning (such as listening, exploring, experimenting, persisting)' 'Confidence to explore, discover, learn from mistakes and develop' 'Wanting to find out, through exploration and experimentation'
	SENSE OF PRIDE AND ACHIEVEMENT	'A sense of satisfaction in one's achievement' 'The satisfactory conclusion of a mental or physical challenge' 'Succeeding at something you have set out to do' 'Awareness that you have made something happen that you wanted to happen, and you know why'
POSITIVE SENSE OF SELF BEING IN THE WORLD	REALISTIC SELF-ESTEEM	'Your personal inner feeling about yourself, based on real life' 'How you see yourself and are perceived by others' 'Feelings about self based on experience'
	CONFIDENCE	'An inner feeling of strength and hope' 'Positive belief in yourself' 'Willing to have a go'

Figure 3.5 Practitioners' definitions of agency

> Sasha was on the move all the time, crawling over to the things she was interested in, and pulling herself up when something was out of her reach. Lara told me that she has started walking, doing a few steps at a time. This ability to move around and get to things that she wants clearly gives her a great deal of satisfaction.

The ability of very young children to make their own decisions about where they want to go is an example of their internal decision making. This is about 'internal locus of control', a term that Gammage explained like this:

> The Locus of Control concept refers to the belief individuals have about their personal power and agency. The beliefs people have about the control they have in their lives, range from those who think that they play an active role in the successes or failures they experience (internals), to those who believe that the things that happen to them are the result of luck, fate or other people (externals).[18]

One last point about the 'influencing' component of agency is about making people laugh ... something from which many young children gain great pleasure. Making people laugh on purpose has all the elements of influencing. It gives us a sense of empowerment, and the knowledge that we have made something happen – it can even have a caring element. Here is Rebecca at 16 months, playing with these possibilities.

> Over by the toys again, with her back to us, Rebecca finds a rigid cardboard spherical toy that makes a deep cow noise when turned upside-down. Rebecca turns this before we have seen that she has it, then waits for the laugh, delighted when it comes. Next she briefly plays with the threading toy, just for 10 seconds or so. Then, with perfect timing, she makes a similar deep noise herself, watching us carefully to see the effect.

Putting the Constructs Together

Returning now to all four constructs of wellbeing we have, felicitously, a readily memorable ABC structure. 'A' for agency, 'B' for belonging-and-boundaries and 'C' for communication. See Figure 3.6 for the completed model.

While it is helpful to consider these constructs one by one, another look at the examples above can serve to remind us how integrated the constructs actually are, and of the need – mentioned at the beginning of this chapter – to think about each one essentially in the context of the others. The observations show how, in real life, there are almost certain to be two or more constructs in evidence at once. While the observation of Edward and his mother Sophie gave us a strong example of communication, the same episode could have been used to illustrate aspects of any or all of the other three constructs. His desire to get things right and the way he made his mother laugh were examples of agency; his attachment to his mother and her refusal to let him spoil her tea was evidence of his belonging-and-boundaries; and he needed to exercise considerable motor control to achieve his eyes, nose and mouth, and to mend the pen.

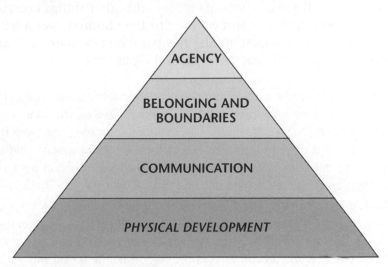

Figure 3.6 The ABC of wellbeing

Here is an example of all the constructs shown in one episode. We see Thomas again, still at 7 months. This extract shows how early all these constructs can be observed, even in the most everyday kind of experiences in the home. Thomas shows us: agency in his persistence with the mirror; belonging in the way he keeps an eye on his mother and his twin; communication in his eye contact and 'conversation' with his mother; and physical tiredness in his eye rubbing.

> While he plays, Thomas is keeping an eye on both Bianca and Jack – now and then checking out where they are. This involves craning around to look over his shoulder. Bianca is keeping an eye on him too, so that occasionally they are looking at each other. One of the suspended toys has a mirror on the bottom of it, and he manages to catch it with his left hand. Then he tries really hard to get it at the right angle so that he can look in the mirror. He persists with this for a long time, although it is too hard to manage on his own. Occasionally he rubs his eyes, evidently feeling a bit sleepy.
>
> Thomas has been making the chatty little noises to the toys all this time, but now he makes a different noise as he looks at Bianca, and she answers straightaway. There follows a brief, turn-taking (and of course unintelligible, except to them) conversation, with Thomas leading and Bianca echoing his sounds back to him.

The last observation in this chapter also shows all the constructs together, in an episode lasting only just over a minute. In this brief episode, Sasha, aged 19 months, is with her mother Lara and one of her brothers, Zeb. Both her brothers have additional needs, although they are very different from each other. Lara is expecting a new baby shortly and the family is planning to move, partly because there is just nowhere to put everything. In the front room there are piles of clothes and other things everywhere. Lara is calm; and responsive and warm with the children. Sasha herself is quite extraordinarily competent. She has baby blonde hair, is wearing a long-sleeved white T-shirt and a nappy, and looks cute.

> Sasha and Zeb are finishing their little bowls of ice-cream. Sasha is sitting on a gap in the floor between the piles of things, with her bowl on the floor between her knees, spooning melted ice-cream in with an adult dessert spoon and hardly spilling a drop. It is quiet in the room except for the click of spoons, and she is beaming at me between mouthfuls. After a while she looks round at her mother, who is sitting on the settee behind her, and they giggle.
>
> Now Sasha gets to her feet, clutching bowl and spoon carefully. 'OK then, don't spill it – do you want Mummy to do the last little bit?' Lara asks. 'I'll get the last little bit out for you … there we go, none left, is there? You going to put it in the kitchen then?' Sasha sets off across the floor, drops the spoon with a clatter, exclaims, and bends down to pick it up, grunting with effort and satisfaction as she stands up again. With her small shoulder she heaves open the door to the kitchen and giggles with satisfaction; but the baby gate across the kitchen area is closed. She tries to heave that too, but can't, and waits for Lara to come and open it.
>
> In the kitchen the dishwasher is open, and we can see that there are dishes in it. Sasha glances at them and turns enquiringly to Lara, making questioning noises. 'No, that's clean in there, that needs emptying doesn't it? Put it up on the side then'. Turning back, Sasha stretches up as high as she can, making effortful sounds. She can just reach high enough to push the bowl and spoon up onto the side next to the dishwasher. Then she turns and comes back through the baby gate, looking and sounding extremely pleased with herself.

The main purpose in having a wellbeing model is to make it possible to think about the best situations and experiences for nurturing resilient wellbeing. This is reminiscent of the three components of agency: being in the world ('sense of self'); exploring and understanding the world ('learning'); and acting on the world ('influencing'). We have started by identifying and exploring the constructs of wellbeing. Yet the ABC model is one half of the Wellbeing Framework. In the next chapter we look at the other half of the Framework, the processes of wellbeing development, and the rich situations and experiences that are most likely to generate it.

Key messages 🔑

- There are four wellbeing constructs: agency; belonging-and-boundaries; communication; and physical wellbeing.
- Agency and belonging-and-boundaries are about states of wellbeing, while communication and physical wellbeing are about determining it.
- This is an integrated model of wellbeing, that brings together how we feel (affect) with how we learn (cognition).
- Physical wellbeing forms the basis of the wellbeing model.
- Communication is the vital determinant.
- Belonging-and-boundaries are two sides of the same coin, and are inextricably linked.
- The three components of agency, the apex of wellbeing, are: positive sense of self; learning; and influencing.

Questions to think about and discuss 💬

1. How do babies and very young children communicate? Give some examples from your own observations. (Please note the exact ages of the children at the time of the observation.)
2. Why is it appropriate to think about 'belonging' and 'boundaries' as two sides of the same coin? How might you explain the idea to young children, and to their parents?
3. Using Figure 3.5 'Definitions of agency', try covering up the right hand column and inventing your own definitions for the elements. Which elements were difficult, and why?

Further reading 📖

LANE, J. *Young Children and Racial Justice: Taking Action for Racial Equality in the Early Years – Understanding the Past, Thinking about the Present, Planning for the Future.* London: National Children's Bureau, 2008.

This thoughtful and comprehensive book is a wonderful resource for practitioners, full of useful information and revealing insights. It is challenging, interesting, and constantly thought-provoking. Lane has a vision for the early years: 'As individuals we cannot make the world free of racism and a safe place to be, but we can do our very best to ensure that our early years settings are small models of what we would like the world to be'. The book is both inspirational and pragmatic. Once you have seen it you won't want to be without it.

BERNARD VAN LEER FOUNDATION (ed.) *Early Childhood Matters: Enhancing a Sense of Belonging in the Early Years.* The Hague, Netherlands: Bernard van Leer Foundation, 2008.

Early Childhood Matters is the Bernard van Leer Foundation's journal, beautifully presented and published twice a year. This issue carries 11 articles, all reflecting on the theme of positive identity and a sense of belonging as it relates to young children. It is a deeply interesting collection, adding many insights into this construct of wellbeing as the context of social inclusion and respect for diversity. Obtainable by visiting the Foundation's website at: www.bernardvanleer.org

UNDERDOWN, A. *Young Children's Health and Wellbeing.* Maidenhead: Open University Press, 2007.

In this elegantly written and highly informative book, Underdown approaches her discussion of wellbeing from the health perspective. She takes a broadly holistic approach to the big issues of health and wellbeing: transition to parenthood; foundations for social and emotional wellbeing; inequalities in early childhood; growth and nutrition; the impact of family change; child public health; children under stress; children's involvement in health; and listening to young children. These themes are comprehensively discussed in a very readable way.

References

[1] BUCHANAN, A. & HUDSON, B. *Promoting Children's Emotional Wellbeing.* Oxford: Oxford University Press, 2000.

[2] ROBERTS, R. *The Development of Resilient Wellbeing From Birth To Three,* PhD thesis, University of Worcester in association with Coventry University, 2007, http//eprints.worc.ac.uk/511/1/Rosie_Roberts_complete_thesis.pdf

[3] CARR, M. *Assessment in Early Childhood Settings: Learning Stories.* London, Paul Chapman, 2001: 43.

[4] MASLOW, A.H. *Motivation and Personality.* New York: Harper, 1954: 236.

[5] STEWART-BROWN, S. 'Parenting, Well-Being, Health and Disease', in A. Buchanan & B. Hudson (eds) *Promoting Children's Emotional Well-Being.* Oxford: Oxford University Press, 2000; UNDERDOWN, A. *Young Children's Health and Wellbeing.* Maidenhead: Open University Press, 2007; ALBON, A., MUKHERJI, P. *Food and Health in Early Childhood.* London: SAGE, 2008; DEPARTMENT for EDUCATION AND SKILLS (DfES) *The Early Years Foundation Stage: Setting the Standards for Learning, Development and Care for Children from Birth to Five,* Nottingham: DfES, 2007.

[6] SPENCER, N. *Poverty and Child Health.* Oxford: Radcliffe Medical Press, 2000.

[7] DEWEY, J. *Democracy and Education.* New York: The Free Press, 1966: 4.

[8] ROBERTS, R. *Self-Esteem and Early Learning: Key People from Birth to School,* 3rd edn. London: Paul Chapman Publishing, 2006: 11–12.

[9] MALAGUZZI, L. *The Hundred Languages of Children.* Municipality of Reggio Emilia: Reggio Children, 1996.

[10] DOWLING, M. *Young Children's Personal, Social and Emotional Development,* 2nd edn. London: Paul Chapman Publishing, 2005: 121.

[11] UNDERDOWN, A. *Young Children's Health and Wellbeing.* Maidenhead: Open University Press, 2007: 41.

[12] DfES *Birth to Three Matters: A Framework to Support Children in Their Earliest Years.* London: DfES, 2003; NEW ZEALAND MINISTRY OF EDUCATION *Te Whariki: Early Childhood Curriculum.* Wellington: Learning Media, 1996.

[13] LANE, J. *Young Children and Social Justice: Taking Action for Racial Equality in the Early Years – Understanding the Past, Thinking about the Present, Planning for the Future.* London: National Children's Bureau, 2008; WALL, K., *Special Needs and Early Years.* London: SAGE, 2006.

[14] DUNN, J. *Children's Friendships: The Beginnings of Intimacy.* Oxford: Blackwell Publishing, 2004.

[15] SHONKOFF, J. & PHILLIPS, D. *From Neurons to Neighborhoods: The Science of Early Childhood Development.* Washington DC: National Academy Press, 2000: 93.

[16] LANE, J. *Young Children and Social Justice: Taking Action for Racial Equality in the Early Years – Understanding the Past, Thinking about the Present, Planning for the Future.* London: National Children's Bureau, 2008: 135, 156–157.

[17] PALEY, V.G. *In Mrs. Tully's Room: A Childcare Portrait.* Cambridge, MA: Harvard University Press, 2001: 24.

[18] GAMMAGE, P. & KRIEG, S. *REFLECT: An Observation System for Teachers of Young Children.* Adelaide, SA: Department of Education and Training, 2001.

Companionable Learning

Companionable Learning: the Mechanism of Wellbeing

Knowing the theoretical constructs, components and elements of well-being does not go far enough to help us in a practical sense. This is only one half of the Wellbeing Framework. The crucial questions for early years practitioners are not only about what wellbeing is, but also about how wellbeing works. What are the situations and experiences in which wellbeing thrives and develops? We need some large signposts towards the ways in which all four interrelated constructs of wellbeing develop.

The main signpost for the development of wellbeing is something that can be called 'diagogy'; or, equivalent but more straightforward, 'companionable learning'. Companionable learning – the other half of the Framework – is the central process or mechanism whereby wellbeing develops. It is about learning in the widest possible sense, i.e. all of a child's development that flows from active engagement with the world and the people in it. It is about the way that a child – however young – and his or her companion learn together, in a mutual state of attention to each other. It is about 'sustained shared thinking' involving child and companion.

'Sustained shared thinking' was described in the Effective Provision of Pre-School Education (EPPE) Project in the following way:

> 'Sustained shared thinking' is where two or more individuals 'work together' in an intellectual way to solve a problem, clarify a concept, evaluate an activity, extend a narrative etc. Both parties must contribute to the thinking and it must develop and extend the understanding. It was found that the most effective settings encourage 'sustained shared thinking' which was most likely to occur when children were interacting 1:1 with an adult or a single peer partner'.[1]

In visual terms, in companionable learning the learners are side by side, with a shared preoccupation. Sometimes both child and adult are exploring something that is unfamiliar to both of them; while at other times the child may be exploring something unknown to him or her, while the companion is learning about that child's response to the unknown. Whichever it is, they are both learning – so that companionable learning essentially involves a state of mutual companionable attention, to each other and to the matter in hand. It is a mutual state of intersubjectivity that involves the child and the adult (or sibling or peer); both learning together in an equal, reciprocal dialogue. In the words of the Akan proverb, 'The hand of the child cannot reach the shelf; nor can the hand of the elder get through the neck of the gourd on the shelf'.

Companionable learning essentially involves communication. As Rogoff says:

> The process of communication, whether verbal or non-verbal, is a social activity that can be regarded as the bridge between one understanding of a situation and another. By its nature, communication presumes intersubjectivity – that is, shared understanding based on a common focus of attention and some shared presuppositions that form the ground for communication.[2]

Shared understanding is very evident in this episode of companionable learning with Dylan, now just two years old, and his father Peter. They are both engaged in Dylan finding out how the watering can works, although for different reasons. They have been clearing the garden and Peter has heavy-duty gardening gloves, one of which Dylan has appropriated. It is an extremely hot afternoon, and now they are just outside the back door in the blazing sun. They have a green plastic watering can, the kind with a long spout and a sprinkler on the end.

> Peter is showing Dylan how to hold the watering can by the handle with one hand and tip it up to make the water come out. They have both been holding the handle, but when Peter lets go Dylan does too, and the can clatters onto the concrete paving. Peter picks it up and shakes it to see if there is any water left in it, which there is – just a little. He stands it upright again. Dylan peers into it and, dropping Peter's glove that he has been holding in his right hand, reaches out with both hands and picks it up, one hand on the handle and the other under

the spout end. Now he can easily tip it, which he does, sprinkling the ground in front of his feet. Peter watches. All we can hear is the sound of water falling on the concrete, together with a woodpigeon nearby cooing gently in the heat.

Dylan tips the can until the very last drop is gone and Peter is saying

'Where's the water, it's all gone!'.

Then Dylan rights the can again so that he can look inside it through the hole in the top. He tips it again but doubtfully, and, as he thought, no water comes. He briskly holds the can up to Peter.

'More' he says, looking at Peter urgently. He points inside the can and says 'There'.

'More?' echoes Peter.

'Water' says Dylan again, now peering into the can again as if he'd like to climb right into it. 'Water'.

'You want some more water? More?' asks Peter. Dylan affirms with a grunt.

'I'll get you some more water then'. He disappears through the door into the house.

Here, Dylan's learning was supported by Peter, in a way reminiscent of Vygotsky's extremely influential theory in relation to children's learning, his 'zone of proximal development'. This refers to the gap between what children can do on their own, and what they can do in the company of someone more skilled or experienced, who might be a child or an adult. Vygotsky described how children can be supported in what they can nearly do by adults whose encouragement enables them successfully to tackle tasks they could almost, but not quite, manage alone.[3] In terms of helping us to think in practical ways about how to support children's learning, this is one of the most useful and far-reaching theories available to us. The distinction between this and companionable learning is one of focus: in the zone of proximal development, the focus is on the child's activity and learning, and the adult's role in supporting that learning. In companionable learning, both child and adult are partners in learning together.

In 2002, Trevarthen used the term 'companionship' in relation to learning, writing that infant research had led him to accept the view taken by Comenius, Vygotsky, Bruner, Rogoff and others, that 'education of the young that fosters enthusiastic learning will be collaborative ... it should grow in consistent relationships of trust and liking'.[4]

Trevarthen explored the concept of the mother as more than a protector, and a secure base from which to explore; but also as a friend and play-mate with whom the child can explore a 'common sense' of their world. 'From birth, a child's learning depends upon sharing his or her impulsive acting and thinking with other familiar persons, who them-selves are experimenters, discoverers, and communicators, eager to share what they think and do'.[5]

Companionable learning is an essentially interactive process. The learn-ers may not be learning the same things; indeed that would be unlikely, as any two people are bound to process incoming stimuli in different ways, depending on their previous knowledge, experience and under-standing. But the learners *will* be jointly involved and focused; and companionably engaged, interacting with each other in the process of their learning together.

Babies' and young children's companions

Who are babies' and young children's companions? They are the people (parents, and other adults and children) who see children regularly and know them well; the people who give them companionable attention, and to whom they are bound by love or affection. Often alternative care-givers, they have been described as 'the "kith and kin" who have remained relatively invisible in the child development literature'.[6]

Here is Dylan again, playing with his mother.

> In the room with the doors into the garden, Mya was throwing the little red bouncy ball towards Dylan, who retrieved it from the floor with a triumphant shout and threw it back to her. He was surprisingly good at throwing, almost always sending it in roughly the right direction – quite an achievement. This was exciting, and he laughed and shouted. Then Mya bounced it lightly on his head ... he shut his eyes tight, completely trusting that it would be fun and not hurt.

A reasonably comprehensive list of young children's possible companions might include: mothers, fathers, partners, siblings, aunts, uncles, cousins, grandparents, key people (in day care), peers, neighbours. In New Zealand, the single Maori word 'whanau' is used to describe all these important players in young children's lives. For some children a family pet such as a cat or a dog can become a companion. We have seen Dylan with his father and his mother, and now we see him with another of his companions, their neighbour's cat.

Earlier, Dylan had wanted Mya to open the garden doors, and when she did he had called through them. Mya said that he had been calling to the neighbour's cat, but it was nowhere to be seen. Now, when Dylan arrived at the doors, there it was, just outside and looking very friendly. Dylan called 'Hiya!' several times. Mya said that Dylan loves it and likes to stroke it gently. They opened the doors and Dylan was very quiet and careful with the cat, stroking it lightly and not making sudden noises or frightening it.

The downside of this moving relationship emerged a few months later, when Dylan and the cat were in the garden. In spite of his mother's and his aunt's best efforts to dissuade him, Dylan persisted in chasing after the cat, who clearly wanted to be left alone. Pursued to the bottom of the garden, the cat turned and warningly bit Dylan's outstretched hand. Dylan was confused and upset, learning that an animal companion cannot be trusted in the same way as a human one. But he still loved the cat!

Similar processes can often be seen between sibling or peer companions. The relationships are inevitably complex, charged with frequent small episodes both of companionship and jealousy, of fun and irritation, of love and loss. These kinds of companions probably do not carry the sort of 'unconditional positive regard' that characterises attachment relationships with parents or key people.[7] And yet sometimes the importance of these companionships cannot be over-estimated.

The twins Jack and Thomas, now aged 11 months, are very securely attached to their companionable mother. As well, they have a very special companionship with each other. While their mother is very careful to protect their individual identities, at the same time she nurtures their companionship with each other whenever she can. They sleep companionably together in a large drop-side cot, one at each end.

It is summer. The two boys, both wearing baby-grows, are sitting facing each other on a rug outside in the sun. Jack's is pale blue, Thomas is in navy. Jack has ear-ache, and later is distressed. Interestingly it is Thomas who is looking unusually solemn and thoughtful – maybe empathising with his brother.

Thomas is lying on his tummy, 'tortoise-like', while Jack is still sitting up. They both lean forward to look at a musical box (it is the kind they can carry around like a little suitcase, with a screen for moving pictures). Bianca has wound it up, and put down beside them. Jack points at it, and they both watch it together. After a minute Jack looks up at me and smiles, while at the same time Thomas gently takes the squashy cube that Jack has been holding – Jack is apparently

(Continued)

unconcerned – and rolls over onto his back to examine it carefully. Now Jack picks up the musical box and holds it on his lap to have a good look at it, but Thomas decides he'd like that too, and starts to reach for it. This time Jack protests, and Bianca comes to the rescue.

Five Companionable Learning Principles

The following five principles of companionable learning point us to the kinds of situations and experiences that children need, to support their developing wellbeing. While the principles themselves are described in this chapter, practical applications for children at home and in settings are explored in Chapter 5 Children's Wellbeing; Chapter 6 All to Play For; Chapter 8 Being Key Companions; and Chapter 10 Wellbeing and Integration.

First principle: companionable attention

Companionable attention is about those times when children feel that they are enjoying the full attention of their companions – a kind of 'mindfulness'. The importance of attachment theory has been well documented;[8] and 'mindfulness' is often a feature of a securely attached relationship. Holmes defines attachment like this:

> 'Attachment' is an overall term which refers to the state and quality of an individual's attachments. These can be divided into secure and insecure attachment. Like many psychodynamic terms, 'attachment' carries both experiential and theoretical overtones. To feel attached is to feel safe and secure. By contrast an insecurely attached person may have a mixture of feelings towards their attachment figure: intense love and dependency, fear of rejection, irritability and vigilance.[9]

While attachment originally referred to the vitally important relationship between the child and the parent – usually the mother – the term is now useful in a wider sense. With the expansion of care and education for the youngest children outside the home, a range of primary carers come into the picture, and the importance of loving and secure relationships not only with parents but also with, for instance, a key person in a setting is recognised. It is helpful that the key person approach is acknowledged in this way, although much needs to be done to bring together the theory and the practice of it. Features of attachment were elaborated by Dunn in relation also to children's siblings and peers.[10] I would argue that aspects of attachment may extend even further, to all a child's companions as defined in the section above.

It is interesting to consider how central the three 'ABC' constructs are to relationships based on mutual companionable attention, whether between child and child (peer or sibling), or child and adult. Both parties' sense of self and ability to influence is confirmed by the other. Belonging-and-boundaries are part of the fabric of the relationship, which takes place by way of communication in a range of forms – the many spoken and unspoken languages of early childhood.[11] Whether at home or outside the home, children constantly demonstrate their fundamental need for companionable attention.[12] They are extraordinarily good at soliciting this; and if unsuccessful in attracting the kind of companionable attention they profoundly need, they would often rather be accorded disapproving attention than none at all. The strength and continuity of this need is astonishing; as are the ways in which children mostly manage to obtain what they need.

Bianca's partner, who had known the twins only for a few months at the time, described their need for companionable attention like this:

> All games are, is paying them attention; and they feel the attention – see it. It doesn't matter what you play with them so long as they can feel the attention … so you don't have to play with them so long as you're looking at them, smiling, talking to them.

Here are three examples of children displaying their need for companionable attention, and their delight in it. We start with Rebecca's need for companionable attention from her father. She is 16 months.

Keith sits on the settee. After a bit more drawing, Rebecca picks up the clipboard with her picture on it and carries it over to where he sits. Putting it on Keith's knee she returns to fetch the pencils. At first she carries on drawing as she had been doing before, while the board rests on his knee and he and I talk over her head. But then she carefully holds a pencil in each hand and tries drawing with them both at once. Keith laughs and says 'Two hands at once!' Not looking at him but secretly smiling to herself – she has won his attention – she carries on drawing. In a while Keith gets up to do something in the kitchen. When he has gone, Rebecca gathers up her drawing things and follows him through. She sits down on the kitchen floor where she can see him, lining up the pencils beside her and balancing the clipboard on her legs stretched out in front of her. It fits just right between her lap and her ankles, perfect for carrying on drawing *and* keeping an eye on her father.

Now we have Hamza, aged two years 11 months, who wanted me – or perhaps, given the fairly recent arrival of his younger brother, needed me – to change my observing role into that of a companion. Here is how he skilfully went about securing my engagement with him – a skill he had developed with the many companions in his family.

> Hamza stands still and thoughtful in the middle of the room, and then says to me 'What shall we do?' After waiting a moment I answer, 'I don't know – what *shall* we do?' At this he looked entirely gratified, and I realise that of course my answer has let him know that I am agreeing that we *will* do *something*. Returning to the pile of toys he selects a large yellow dumper truck, and coming back says, 'Look this one, a big giant one'. Then he shows me how the dumper works, and the bit on the front where, 'Look, steam come out'. Then, whizzing past his mother on the way to fetch something else he says, 'Mum, I'm playing with her' – in much the same way that one adult might say to another, 'I'm going to be busy for a while'.

And here is how Jack, at seven months, succeeds in distracting his mother from her preoccupation with getting ready to go out.

> Bianca, who has been busy getting things together to go out, comes into the room and stands in front of their (the twins') chairs. She is looking around and apparently thinking about what she needs to take. Jack watches her, smiling broadly at her although she is not yet looking at him. But soon she sees him, and her face lights up as she greets him. Then he smiles even more delightedly, and chats back to her.

The observations in these chapters are taken from the data collected in the Companionable Learning study (explained in the Introduction). In all the hours of watching and filming there was hardly an observation where this (often mutual) need for companionable attention was not fundamentally the 'driver' of the responses that child and companion made to each other. Companionable attention was particularly rich for the development of all the wellbeing constructs. It was abundantly clear that children need familiar, affectionate, attentive companions, and they need regular time together with them in a safe environment where they can be comfortably, companionably together.

Second principle: agency in companionable play

Agency is at the apex of children's wellbeing – how they see themselves, the way they learn, how they make things happen. Consequently we need to see, as clearly as we can, how agency develops. This is especially important in relation to young children, whose situations and experiences in early childhood we know make such an impact on their later lives.

Extensive observation of young children's play proves to be very revealing in this respect. It is in play with their companions that they discover their sense of themselves. It is in playing that their learning dispositions take shape. And it is in their play that they experience what it means to influence what happens, both for themselves and for other people.

In fact, in children's play with their companions, two wellbeing constructs are strongly represented: the process of communication, as well as the development of agency. We can see them both clearly in this episode with Edward, aged two years three months, with his father Michael and his brother James, aged four years six months. Michael is permanently in a wheelchair, his companionship with the boys complicated by the challenge of working out his role as their father in this situation. Edward is sitting in front of the computer, wanting to play a game. We see how Edward's play, with its developing agency and communication, is rooted in his companionship with Michael and James, rather than his use of the computer itself.

> Edward was joined by Michael (his father), looking over his shoulder at the screen. James dragged his chair over to sit beside Edward, and just watched for a little while as Edward started on a game, and soon they were sharing it. After an instance of mouse skill on Edward's part, James said 'That's very good, baby!' in a genuinely admiring voice. A short while later, Edward said to James: 'You have a go', and let go the mouse for him; once again it was James's turn. When he came to the end of a sequence, Edward – who had been watching closely – remarked 'Ah!'. James asked 'What's happened now?' Edward replied 'Haha, what's happened now?' in the very same intonation, and then added 'Nice one!' To which James replied 'Nice one, baby!'

This is a lovely picture of a companionship in which the boys are playing with their identities using language, made all the more special in the context of what is sometimes quite a stormy companionship. Here is another glimpse of Edward and James, with their mother Sophie; this time not getting on so well. We see them battling for their agency, and we also see how that battle can adversely affect what is normally a very articulate relationship. Although as practitioners we often talk about children *playing* with activities such as jigsaw puzzles, we can see that this is not in fact play in the sense of child-initiated, spontaneous, imaginative, creative first-hand experiences.

> James and Edward are engaged in putting together a circular floor puzzle consisting of probably 50 pieces or so. James would like to do it all, but Edward wants to choose which bits he will do. Really, both children would like to have all the pieces to themselves.
>
> Soon Edward is looking dispirited, and James suddenly says he can do no more – perhaps they can both see that they are not going to get what they want. Sophie can see that if they join up both their efforts so far, they will at least have completed the edge of the puzzle, except for one piece; so she puts the two bits together for them.
>
> *(Continued)*

'I did the most' says James.

'No, I did the most' puts in Edward.

'Did you?' their mother asks.

'No he didn't' says James, shaking his head and looking worried.

Meanwhile Michael has wheeled his chair over to watch them.

'I think Edward probably did as much as you, James' he says. 'Where's that last bit, Edward?'

James quickly picks it up, Edward tries to take it from him, James holds on to it, Edward cries and hits out.

'James, don't be so rotten' says Michael. 'Let him have a go, please'.

James holds on to the piece.

'No, it's mine' wails Edward.

Between James putting the piece into the hole, and Edward trying to get it out in order to put it in himself, Edward's fingers get squashed. Now he is crying in earnest and recriminations ensue, with both companions looking miserable. Only a complete change of scene can cheer them up, and everyone is feeling rather ragged. In terms of wellbeing, no one's agency feels good, belonging-and-boundaries are frayed, communication has not helped, and Edward's fingers are hurting.

I am left with the thought that although jigsaws may be important for young children's development, they might sometimes cause more frustration than they are worth.

In the context of children's imaginative play, a child's companions may not be only family members, friends and neighbours, but also the 'persons' of the child's imagination – those actors in the alternative worlds constructed by the child. It is in this kind of play that agency really thrives: the heightened sense of self, the unconscious employment of learning dispositions, and the sense of purpose in action. Here is Sarah, aged four years six months, with her life-long companion Lion, clearly a sweet-natured and now rather threadbare-looking creature of only a few centimetres, with long dangly arms and legs and big paws.

Lion is grounded – he is not allowed out. This is because he is so precious a companion to Sarah that she would be intolerably miserable by day and unable to sleep at night if he were to go missing. Sometimes he is installed in splendour in an old pewter goblet in the middle of the kitchen table, legs dangling over the edge; and sometimes he is ruthlessly abandoned, falling to the floor as Sarah pursues other compelling interests. There is often an urgent search towards the end of the day when he has disappeared, having been discarded in some obscure place. Occasionally he is to be found sitting on the shelf opposite the door of the flat, waiting for Sarah's return.

But when Sarah is out, Lion is sometimes with her nevertheless. 'He's bounding along behind us – can you hear him roaring?' she asks. Then a roaring sound comes from the general direction of Sarah, and she says 'There he is!' When she gets home she has 'a moment' with Lion, holding him up to her face and pushing his paw against her nose, breathing in the precious smell of him with a far-away look.

Sarah's play with Lion is richly imaginative and complex. In it she is experiencing agency, learning much about belonging and boundaries, and exploring communication in which she uses two voices, her own and Lion's.

Not so long ago, 'play' was held by many to be a time-wasting alternative to the more important activity of learning. Now, play is acknowledged to be of vital importance for children's development; and yet, the reason *why* this should be the case is for many people, even early years professionals, sometimes not easy to articulate.

We are familiar with the idea that play is how children learn. The Early Years Foundation Stage Practice Guidance tells us that through play children can:

- explore, develop and represent learning experiences that help them to make sense of their world
- practise and build up ideas, concepts and skills
- learn how to understand the need for rules
- take risks and make mistakes
- think creatively and imaginatively
- communicate with others as they investigate or solve problems.[13]

We are less familiar with the idea of play as a prime mechanism for the development of young children's wellbeing – in particular their sense of agency. This 'bigger' idea incorporates within it the fundamental processes of learning. Learning relies heavily on a positive sense of self, and on the dispositions we bring to it; and our need to influence people and events is an insistent learning driver. Why is play – child-initiated, creative play – so important for children? Because, we can argue, it is a powerful way in which children develop the strong positive sense of agency that they need for their wellbeing. Play is an absolutely fundamental activity in which children's agency develops and thrives. If children are to develop a sense of wellbeing, they need to play. Chapter 6 All to Play For, elaborates on this argument.

Third principle: 'anchored' children

The things that children's companions say that their children most enjoy doing with them can be categorised almost entirely as situations that guarantee the companions' continuing physical presence, for instance going out for a walk, or bath time. Equally fascinating, is that they say their own best moments with their children are about situations that fall into the same category. On reflection this principle is hardly surprising, at least in relation to the children, given their need for companionable attention; as these 'anchored' situations guarantee companionable attention.

Figure 4.1 shows the answers that mothers gave to the questions, 'What are your child's best moments with you?' and, 'What are your best moments with your child?'

Children	Mothers	Other companions
• Doing things together, thinking together, helping mummy out. • Going out and running around. • Tickling games and stuff like that. • Chasing and cuddles. • Having a bath, having a massage. • Feeding herself. • Physical things. • Singing songs, rough and tumble. • Nappy changes, being bathed.	• Whatever he enjoys. • When he wants to do things with me. • Playing and making him laugh. • Things we do together. • Same as hers – when *she's* happy are my best moments. • Each others' undivided attention. • Seeing her enjoy herself. • Chatting with them, making them laugh.	• Going out together. • Playing in the park. • In the back-pack, watching what I'm doing. • Lovely cuddles. • TV or books together. • Football, TV, stories, rough and tumble. • Having my undivided attention. • When we play together, rather than when I play with her. • Bedtime games.

Figure 4.1 Children's and companions' best moments with each other

Almost all of these 'best moments' are companionable ones. This is how one mother described first her child, and then herself.

About her child:

> he enjoys when we do tickling games and stuff like that, he enjoys that – he enjoys it when I actually give him attention and play with him, do eye contact and peek-a-boo and tickle … often he's not really that interested in doing them unless you're doing it with him. Basically he wants your attention.

And about herself:

I enjoy the playing and being silly, and larger than life, and making him laugh. We are quite similar really.

Very often these companionable situations and activities took place at times when the adult was 'anchored' to the child, for instance at mealtimes, in the bath, or when sharing books. Here is a glimpse of Ivan's bath time with his mother Kathleen. Ivan is nine months old.

> Ivan has been in his bath for a while, with Kathleen seated on a low stool beside the bath so that she sometimes reaches in to play with him, and all the time is completely focused on what he is doing. He is lying back in the water, and has a little yellow plastic duck in the bath with him, which he has been trying for several minutes now to pick up – with his feet. Kathleen watches his efforts quietly, not attempting to help him with the task that he has so determinedly set himself. Eventually she plays 'This little piggy' with his toes, but although he seems politely to indulge her, he is not to be deflected from the duck. At last, hooking his right foot under it, he manages to lever it up just far enough for him to grab it triumphantly with both hands.
>
> 'Well *done!*' says his mother.

This kind of 'anchored' companionable learning is exactly what the youngest children desperately want and need.

Fourth principle: companionable apprenticeship

'Apprenticeship' may be the best-kept secret in early childhood care and education in relation to wellbeing. Apprenticeship is about cooking together, laying the table together, shopping together, rather than under sufferance, helping put the washing into the machine, joint efforts with the Hoover. For homes and settings fortunate enough to have a patch of earth it means digging and planting and watering and weeding – and harvesting. Children's routine involvement in real-life tasks is a wonderfully rich context for *all* the wellbeing constructs. 'Apprenticeship' situations do not just have great value for cognitive development in the conventional sense; they are a rich source of opportunities to develop all kinds of agency, a feeling of belonging and the consequent boundaries, a great deal of communication, and often the need for considerable physical skill.

Freddie is keen on apprenticeship. Now 21 months, he is seriously helpful, especially if it involves doing something together with a companion; things like washing up, tidying things into the place where they belong (usually), carefully opening and shutting doors for people, working the DVD, packing his bag – or feeding the cats.

Freddie is home from his child-minder, and his first job is to feed the cats. (This is not something he is likely to forget, as they tend to hang around under his feet when they are hungry, looking hopeful.) Dropping his bag on the floor of the passage he goes into the kitchen, to the low-down drawer where the cat food lives. The cats follow. Taking two pouches out of the box, he heads over to his father for help with opening them, then drags him to the cats' dishes on the floor of the lobby.

'No no' he says to the cats as they try to crowd in before the food is in the dishes.

He and his father together squeeze the cat food out of the packets into the dishes (Freddie is getting better at it) and then he stands back and watches them for a minute as they eat. Looking satisfied, he turns away, climbs on to the little truck nearby, and scoots away down the hall, grinning broadly.

'Apprenticeship' situations are anchoring, too. It seems that as a society we have adopted a view of household tasks that relegates them to chores to be minimised. This has happened in conjunction with the idea that children need a lot of stimulating activities for their development, and unfortunately 'apprenticeship' situations are not perceived to fall into this category. But although we ourselves might like to dispense with the 'chores' of daily living, this is certainly not the case for very young children. 'Apprenticeship' is quite the opposite for them, as it entails the very things in which children are most interested: being involved for the duration of a task with someone they love, doing important things just like they do.

This is not a new perspective, as we know from Isaacs, whose work early in the twentieth century led her to write:

> His efforts to understand the activities of the grown-ups and, above all, his interest in the primary biological processes of the household – the shopping and cooking and preparation of meals, the washing and cleaning and use of fire and water – form the nucleus of his intellectual interests. From these develops his wish to read and write; his later understanding of number and geography and history, of literature and the human arts, is rooted in these primary interests in the life of his family and home.[14]

In the context of increasing numbers of very young children spending long hours in day care this is a thought-provoking perspective. Children's companions at home – parents, extended family, even child-minders – who appreciate the potential of apprenticeship find it comparatively easy to explore this way of supporting the development of their children's resilient wellbeing. Making apprenticeship work in institutional settings may be experienced as more of a challenge.

Rogoff defined apprenticeship as 'children's routine guided

participation in socio-cultural activity'. She writes:

> The concept of guided participation refers to the processes and systems of involvement between people as they communicate and coordinate efforts while participating in culturally valued activity. This includes not only the face-to-face interaction, which has been the subject of much research, but also the side-by-side joint participation that is frequent in everyday life ... The concept of participatory appropriation refers to how individuals change through their involvement in one or another activity, in the process becoming prepared for subsequent involvement in related activities ... participatory appropriation is the personal process by which, through engagement in an activity, individuals change and handle a later situation in ways prepared by their own participation in the previous situation. This is a process of becoming, rather than acquisition.[15]

This model of activity – apprenticeship – is strikingly appropriate in relation to the lives of the youngest children at home; and as such is of great potential interest not only to parents but also to family day-carers, child-minders and any practitioners who work in homes to support families with very young children. The idea of apprenticeship carries considerable potential for settings too. Although it may be more challenging for practitioners in the context of a setting, to small children it is the same idea, and they love all the opportunities they are given, to be needed and to be real helpers.

Fifth principle: children's personal time and space

It was no surprise to be told by very many mothers, of the importance of their own personal time and space. Even a cursory reflection on the challenges of meeting a baby's needs in the first year is enough to generate a sense of wonder that so many mothers manage to enjoy that pressured and difficult time; and a reminder that so many others are seriously in need of a great deal of support. But it was thought-provoking to find that children, too, need their own personal time and space.

This principle relates, for example, to children's frequent insistence on doing things in their own time. We know that when we allow very young children to set the pace, it will be different from our own; altogether slower than our own, with a great deal of 'processing' going on. Here is Ivan, taking a good half an hour to walk once around the room, 'processing' as he goes.

Kathleen had told me about Ivan's exciting progress, that he is on his feet (never having crawled), able to make his way around the room by holding on to things – hence the arrangement of trucks, chairs, toy box, etc. Now Ivan looks with a great deal of interest at the inviting array of toys arranged in the room. Kathleen

(Continued)

puts him down standing on the floor holding on to the sofa seat at the far end. From there he surveys the room, apparently planning his route. He edges his way along the sofa in my direction, heading for a chair with a pop-up toy on it and clearly concentrating hard. But on arrival he ignores the toy and keeps going towards his chair, which is almost within reach. Continuing past the chair via the bars of the playpen, he finally makes it to the front of the fire-guard, which is very easy to catch hold of. He turns to Kathleen with a look of triumph, and she smiles broadly at him and says 'You *did* it!' He looks enormously pleased.

There follows a period of travelling from object to object, with Ivan eventually reaching the other end of the room via the other end of the guard, the little armchair, the baby-walker with bricks, and finally to the toy box. And with each arrival he seems immediately to be thinking 'Which way next?'. It is as if he is wholly engaged in relishing and developing the ability to make his own choices, and the skills involved in moving around on his feet – and he seems to be in a kind of bemused ecstasy about the process.

For some children, being able to reflect on and to 'process' their experiences was a normal element in the progress of their day; this was one kind of companionship – one style of interaction – that respected the children's need for this processing time, and the space to do it. But for others, throughout the day there would be a relentless stream of events, experiences, interactions and expectations which left them no time to think. The children's way of dealing with this was often a kind of frozen mental and physical stillness or 'absence'.

Some children's ready use of this strategy is concerning. This is their learned response to certain situations, the result of an over-emphasis on stimulation that was thought to benefit children's optimal development in the early years. Yet what will be the effect, in the primary classroom or indeed the playground, of this learned response? Will these children habitually employ this now-familiar strategy of 'switching off' in the face of an overload of stimulation?

Here is Brianna at 19 months, taking plenty of time to think about her doll.

Brianna carries the doll over her shoulder, walking to the far end of the room and turning around to sit down on a cushion facing me. After letting the doll fall to the floor, she expertly scoops her up again to her shoulder with one hand, while she examines the mobile phone she is holding in the other hand, exactly in the same way that she has seen her mother reading a text message. Putting the phone to her ear she 'listens' with a far-away look in her eyes, then with a little sigh turns back to the doll and puts it down again beside her. She pats its knee thoughtfully and seems to be considering for a while what to do next. The TV is on very low in the background but otherwise the room is quiet and there is no sense of rush. Brianna herself is taking her time.

After a minute or two of patting and thinking she leans over and looks carefully into the doll's face. Then she straightens up, and 'phones' again briefly, watching the doll as she does so, as if asking for advice. Then picking up the doll again with the same confident one-handed movement, Brianna stands up and walks back across the room with it.

As adults we sometimes use reading – or at least, appearing to read – as a kind of 'cover', to give ourselves time to think. Here is Alena doing just that. She is two years and two months, and is in her day nursery with her key worker, Julia.

Alena gives the 'Postman Pat' book to Julia expectantly, clearly wanting her to read it. Julia does this, telling the story simply to Alena, who is sitting on her right. Then, aware that she is needed by another of her children, she hands the book back to Alena, who seems still to be thinking about the story she has just been told. Standing in the middle of the room but apparently unaware of the busyness of small children and adults around her, she idly balances the spine of the book in her left hand while she flicks through the pages by running her thumb gradually down the right-hand cut side of the pages – a gesture most often to be observed in bookshops and libraries, by people who have had a lifetime of flicking through books to find the page they want.

Children need time to 'process' their experiences, just as we do. It is this reflective activity that generates an internal locus of control, and a sense of empowerment. It also enables children – and adults – to develop a sense of purpose. These things are important elements of wellbeing, and result from those inner conversations that are one of the vital aspects of communication – communing with oneself.

Key messages

- Wellbeing develops through the mechanism of companionable learning.
- Babies' and young children's companions are all those who see them regularly and know them well; and to whom they are bound by love or affection.
- Babies' and young children's wellbeing depends on companionable attention.
- Children's agency develops in companionable play.
- Companionable learning is *most* satisfying for both children and adults in 'anchored' activities.
- Companionable 'apprenticeship' in frequent 'real life' situations helps resilient wellbeing to develop.
- Children need personal time and space as well as companionship; just as adults do.

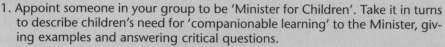

Questions to think about and discuss

1. Appoint someone in your group to be 'Minister for Children'. Take it in turns to describe children's need for 'companionable learning' to the Minister, giving examples and answering critical questions.
2. Describe one of your observations of a child playing, where you could see agency developing. Give the child's age, and explain what you mean by agency.
3. What are your own favourite 'anchored' situations in your work with young children? Can you think of others that you could introduce?

Further reading

CSIKSZENTMIHALYI, M. *Flow: The Psychology of Happiness*. London: Rider, 1992.

The author of this fascinating book, an American psychologist, focuses on the positive aspects of human experience – feelings of concentration and enjoyment that he calls 'flow'. His exploration of what it is that generates happiness in the human condition resonates with the companionable learning processes described in this chapter.

DUNN, J. *Children's Friendships: The Beginnings of Intimacy*. Oxford: Blackwell Publishing, 2004.

With many vivid observations of children's relationships drawn from extensive research, Dunn documents the peer companionships of early childhood; showing how their imaginative play with each other helps them to explore their own and alternative worlds. This lovely book portrays children as companions to each other.

HUGHES, S. *Giving*. London: Walker Books, 1993.

This magical book for children shows the young heroine with a series of companions with whom she exchanges 'presents': a kiss and a cuddle, a painting and a piggy-back, a cross look or a smile, or a seat on the bus. Enlivened with Hughes's unmistakeable illustrations, it is a superb glimpse of companionship in action.

References

1 SYLVA, K. *The Effective Provision of Pre-School Education (EPPE) Project: Findings from the Pre-School Period*. London: University of London Institute of Education, 2003: 3.
2 ROGOFF, B. *Apprenticeship in Thinking: Cognitive Development in Social Context*. Oxford: Oxford University Press, 1990: 71.
3 VYGOTSKY, L.S. *Mind in Society: The Development of Higher Psychological Processes*. Cambridge, MA: Harvard University Press, 1978: 84–87.
4 TREVARTHEN, C. 'Learning in Companionship', *Education in the North: The Journal of Scottish Education*, New Series 2002, 10 4.
5 TREVARTHEN, C. Stepping Away from the Mirror: Pride and Shame in Adventures of Companionship: Reflections on the Nature and Emotional Needs of Infant Subjectivity, in C.S. Carter, L. Ahnert, K.E. Grossman, S.B. Hardy, M.E. Lamb, S.W. Porges & N. Sachser (eds) *Attachment and Bonding: A New Synthesis*, Vol. 92, Dahlem Workshop Report. Cambridge, MA: The MIT Press, 2005: 58.
6 WERNER, E. Protective Factors and Individual Resilience, in: J. Shonkoff & S. Meisels (eds) *Handbook of Early Childhood Intervention*. Cambridge: Cambridge University Press, 2000: 123.
7 ROGERS, C. *On Becoming a Person*. London: Constable, 1961.
8 BOWLBY, J. *Attachment*. London: Penguin Books, 1969.
9 HOLMES, J. *John Bowlby and Attachment Theory*. London: Routledge, 1993: 67.
10 DUNN, J. *Young Children's Close Relationships: Beyond Attachment*. London: SAGE, 1993; DUNN, J. *Children's Friendships: The Beginnings of Intimacy*. Oxford: Blackwell Publishing, 2004.
11 MALAGUZZI, L. *The Hundred Languages of Children*. Municipality of Reggio Emilia: Reggio Children, 1996.
12 TREVARTHEN, C. 'Stepping Away from the Mirror: Pride and Shame in Adventures of Companionship: Reflections on the Nature and Emotional Needs of Infant Subjectivity, in C.S. Carter, L. Ahnert, K.E. Grossman, S.B. Hardy, M.E. Lamb, S.W. Porges & N. Sachser (Eds) *Attachment and Bonding: A New Synthesis*, Vol. 92, Dahlem Workshop Report. Cambridge, MA: The MIT Press 2005: 58.
13 DEPARTMENT for EDUCATION AND SKILLS (DfES) *The Early Years Foundation Stage: Setting the Standards for Learning, Development and Care for Children from Birth to Five*, Nottingham: DfES, 2007: 7.
14 ISAACS, S. *The Educational Value of the Nursery School*. London: The British Association for Early Childhood Education, 1954: 20.
15 ROGOFF, B. *Apprenticeship in Thinking: Cognitive Development in Social Context*. Oxford: Oxford University Press, 1990: viii, 142.

Part 3

EVERYDAY WELLBEING

5

Children's Wellbeing

The last chapter was about companionable learning, the mechanism for wellbeing development. This chapter is about everyday companionable learning, drawn from evidence collected across a range of homes and settings. Taking a universal perspective, it is also written for people who live and work with 'looked after' children, and those with additional needs and heightened vulnerability. All four 'A's of everyday wellbeing have particular relevance, too, for those children whose behaviour sometimes challenges us.

When they are awake, and whether they are alone or with others, children are learning all the time – although not necessarily learning what we imagine, or what we would like them to be learning. Here we explore daily wellbeing situations and experiences for babies and young children, at home and in settings.

The Four 'A's of Everyday Wellbeing

These four 'A's of everyday wellbeing are the structure around which most of the rest of this book is built. They are applicable in a range of situations, reflecting the observations and structuring of wellbeing and companionable learning in Part 2 that underpin the Wellbeing Framework. The four 'A's are about anchored attention, authority, apprenticeship, and allowing children the time and space they need.

Anchored attention

The idea of anchored situations was introduced in Chapter 4, with examples given by mothers about themselves and their children at home. Anyone living with a very young child will recognise their need to stay with you, wherever you go; and to their delight in opportunities to 'pin you down'. This process of anchoring is at the heart of the 'belonging' half of the belonging-and-boundaries construct of wellbeing, as anchored situations directly feed children's and companions' sense of belonging.

Because babies and young children thrive on 'anchoring' with loved companions – indeed, we might say so does the child in every adult – the idea is also important for children when they are in settings. Children (and companions) do not necessarily need to be physically anchored, as after a while anchoring can work as a mental process. To be 'camped out in the key person's mind' is the wonderful phrase for it invented by Elfer, one of the three authors of *'Key Persons in the Nursery'*.[1]

The situations and experiences described in this chapter are recognisably a collection of the youngest children's favourites, and this has much to do with their anchoring potential.

Authority

Like the other three 'A's of everyday wellbeing, this one only works appropriately in the context of companionable attention. This element of everyday wellbeing is absolutely not about a rigid, authoritarian approach to young children. It is about an authoritative 'gentle but firm' style of companionship with children that can be an especially helpful foundation for children's sense of belonging-and-boundaries. It reflects the 'boundaries' half of the belonging-and-boundaries construct.

Authority involves a companion's 'sure touch'. It is about companions being reliable, regular and consistent; and trying always to do what we have said we will. Underpinning it are the processes of establishing routines and rules, and gently but firmly sticking to them as long as they are appropriate. It is about saying yes as often as we can (this is very important); but when we say no, meaning it. In families and communities it involves being clear about values and what they mean in practice.

None of this is easy to achieve, and for companions supporting developing wellbeing it is always likely to be a journey. But thinking about belonging and boundaries as essentially interdependent does make it easier for everyone. Using 'authority' in this companionable sense means that many of the situations described below can help develop and support the wellbeing of everyone involved.

Apprenticeship

Another aspect of companionable learning introduced in Chapter 4 was apprenticeship – children's active companionable involvement in everyday tasks that they normally see adults doing. It is often referred to as 'helping' by the children themselves.

Clearly relevant to everyday life at home but also extremely helpful in settings, this concept is a good example of the potential strength of child-minders in family day care. Child-minders are well placed to involve children appropriately in everyday real-life activities such as cooking and cleaning, gardening and fixing things. Larger settings, too, can build up children's participation in this way. Apprenticeship does, of course, involve anchored attention. Again, many of the situations described in the sections below will be apprenticeship ones, especially when they are approached in a way that involves the idea of companionable learning.

The examples in Figure 5.1 help to explain what apprenticeship is, and what it is not. Those in the right-hand column may have valid purposes, but they are not about apprenticeship.

Across the diverse cultures in our society, it would appear – as a generality – that the more westernised a culture, the less likely is it to contain apprenticeship as part of its child-rearing practices. In westernised cultures there is a much more explicit division between those things that are appropriate for children, and those that are in the domain of adults. In relation to expanding day care for children in the west, apprenticeship activities – even when their importance is understood – are harder to organise in institutional day care settings. Perhaps one of the reasons why apprenticeship is not, at present, an important part of childhood in the west, is the insistent focus on children's independent achievements, rather than on their companionable ones. Going some way towards redressing this imbalance would be helpful for children's wellbeing.

Apprenticeship is ...	Apprenticeship is not ...
A child helping a companion with real washing-up that needs doing.	A washing-up activity by the children in a water tray; 'pretend' washing plastic plates and cutlery from the home corner.
Children and companions tidying up together.	Encouraging a child to do something useful, such as tidying up, while the companion watches.
A child and companion going shopping together, with a shared purpose relating to the child's experience, and a good deal of interaction between them.	A companion taking a child to the shop, but the child does not know the purpose and is not included in the processes involved.
A child and companion mending a broken object together.	A child waiting while a companion mends something the child needs.

Figure 5.1 What apprenticeship is, and what it is not

Allowing children time and space

The first and most importance 'allowance' of this kind that children need is time to play. This aspect of wellbeing has a chapter all of its own in Chapter 6 All to Play For.

Both at home and in settings, children need 'somewhere to call their own' – even if only their own peg and shoe bag, or a particular area of the bedroom. Many children treat their buggy and – if they have one – their car seat as their own space too. For them, being in these places can often involve 'down-time', the mental space to process what has been happening. This idea was introduced in Chapter 4 too.

Listening and looking are important ways in which children learn, but often they do not have enough time to do these things in worthwhile ways. Figure 5.2 highlights what worthwhile looking and listening involves.

Worthwhile looking means ...	Worthwhile listening means ...
... taking it slowly	... taking it slowly
... talking about what you see	... asking questions, not just answering them
... looking again and again	
... looking at details	... listening to your friends
... looking at mysterious things	... listening to yourself
... looking at beauty	... listening to difference
... looking at pain	... listening to agreement
... looking with your hands as well as your eyes	... talking about what you hear – not the sounds but the meanings
	... listening with an open heart

Figure 5.2 Worthwhile listening and looking (derived from Rich et al.)[2]

Reflection is an essential part of any learning process. Mothers are sharply aware of their own need for this kind of reflective mental space, perhaps because usually they do not get enough of it. There is less acknowledgment of children's equally pressing need for 'time to call their own'. Sometimes these needs can be solved in one go. Here are Freddie (two years 11 months) and Ellie (14 months) with their mother Kathy.

Freddie is lining up his lorries and trucks across the kitchen floor. Ellie (to Freddie's irritation) has been very actively trying to help, but now she is in the green sling on her mother Kathy's back. Kathy has been miles away for a few minutes, chopping up vegetables for soup, and Ellie also has that dreamy far-away look that is not so much about being sleepy as being miles away too. Now Kathy finishes chopping and tells me that Ellie seems to need this mental space. Sometimes, like today, they don't go out, and she has found that if she doesn't put Ellie in the sling for a little while now and then, Ellie becomes frantic and wild. I ask if Kathy gets back-ache, and she says no, because she has used the sling all along and her muscles are used to it. She says it gives her quiet moments too, knowing that Ellie is safe. Sometimes Ellie drops off and then Kathy can put her down in her cot; but sometimes a little 'dream time' is all she needs and then she's ready to play again.

When children	experience the four 'A's, they ...
... feel anchored	... experience a sense of belonging ... have an attentive companion with whom to share communications about their world
... live with *companionable* authority	... are likely to feel good about themselves ... develop an understanding of the need to respect people and places ... are aware of expectations, familiar with routines and rules, and understand the reasons for boundaries
... are engaged in everyday apprenticeship	... are likely to learn useful skills and feel proud of their achievements ... become appropriately involved in routine household tasks ... can learn about making decisions and making things happen ... can learn about caring for themselves, and caring for others ... understand about the occasional need for 'a right way' to do some things ... want to learn looking and listening skills because they need them
... are allowed time and space	... can think about what they want to do ... can think about themselves and others ... can develop a sense of belonging to place ... find self-regulation more manageable ... can listen, look, touch and smell, at their own pace ... can think back over what has happened have time for feelings of awe, wonder and mystery

Figure 5.3 When children experience the four 'A's

Figure 5.3 demonstrates that when children experience the four 'A's, their agency, belonging-and-boundaries and communication are all most likely to thrive.

About Food

Now we come to three groups of practical examples of everyday well-being. The first group, about food, is relevant both in homes and in settings. In these examples, anchoring and apprenticeship are the main characteristics, and routines will also be important. A certain amount of 'down time' waiting for results may be involved too.

What children eat, and where their food comes from, is one of the most fundamentally important aspects of their early childhood. From breast or bottle feeding to discovering what their favourite meals are made of; from learning where the ingredients come from to how to cook them; and from laying the table to clearing up, young children are usually deeply interested in being involved. This is seriously real life on a day-to-day basis, and they can join in with so much. But the satisfaction of the four 'A's is not necessarily automatic. It is less a question of what children are doing, more about the companionable ways in which these things can be done together.

Shopping

Here is Jimmy, aged nearly three years, at the supermarket with his mother Angela.[3]

Jimmy and his mum have had fun choosing their shopping together, and now they are at the check-out. Jimmy is sitting in the front of the trolley. They have a conversation about having to wait patiently in the queue.

'Now finish shopping?' says Jimmy questioningly.

'Yeah, we have to wait' his mum replies. 'We can do our shopping in a minute. Mummy's going to put them on here first' (indicating the conveyor belt).

'When we get to the other end' she says, pointing, 'You can help me pack them'.

After a while the shopping has been packed into bags and paid for. Angela picks up a heavy bag in each hand and says to Jimmy 'Come on, let's go'. But Jimmy is holding up his arms to be carried.

'I can't carry you Jimmy' she says.

Jimmy, sounding tired, suddenly weeps loudly.

'I can't carry you' Angela repeats, and holding out one of her already laden hands, she suggests 'Hold my hand'.

Jimmy ducks the bags and nearly manages to grab hold of her around the waist.

'No, listen' Angela says. Surrounded by trolleys and other shoppers, she crouches down and talks to him calmly. Later I see them walking contentedly side by side through the car park.

When they get home they will unpack the bags, decide what to eat today, and start to get it ready. Jimmy and his mum have always done things together, and he knows all about feeling anchored and engaged in everyday activities. This glimpse of supermarket shopping shows how hard it can be with small children though.

Here is another way of managing doing the shopping, especially with a younger baby. We glimpse Ivan at nine months with Kathleen, off to the supermarket. What we see also supports wellbeing, but differently. Here, it is about the opportunity for 'down-time' in his very own space, the pushchair. The brief observation note tells us that

> Ivan is very at home in his pushchair, and more observational and reflective than interacting.

A trip to the corner shop, while not actually getting the main shopping done, can be a good experience for wellbeing.

> Freddie is excited because his father has promised to be home earlier than usual from work, so they can have tea together. But Kathy has realised that they are out of milk and there is nothing at all special to eat, so they are off to the corner shop.
>
> 'Hold on to the pushchair Freddie' says his mum.
>
> It is only five minutes' walk away, and with Ellie in the pushchair they are walking slowly along the pavement, chatting about the birds they can hear in the hedge. Then Kathy says, more to herself than to Freddie,
>
> 'If only we had thought about this earlier, we could have made some cookies for Dad'. But Freddie says, 'Can I pay?'
>
> Freddie, who knows where in the shop Dad's favourite biscuits live, goes to fetch them, while his mum picks up the milk and some bananas. In a moment they are at the counter, and mum gives Freddie the money to pay. The lady behind the counter knows Freddie very well, and smiles at him cheerfully.
>
> 'Having a party then?' she asks.
>
> 'Dad' explains Freddie.
>
> 'Ah I see' she says, now smiling at Kathy and handing her the change.
>
> 'Hold on to the pushchair Freddie' says his mum. 'We don't want to be late'. They walk more briskly back up the road, and when they get home there is Dad just crossing the road from the bus stop.

Here, Freddie was anchored to holding the pushchair and helping his mum with a real task. In the slow walk down to the shop they had time to think about what they are doing – Kathy to regret not having thought about tea earlier, and Freddie to make sure he gets to give the money to the lady in the shop.

Growing things to eat

Growing things to eat can be quite straightforward so long as the project does not become too ambitious, at home as well as in settings.

Most settings are fortunate in having space somewhere outside, even if only enough for a few grow-bags for tomatoes. A minor harvest of herbs can be grown on a window sill, and bean sprouts are easy and cheap if there is space in a warm, dark cupboard. Children love being companionably included in this kind of simple food-growing. They love talking about what they are doing, having to do it properly, and the achievement of having helped to grow something that everyone can eat, too. At best, growing things involves all four 'A's of everyday wellbeing.

Here we see Adam, aged 26 months, in the Children's Centre with his key person Jen. Adam's satisfaction is almost tangible.

It's Adam's turn to look after the tomatoes this week, and he and Jen are getting ready to water them. Adam has fetched the watering cans and now he climbs up on the stool beside the sink. While Jen holds the can steady under the tap he watches the water level rising in the can, turning off the tap at exactly the right moment.

'Good – there!' she says to him. 'Shall we pick the other one up too? Yeh, yeh?'

Adam watches while Jen swaps the two cans over and holds the second one steady, waiting for Adam to operate the tap.

'Yeh, yeh?' asks Adam, turning to look at her and using exactly the same cadence that she just has.

'More – yeh!' she says encouragingly. They watch the water until Jen asks 'Turn it off?' and Adam carefully does so.

'Well done' she says.

'Yeh, yeh' he says again, climbing down from the stool. Jen carefully hands him the can while he continues his now triumphant 'yeh, yeh, yeh'.

Once he has a firm grip on the can he smiles broadly and walks away with her towards the door.

Preparing for meals

A few weeks later, about the time Adam's tomatoes are ready to eat and he is busy arranging tomato slices on a plate to share around the group, Harriet, aged 20 months, and her child-minder are making cheese sandwiches for lunch.

Harriet is sitting in her high chair with her bib on, a chopping board on the table in front of her. Susan uncovers the bowl containing the chopped-up cheese and holds it out to Harriet saying 'D'you want some?' Harriet takes a few little bits in her fingers and puts them in her mouth, suddenly looking very cheerful. When she has swallowed them, Susan helps her spread margarine on two slices of bread. Then Harriet adds a few small pieces of cheese.

'Oooh, lots more, Harriet!' says Susan, adding a big heap of cheese to Harriet's tiny one. Harriet gets the idea and picks up a fistful. Soon there is plenty of cheese, and Susan points to the second slice of bread.

'Now … that one needs to go on there … that's it, pick it up!'

Harriet seizes the bread in both hands, consequently finding it right in front of her face.

'Ah!' she says, taking a bite. 'Ah' says Susan too. Between them they manage to get the slice into the right place, and pat it down. Susan carefully cuts the sandwich into four smaller ones, and says

'Now we need a plate, don't we?'

Putting the plate down next to the chopping board, she says 'Pop them on there' and 'Woops!' as the first sandwich falls apart in Harriet's grip. Exercising admirable restraint she encourages, but manages not to take over, until eventually the transfer process has been completed entirely by Harriet.

'Lovely' Susan says. 'D'you want to eat them now?'

She laughs as Harriet takes a big bite.

'Mmm' says Harriet happily, her eyes sparkling and her mouth very full of cheese sandwich.

Laying the table is full of possibilities, too. What with counting up how many people will be eating, finding the right amount of the appropriate cutlery and plates, collecting things to drink out of, and getting it all on the table in the right place, there is much to think about. It can be a very satisfying companionable task. This is how it was done in Maria Montessori's school in Rome in 1913, described through the – initially rather critical – eyes of American Dorothy Canfield Fisher.

I was watching the four little girls who had now at last finished their very leisurely meal and were preparing the tables for the other children. They were about four and a half and five years old, an age at which I should have thought children as capable of solving a problem in calculus as of undertaking, without supervision, to set tables for twenty other babies. They went at their undertaking with no haste, indeed with a slowness which my racial impatience found excruciating. They paused constantly for prolonged consultations, and to verify and correct themselves as they laid the knife, fork, spoon, plate and napkin at each place. Interested as I was, and beginning, as I did, to understand a little of the ideas of the school, I was still so under the domination of my lifetime of over-emphasis on the importance of the immediate result of an action, that I felt the impulse to snatch the things from their incompetent little hands and whisk them into place on the tables.

But then I noticed that the clock showed only a little after eleven, and that evidently the routine of the school was planned expressly so that there should be no need for haste.

The phrase struck my mental ear curiously, and arrested my attention. I reflected on that condition with the astonished awe of a modern, meeting it almost for the first time. 'No need for haste' – it was like being transported into the timeless ease of eternity.[4]

That impulse to 'snatch things from their incompetent little hands' is surely one that afflicts us all from time to time. We saw Susan overcome it as she wisely waited so that Harriet could struggle successfully with her collapsing sandwiches.

Companionable meals

When people sit down to eat together they are – for the duration of the meal – anchored. Unhurried mealtimes are not only better for the digestion, they enable companions to think and talk as well as eat together. Table manners can be a battleground with young children; but this is often because good manners are expected too young, before children have had enough opportunities to understand the boundaries involved – and possibly because it is so easy to forget that children learn from what we adults do, far more than from what we say. Regular (not necessarily daily) mealtimes for the youngest children and adults together, right from the start, can be very good for wellbeing. This is an easy way for children to absorb the cultural life of the families and communities to which they belong.

Here is nursery dinner time in a New Zealand Children's Centre. We see educators Shelley and Linda with a group of three-to-five-year-olds. The sense of collective wellbeing around the table today is very strong.

The children – about eight of them – have washed their hands and are sitting down around two tables pushed together in the playroom. A delicious smell comes from the kitchen. Shelley hands around bowls of macaroni Bolognese.

'Yum' she says enthusiastically, so that the children join in. 'Kate's made a special'. Before they start eating, Linda asks Max 'What's that song you were singing, that you said you'd got at home?' Max stops the show with a wonderful Maori clapping chant, ending with everyone cheering and clapping together. 'Yeah, cool Max!' says Linda.

Shelley explains that they give the children responsibilities – things like returning and scraping their plates, helping to tidy up, sweep, wipe tables. She and Hau have been talking about dogs, while the others listen. Now Shelley says to them all: 'D'you know, Rachel's got a dog', and to Rachel she says, 'You tell Hau what your dog's name is?'

'Sammy' says Rachel, and 'Sammy' echoes Shelly – 'and what colour is Sammy?'

But before she can answer, 'I'm frightened of dogs' Hau interjects.

Several children chime in now, but Shelley says to them firmly, 'Hau's telling you that he's frightened of dogs'. And turning back to Hau she adds:

'But you weren't frightened when Kate from the kitchen brought her little puppy in – you weren't frightened'.

Hau holds up his hands to show how small the puppy was, and says 'I'm frightened of *big* dogs'.

'Right' says Shelly, nodding. 'You're frightened of *big* dogs'. And listening to his rather uncertain reply, she guesses 'You'd be frightened if you saw a dog at the beach?'

Hau nods vigorously. 'Swim away' he says cheerfully, making arm movements.

'Ah, you'd swim away – yeah', Shelley confirms, smiling and nodding too.

They are still sitting around the dinner table, tucking into bowls of creamy rice pudding. It's nearly rest time. Linda says 'I'm really tired – gosh I'm tired, I need to have a sleep too. Who will give me their bed?'

'You can have my bed' says Robbie, smiling at her. Linda says

'Oh Robbie, you are so kind. Thank you. Can I?'

Robbie nods, looking proud.

'Will you sleep in it too?' Linda asks him. Robbie nods again and she adds 'It'll be that squashed! Who will tuck us in and pat our back?'

'Mummy' suggests Robbie confidently.

'But Mummy isn't here!' says Linda. They all look thoughtful. 'Maybe Pat will – maybe our friend Pat will tuck us in and rub our back'.

Picnics

Eating outside is wonderful for all the four 'A's. Having a picnic need not involve a major expedition; just stepping out into the garden or the park works well. In changeable or cold weather, eating just outside the house or flat means it's easy to run for cover. With this approach, picnics can be quite frequent happenings.

Picnics can be very good for all the four 'A's. Getting picnics ready and clearing them up can be done in an 'apprenticeship' way. Children who especially need to feel anchored will be happy sitting in their pushchair to eat, or close to people on a rug, and if they want to wander around while they munch, that's good time and space for them. Of course that is only alright if they are safe, which brings in the need for authority.

Here is Mrs Weston with a small group of four-year-olds, outside on a summer day.

It is warm and mostly sunny today. In the sky over the nursery garden there are huge white clouds. 'Come on then Shane – don't get left behind' calls Mrs Weston as she leads them over the grass in a little line towards the hill. (This is not really a hill, just a heap of earth that the builders left behind one time, and then the grass grew over it. It is a small, round, flat place that has been the scene of many stories, games and picnics). The children and Mrs Weston are each carrying a little package wrapped up in foil and sealed with a label on which they have written their name. At last they are all sitting on a rug on the top, and can see over to where some of the other children are playing. They unwrap the sandwiches – one each – that they only wrapped up a few minutes ago after they had finished making a huge pile for the visitors coming later. 'Can't get mine out' says Shane after a moment. 'Oh no!' says Mrs Weston. 'Can anyone help Shane?'

While they eat, they talk about their morning and all the things they did to make the sandwiches – and Mrs Weston tells them about the visitors who are coming later. After they have put all the bits of foil and unwanted sandwich into the rubbish bag she says

'We'd better go back in soon. Joanne might need a bit of help with the clearing up, don't you think? Tell you what though, let's do something special first. Just look behind you – is there a space for you to lie down carefully on your back? You need to have the sun behind you.'

With her back to the sun she lies down herself, adding 'Like this'. The children all lie down too, and there is a little silence. Then Mrs Weston says 'I can see three big clouds and a little one'. And then after a moment she says 'What a funny thing! What does that little cloud remind you of?'

Lost 'food' opportunities

What might be lost wellbeing opportunities in relation to food? An obvious item for this section is the dearth of opportunities for children to eat companionably, from their earliest years and throughout their school lives – possibly their whole lives. The television has done much to militate against companionship at mealtimes. All too often family furniture no longer includes a family-size kitchen table, the focus of much apprenticeship and around which families could sit for meals. Now, all too often, the focus is the television.

Reasons for eating together at home are about opportunities to involve children in companionably preparing for a meal and clearing it up, families having thinking and talking time together, and chances for children to experience some of the pleasures of belonging in the family, and the consequent boundaries.[5]

For settings, the point is made in the New Zealand anecdote above, where the nursery dinner described was so very different from the hectic noise, haste and impersonality of school hall 'canteen' dinners.

Old Friends

'Old friends' refers to objects and familiar activities as well as people. This is about children and their long-time companions feeling anchored with each other; and also about deeply familiar books and stories, songs, rhymes and music.

Companions

For many children old friends do, of course, include grandparents and other older family companions. These people are often in an optimal position to offer anchored companionable attention, not usually having to juggle quite so many things at once, in the way that parents do. One of the greatest joys of these relationships for many older companions is to find themselves comparatively frequently (compared, that is, with when they themselves were parents) in a position to offer the kind of anchored companionship that most young children eagerly welcome.

Here is Sarah, aged three years, on holiday with her family and anchored to her granny.

Sarah's granny Rachel has come on the holiday too, and they are up and out in the lane early because Rachel says if you're quiet that's when you see rabbits. On the way out Sarah has picked up Rachel's belt, and now, holding one end firmly, she attaches the other end to a loop on Rachel's trousers. It is like a dog lead. 'Now I've got you' she says as they walk along. 'You can't escape'.

The next day everyone walks over to the next village, and Rachel is still allowing herself to be anchored. Sarah loves being completely in control of her, and sets the pace. Sometimes Rachel is allowed to take the strap off her trouser loop (where, actually, it is not entirely comfortable) and hold it in her hand; but always Sarah has one end, and she the other. This game persists spasmodically throughout the holiday, and for some weeks at home afterwards. Fortunately, Rachel is quite happy being anchored to Sarah, who knows that being good company is the way to keep her granny happy and so to keep the game going.

Books and stories, songs, rhymes and music

Babies and young children sharing books with their companions is a widely recognised strategy for anchoring – recognised by small children, that is. How familiar is the peremptory, relentless and sometimes puzzling request to 'Read it!' Often this is not only about the book itself, but also – or sometimes even mainly – about needing anchored companionable attention. Children learn very quickly 'what works' to anchor their companions. If that's what they need, then books and stories usually work a treat.

Experiences with books, stories, songs and rhymes often involve a reflective element, and in these favourite companionable situations the establishment of routines and consistency can be a major source of pleasure for children. In the aftermath of caring for a pet, or when sharing a favourite book, opportunities often arise to discuss values such as caring and trust, responsibility and reliability.

A great deal of information is available about the importance of regularly sharing books and stories, songs and rhymes with babies and young children right from the start.[6] These experiences with 'old friends' are centrally relevant to everyday wellbeing.

Dylan does lots of book sharing with his mum. Here he shows his resulting ability to choose and use books himself, and his understanding of how important it is to look after them. He is 19 months.

Dylan has been playing with the posting box but then, finding a boy beside him holding a book, he tries rather tentatively to take it. Naomi kindly says 'No, no Dylan', and reaching into the book box she takes out another book and hands it to Dylan instead. After both she and the other child have moved away, Dylan goes over to the book box, puts the book back, and takes out another – one of his favourites that he often chooses when he and Naomi cuddle up and look at books for a while together. Holding it carefully, he sits down with his back to the wall, turns it around so that it is the right way up, and opens it at the first page. After looking at the book for several minutes he gets up to put it back into the box (at the same time picking up one that is lying on the floor and returning that too) before he chooses another one.

Sitting down again in the same place as before, he discovers that this book has a slightly torn page with a loose bit, and he begins curiously to pull it several ways, tearing it a little more in doing so. Then he seems to be thinking about mending it, trying to fit the torn but still attached shape neatly back into the gap it has left. At this point Naomi notices what is happening, and calls over to Dylan not to tear it. He waves at her in response, and she comes over and takes the book from him quite briskly, saying it needs mending. Dylan is completely accepting of this, and watches her as she takes it over to the worktop to fix it.

After a moment, Dylan gets up, moves over into the middle of the room, and stands watching the mending process. Eventually it is done, and Naomi hands the book back to Dylan saying 'There you are, all done'.

Book sharing is a far cry from story times with all the children on the carpet around the teacher's chair. Group story time is a very different experience for children from book sharing, which is characterised by a close intimacy. 'Book sharing brings you close. It's a very nice feeling to hold a very small baby and read to them'. 'They like the rhythms and sounds of your voice'.[7] Songs and rhymes, which have a very special value of their own, can be about anchoring too.

As well as opportunities for anchoring, books, stories, songs, rhymes and music can be 'old friends' in their own right. Once they become firmly established in a child's experience they provide a familiar, predictable, pleasurable security. As the song goes: 'Make new friends, and keep the old; one is silver and the other gold'.[8]

Pets

Sometimes a pet becomes something much more for a child – a real companion. The definition in Chapter 4 of children's companions is relevant here: people whom children see regularly and know well, who give them companionable attention and to whom they are bound by love or affection. Many family dogs and even some cats fit this 'companion' definition.

Helping to care for creatures is mostly something very young children do with a companion, and helping take responsibility for pets can be about apprenticeship. Creatures – from rats and hamsters to chickens and goats – can be a strong element in the life of a setting. Being on a rota of shared responsibility for the unhurried care of each creature involves all four 'A's, and can be an important and sometimes memorable experience for children.

Sometimes burials are needed. Here are Kelly and David, aged four, with Mrs Weston, helping her to bury Furry, the nursery hamster.

Kelly and David have found just the right box for Furry in the junk drawer. They line it with a special piece of paper, and Mrs Weston puts Furry carefully in. 'That looks just right for him doesn't it?' she says. 'On with the lid?'

(Continued)

This morning they had a talk about Furry being dead, and what that means. It has been Kelly's and David's turn to look after him this week, and Mrs Weston says it's not their fault that he has died. She says he was very old, and hamsters don't last very long so she had thought he might die soon.

Mrs Weston says that now Furry's gone, she could just wrap him up gently and pop him in the bin, but Kelly and David don't want her to. David helped once before when the goldfish died, and they buried it in the special place in the little side garden under the tree by the hedge. They decide that the best thing is to bury Furry there too, and Mrs Weston says that if they do that he will gradually become part of the garden earth. 'If we put him there we can go and think about him when we feel sad' says Kelly.

Looking very solemn, Kelly carries the box carefully outside and Mrs Weston and David follow with the spade and trowel. They go across the garden and through the little gate. Over by the hedge Mrs Weston has already dug a deep little hole. They crouch down round it. 'In he goes then' says Mrs Weston, looking expectantly at Kelly. David says 'I want to do it'. Mrs Weston says, 'Why don't you both do it?' So between them they put him down into the hole, and look up to see what Mrs Weston will do next.

'Now we need to cover him up', she says. 'But first shall we have a little moment to say goodbye to him? You can shut your eyes and think about holding him and what his fur felt like, and remember him how he was. Would you like to do that?' They shut their eyes, and for a minute it's very quiet under the tree with the distant sound of the other children playing beyond the gate. Then Mrs Weston hands the trowel to David and says 'Would you like to do the first earth?' He scoops a trowel-full from the earth pile beside the hole and drops it in. 'Kelly's turn now' she says, and he hands her the trowel. After she has dropped in some earth, Mrs Weston says briskly,

'Right. Now I'm going to finish covering this hole, and then we can make a special sign saying Furry is buried here. Off you go and play now, and I'll call you when I'm ready'.

Mrs Weston's quiet authority about what to do gave David and Kelly the opportunity to 'process' the death of the hamster. She held the situation together for them while they sorted out what they felt and what they wanted to do. This was a healing, containing episode for them, when it might have been a distressing and confusing one; and they were able to feel that they had discharged their responsibility for Furry honourably. In the ABC of wellbeing terms it had been a rich experience.

Odd jobs and fixing things

'Odd jobs and fixing things' has an apprenticeship element too. A leisurely time at home with Kathy doing useful jobs and fixing things is

Freddie's favourite kind of morning. Freddie is two, and likes not having to rush out, not having to manage without her – and he likes the satisfaction of finding out about things and making them work. Here they are on one such morning. Ellie, who is still a baby, is having a nap.

Kathy and Freddie are in the kitchen, having just finished hoovering the hall. Freddie helped. Kathy has put the kettle on (Freddie hopes this means a biscuit) and he has tipped his wooden train track onto the floor. He fits together some of the pieces, and finds the bag with the engines and trucks.

'Would you like me to give you a hand with some of that track?' asks Kathy. He nods, and watches while she does the tricky bits, then helps her complete a figure of eight track with a bridge over the top and the track underneath.

'There you are' she says. 'Try not to break it'.

Freddie gets the bag with the engines and trucks, and sorts them out on the track so the magnets work. Soon he has a train that is heading for the bridge. Over it goes, round the bend, and back underneath. But no, the biggest, best engine, that has come from another set, does not quite fit under the bridge. Kathy sees the problem and decides to offer help quickly before frustration sets in. She looks carefully at the underside of the engine and says 'Look, there are screws here. If we unscrew the top bit, it would fit under the bridge, wouldn't it? Would you like me to do that?' Enchanted at the prospect of a screwdriver, he nods. 'Sure?' asks Kathy. He nods again.

'OK then' she says. She fetches a screwdriver from the pot on the shelf, and carefully unscrews, while Freddie looks over her shoulder, breathing heavily into her ear.

'There you are' she says. 'Under it goes! OK?'

But Freddie, after only a moment, collects up the bits and the screwdriver, and hands them to Kathy expectantly. 'Back?' he asks.

Kathy is puzzled and faintly irritated – but then realises that this isn't really about the train. It is about her and him unscrewing things – and now screwing them back up again.

Lost 'old friends' opportunities

What are lost wellbeing opportunities in relation to old friends? Watching television a lot can get in the way of the kind of reciprocal companionship that children need for their wellbeing. A small amount of companionable television-watching can be fun and instructive for children – and undeniably children watching on their own can be a life-saver for hard-pressed parents. But here we are considering the wellbeing of children, and although we know it's always best for children under five to watch TV with a companion, so that they can talk about what they see, this mostly does not happen. Indeed, television and video games have done much to militate against children's well-being in general. Watching television is often promoted as good for children's developing language, but this only relates to half the process: the benefits of hearing speech, but not those of using it. In reality, children learn to speak by speaking. In all the hours of screen-watching, especially when television is allowed in a child's bedroom, opportunities for wellbeing development – from agency to a good night's sleep – are extremely sparse.

Widely-held concerns about a lot of TV watching in the early years relate to long-term health problems such as obesity; to increased aggression through exposure to violence; and to children's vulnerability to manipulative advertising. Many parents' stated belief is that watching television has a positive effect on their child's development; yet in 2001 the American Academy of Paediatrics recommended no more than one to two hours total media time per day, and that paediatricians should discourage all television viewing for children younger than two years, and encourage more interactive activities.[9]

Given child viewing statistics in the UK, this is worrying enough in itself; and solitary hours in front of the television are lost hours in other ways, too. Young children watching TV alone are not experiencing real anchoring, or companionable authority, or apprenticeship, or quiet times and physical space for their own thoughts and reflective play. The variable content and often frantic pace of many children's programmes and cartoons may be amusing and fascinating for children, but watching television comes very low indeed on the list of wellbeing generators.

Extensive use of a dummy represents other lost opportunities. A calm-inducing, sleep-encouraging dummy seems like a good solution to many 'at-home' difficulties with babies and young children, as a baby with a dummy is most likely to be in a passive state – indeed, achieving a passive state is often the point of using one. With resolution and determination, it is possible for a dummy to be used just to help a baby to sleep, and a dummy can become associated for a baby or young child only with the crib, cot or bed. But often dummies are used to comfort in other crises, as well – indeed they are often marketed as 'comforters'. Yet this is a substitute for what is usually needed to restore a child's wellbeing – a companionable cuddle. Many mothers' lack of confidence in themselves may have something to do with this. Uncertainty about being a 'good' mother often means having little faith in being able to make things alright again with a cuddle. And sometimes too, in reality, perhaps a child with a dummy represents a much-needed break. But all too soon it becomes unwise to go anywhere without the dummy, which has become a substitute for the anchored companionable attention that children fundamentally need.

The debates around young children and television, and the use of dummies, are often framed in terms of class, but everyday extensive dependence on a dummy comes at a price which has nothing to do with class. As well as possible harm to teeth, for dummies as for television there is the issue of delayed language and all-round developing communication, which we know to be the basic process of wellbeing development. This is serious; and yet understandably for many mothers the idea of doing without both television and dummy, and consequently being more available to their children, is extremely challenging and carries major parenting implications. It is an important but undeniably unpalatable message, and it will need concerted and far-reaching efforts and support to families before it becomes established and accepted.

Going Out

Going out with young children these days is liable to be fraught with worries about dangerous traffic, strangers, children's behaviour, and so on; but in spite of the consequent restrictions for children, unexpectedly there is one advantage for them in this situation. Taking responsibility for children outside the home these days means we can never take our eyes off them, and this can generate more of the very attentive companionship in which they thrive. Aside from the frequent changes of scene and activity that the youngest children often need, this may be one reason why they always seem to love going out. The examples below are all about anchoring, with moments too for children's own time and space and quiet moments. They experience the security that comes from anticipating and experiencing boundaries and – mostly – understanding why they make sense.

Getting around

For children, a key element of going out is the mode of transport. Are we walking? Where's the buggy? Lost the car keys! Hurry up, we'll miss the bus/train … Decisions about how to get there are usually dictated by considerations of convenience, speed or expense; but sometimes, if there is a choice, other factors can be taken into consideration. Children usually love going out, and even the ways of getting around can make an impact on the four 'A's.

	Anchoring, authority, apprenticeship, allowing time and space
Sling	This is about firmly feeling anchored – and allowing the babies their own time and space too.
Buggy	Not-too-long spells in the usual forward-facing buggies can be good for time and space, if that's what a child is needing. (But see 'Lost "going out" opportunities'.)
Walking	Can be very good for everything – holding hands, involving children, 'wandering and pondering', keeping safe.
Bus	Small children usually get anchored on the inside seat. They can pay. They can look out of the window and dream. They need to know the rules.
Train	As for buses, but often even better. Usually requires some form of packing to get ready as well – children love doing their own packing, and being real travellers. Maybe a picnic will be needed. The need for books and games on trains (surely mad to risk the boredom of nothing to do?) means lovely anchored times, too.
Car	Probably least good for wellbeing, as being driven along doesn't involve anchored companionable attention (unless the driver is not paying attention to driving), authority or apprenticeship; although the car seat can work like a buggy for children's own time and space.

Figure 5.4 Getting around for children's wellbeing

Everyday expeditions

Here are some common everyday – or maybe every week – expeditions from home: bringing in the washing from outside, walking to the corner and back, going to the shop, a trip to the park, dropping off and picking up siblings from school, visiting other people's houses, attending a local group, going swimming. These can be completely satisfying for all concerned, although undeniably sometimes we wonder why we bothered to go out; and usually our feelings are somewhere in between. How near to ideally satisfying expeditions prove to be – whether for 20 minutes to the corner of the street or two hours to the swimming pool – probably has a lot to do with how many of the four 'A's were involved.

Unfortunately, expeditions from settings have become increasingly difficult to organise. Many settings take the view that although going off the premises may be a 'good' thing, expeditions are now likely to be more trouble than they are worth. It may be helpful to make a distinction between major one-off events that take a very great deal of planning, and more everyday or weekly expeditions that can become part of routine organisation.

'Routine' expeditions from settings might include going to a nearby shop, into the park, little picnics, visiting other parts of a setting, swimming, or involvement with Forest Schools. Sometimes the wellbeing value lies as much in the process of getting out and back again, as it does with the destination.

Lost 'going out' opportunities

What might be lost wellbeing opportunities in relation to going out? The scarcity and expense of buggies where child and companion face each other represents a host of lost opportunities for wellbeing. It would be so much better for children's wellbeing if buggies designed this way were more widely available, at reasonable prices. Children's wellbeing would blossom at double the rate if children in buggies and their companions could more easily make eye contact, talk about what they see and what is happening, sing songs, and so on.

Other lost opportunities already mentioned are all those times that expeditions from settings do not happen because the health and safety and organisational requirements have been set up for major outings, rather than for 10 minutes in the park or going to the corner shop. Also already mentioned is the use of a dummy, which seems especially constraining when a child is out and there is so much to talk about. A dummy in the mouth on an expedition signals 'passive' mode to a child; and this can occasionally be appropriate, if the child in a buggy, bus, train or car seat has become exhausted and genuinely needs a nap. But our understanding of agency, belonging-and-boundaries, communication and physical wellbeing is that these are very rarely 'passive' constructs, and so a dummy is likely to be a constraint on wellbeing opportunities that would otherwise arise from the companionship of going out.

The structure at the beginning of this chapter on everyday wellbeing was provided by the four 'A's: anchored attention; authority; apprenticeship; and allowing children time and space. In the next chapter the same structure is used, along with others, to think about wellbeing play.

Key messages 🔑

- In addition to play, babies and young children's everyday wellbeing is about the four 'A's: anchoring; authority; apprenticeship; and allowing time and space.
- Many everyday wellbeing experiences are associated with food – as well as companionable mealtimes, growing it, shopping for it, preparing and cooking it, and companionably clearing it up.
- Lost 'food' opportunities for wellbeing can be caused by fewer and fewer opportunities to eat companionably, for a variety of reasons.
- 'Old friends' can be family companions; books and stories, songs, rhymes and music; and pets. Unhurried times with old friends, doing odd jobs and fixing things, are good for children's wellbeing.
- Watching a lot of television can result in lost 'old friends' opportunities for wellbeing.
- Ways of getting around can make a positive impact on children's wellbeing.
- 'Going out' is important for everyday wellbeing, and can be easier than we think.
- Lost 'going out' opportunities for wellbeing can be caused by dummy dependency – and forward-facing buggies.

Questions to think about and discuss 🗣

1. Think of a child you know whose behaviour you find especially challenging. Now look at Figure 5.3 When children experience the four 'A's. Which items in the right-hand column might be relevant to the needs of that child?
2. Mrs Weston has spent a morning helping children to make sandwiches, put them ready for visitors, wrap up their own, take them outside to eat them on the hill, talk about their morning and watch the clouds. What has the morning done for the children's wellbeing?
3. It is suggested that reasons for lost opportunities for children's wellbeing include the following: fewer opportunities to eat companionably; watching a lot of television; dependency on dummies; forward-facing buggies. Such issues often tend to be culturally related. What do you think about this list? What would you add?

Further reading 📖

AHLBERG, J. & AHLBERG, A. *The Baby's Catalogue*. London: Puffin Books, 1982.

This lovely little book for sharing with young children is a trip down memory lane for them; and is wonderful for helping them with naming favourite things and talking about them. It is a skilfully diverse collection of everyday baby objects that can keep them and their companions happily fascinated, speculative and nostalgic for hours.

HOBAN, R. *The Mouse and his Child.* London: Faber and Faber, 1967/2005.

Written in 1967 and republished in 2005, *The Mouse and his Child* is sometimes terrifying, sometimes funny, always spellbinding. It is the story of a clockwork mouse and his child on their journey to achieving agency – and on another level, a story of love and loss, colonialism and slavery, desperation and despair, and the final triumph of courage and hope. Although written for older children (definitely not the youngest ones) it works on many levels, and can be taken as a metaphor for the meaning of life – and what having wellbeing might mean. It is a moving and exciting book for adults too, the analogy working especially well perhaps for practitioners who live and work with young children.

RICH, D., CASANOVA, D., DIXON, A., DRUMMOND, M.J., DURRANT, A. & MYER, C. *First Hand Experience: What Matters to Children.* Clopton: Rich Learning Opportunities, 2005.

Here we find direct experience placed at the heart of children's learning. The authors use an alphabet of practical, theoretical and philosophical ideas to explore what really matters to children. In 'D is for doors', we find 'Questions worth asking: Is a gate a door? Is a letter box a door? Has a suitcase got a door?'; and Big 'door' ideas: diversity, form and function, fitness for purpose, human ingenuity; and 'Door things to collect: other things that open and shut – inkwells, umbrellas, suitcases ...; and from George Macdonald, "Every question is a door handle"'.[10]

Or take 'U is for Under', where we find Words to collect: underpants, under age, under cover, under fire, under dressed, under hand, under canvass, under a spell ... and so on. The problem is how to stop – absolutely compelling reading.

References

1 ELFER. P., GOLDSCHMEID, E. & SELLECK, D. *Key Persons in the Nursery: Building Relationships for Quality Provision.* London: NEYN, 2002: 18.
2 RICH, D., CASANOVA, D., DIXON, A., DRUMMOND, M.J., DURRANT, A. & MYER, C. *First Hand Experience: What Matters to Children.* Clopton: Rich Learning Opportunities, 2005: 54.
3 PEEP video series *Learning Together with Twos.* Oxford: Peers Early Education Partnership, 2001 (www.peep.org.uk).
4 FISHER, D.C. A 'Montessori Mother', London: Constable, 1913: 22–24, in Rich, D., Drummond, M.J. & Myer, C. *Learning: What Matters to Children.* Clopton: Rich Learning Opportunities, 2008: 93.
5 ROBERTS, R. *Self-Esteem and Early Learning: Key People from Birth to School,* 3rd edn. London: Paul Chapman Publishing, 2006: 116–118, 119–120.
6 NATIONAL LITERACY TRUST http://www.literacytrust.org.uk
7 PEEP *The Learning Together Series: Learning Together with Babies: Books for Babies.* Oxford: Peers Early Education Partnership, 2000: 26 (www.peep.org.uk).
8 GADSBY, G. & HARROP, B. (eds) *Flying a Round.* London: A&C Black, 1982.
9 AMERICAN SOCIETY OF PEDIATRICS *Children, Adolescents, and Television, Pediatrics,* 2001, 107· 423–426.
10 MACDONALD, G. *Castle Warlock,* London: Samson Low, 1982.

All to Play For

What Sort of Play?

There are so many different kinds of play – exploring, pretending, rough and tumble, fantasy, games with rules, solitary or social. This chapter does not attempt to cover the important issues about play in general, which has been excellently done by others.[1] It is about the kind of play that is particularly rich in opportunities for wellbeing, explored through the structures of the four 'A's (introduced in the last chapter); the roles that children's companions can take; and the ABC of wellbeing.

Wellbeing play

What is wellbeing play, and why is it so important? Wellbeing play is child-initiated, open-ended and un-rushed; with adaptable resources and spaces that are not changed too frequently.[2] Wellbeing play is not externally motivated, not initiated or guided by adults, not constrained by time, not characterised by attention to the end product, not bound by rules. These constraints may have a place in early childhood, and occasionally even perhaps in the development of wellbeing, but they do not characterise wellbeing play. Wellbeing play is characterised by intensity, and intentionality. It is leisurely, creative, full of freedom and imagination, with real or imagined companionship. It is profoundly satisfying.

Freedom to play

It seems that, as for the price of freedom (eternal vigilance), the price for children's freedom to play in this way is our eternal vigilance. Wellbeing play still needs defending – more than ever, some would say. In answer to a call for greater control over children's play with the well-meaning intention of containing children's fears following the 9/11 attack, Paley's response was to argue:

> I would have to disagree. There is no activity for which young children are better prepared than fantasy play. Nothing is more dependable and risk-free, and the dangers are only pretend. What we are in danger of doing is de-legitimising mankind's oldest and best-used learning tool.[3]

Clearly Isaacs would have agreed with her.

> If we were asked to mention one supreme psychological need of the young child, the answer would have to be 'play' – the opportunity for free play in all its various forms. Play is the child's means of living, and of understanding life.[4]

A surprisingly short time ago, child-initiated play – 'just playing' – was generally suspected to be a time-wasting alternative to 'the more important activity of learning'. While we have come a very long way since then, these days 'play' is still often promoted primarily for physical wellbeing and development. Alongside the progress that has been made there remains a still widely-held belief that after a spell of 'work' children need to go outside 'to play, to let off steam'. Children's physical development does in fact mean a great deal to them.[5] Being able to get around – crawling, then walking, then running – opens up new worlds to them; and increased motor skills enable them to take part in daily family life in ways they had previously only dreamed of. Many of them work incredibly hard at these skills, with iron determination. They need to run and climb, and there is no stopping them. Their physical confidence – or lack of it – makes a significant impact on their play with other children. And their physical development affects assumptions that people make about them, and expectations about their capabilities.

Nevertheless, now play is universally acknowledged to underpin not just physical development but all development and learning for young children.[6] But the reasons for this holistic value are still not clear to many people, even in the early years sector. Explaining to sceptical parents and sector colleagues about the reasons for the over-riding importance of 'real' play can still be challenging.

Progression towards Play

Knowledge and understanding of individual children, together with a more general professional knowledge and understanding of children's play, helps us to plan appropriately. Being clear about children's progression towards play is one way to make sense of what children are doing. We can think of play as a continuum of three interlinked stages: watching and exploring; practising and representing; and creatively playing.

With each new concept, interest or situation, in each area of learning, children will move through these stages. Each stage is characterised by a different internal question. First, 'What is this?' Second, 'How can I learn it?' And third, 'How shall I play with it?' As in all progress there will be the metaphorical one step forward and two steps back, and in different situations children will be at different points along the continuum. The continuum carries on into adult life.

Chris Athey, director of the Froebel Early Education Project from 1973 to 1978, explains the first stage more in terms of struggle than exploration, emphasising that the process from struggle (self-motivated, not imposed) to play is a human characteristic of learning. She points out that if mere 'competence' is seen as an endpoint to knowledge, playfulness is lost. Here is how she explains struggle through practice to playfulness, and beyond competence to fun.

> Several important thinkers have embraced the idea that the processes of thought occur on a learning continuum – not a developmental continuum as in cognitive stage levels, but on a psychological continuum. This continuum starts with struggle (accommodation to the new). Everybody knows from personal experience the struggle which accompanies new learning. With practice, the struggle lessens and competence and confidence take the place of struggle. Everybody knows the saying 'Practice makes perfect'. The final part of the learning process, which is sometimes left out of schooling, is the part when children can have some fun with their knowledge.

Philosophers and psychologists who have written at length about the process of learning going from struggle through practice to playfulness and fun include Immanuel Kant (the father of modern philosophy), Karl Buhler (who invented the term 'function pleasure' to describe the function of humour), Freud and Piaget, Arthur Koestler (in his book *The Act of Creation*), Huizinga (who wrote a book called *Homo Ludens* (playful man) in 1949) and Chukovsky (1966).

Chukovsky in his wonderful little book *From Two to Five* described the end of this continuum at its most simple and direct. He described the position of playfulness in relation to the other aspects of learning: 'When the child has become so sure of truths that he can even play with them'.[7] Well-assimilated concepts can be thought of as 'toys of the mind'.[8]

The first level of play: exploration and struggle

The first stage of play is about watching and exploring. Implicit in this stage is the question 'What is this?' At this stage children investigate and hypothesise; they are often on the move, and often new to the situation. They find out about the world and struggle to adjust to it. Struggle – both mental and physical – is a feature of this level.

We see this level in children when they hover watchfully on the edge of other children's play. The play levels we observe in children are not so much about their general levels of development, as about how much experience they may have had with this particular thing or situation. When Freddie is 20 months, he is given a new wooden train set. (It is the one mentioned in the previous chapter in relation to 'odd jobs and fixing things'). Here he is, unpacking it with his mother, Kathy.

Ellie is asleep in the buggy in the hall, and Kathy and Freddie are laying all the bits of track side by side on the kitchen floor. Next they unpack the little engines and carriages, the station buildings and pretend trees. Freddie seems to like the look of these, especially the carriages. Kathy shows him how they join together with little magnets, but he can't seem to get the hang of them, and doesn't seem very interested.

'Shall we make a track for the train now?' she asks, secretly rather enjoying the train herself – the feel of its wood, and the satisfying 'click' of the magnets. Freddie watches as she connects the pieces of track end to end in a figure of eight, so that the train can go first under the bridge, and then round and back over it.

'Look' she says. 'Isn't that clever?'

Freddie, sitting on the floor, watches while she makes a 'ch-ch-ch-ch' noise as she pushes the train along. But they can hear Ellie waking up, so Kathy takes the little engine off the track and pushes it towards him.

'Look, you can push it along the floor if you like. Ch-ch-ch-ch'.

(Continued)

She gets up and goes out into the hall. A few minutes later, coming back carrying Ellie, she finds Freddie standing in the middle of chaos, holding up a bit of track with several bits still dangling off it, trying to shake them apart. He looks quite near shrieking.

Hastily Kathy says 'Shall I find a bag for the train? Then we can put it away'.

She puts Ellie in her bouncy chair, goes next door and comes straight back with two bags. One is made of blue flowery material, an old shoe bag with a draw string.

'Look, we could keep the track in here' she says to Freddie. 'It can hang on the back of the cupboard door'.

The other bag is a stiff plastic see-through one with a zip around the top – little wooden bricks are supposed to fit in it, but now they live in a cardboard box, which is easier.

'Shall we put the train in here?' she asks, holding out the see-through bag.

While she holds it open, Freddie pops in the engine and the carriages and bits and pieces – except for the milk train. Next Kathy pulls the shoe bag open, and holds it while she and Freddie post in the bits of track, until they are all done.

'I think it's time for tea' she says, going to fill up the kettle.

Suddenly behind her there is a crash. Turning around, she sees Freddie has tipped out all the bits of track out again onto the floor. She decides to say nothing and see what happens. Freddie looks at the jumbled heap for a moment and then looks at her.

'Biscuit?' he says hopefully.

Adults operate in this way with new experiences too, though perhaps generating less chaos and mess than young children often do. For instance, our first step when cooking something for the first time may be to watch someone else doing it. Or perhaps we read the recipe, before eventually getting everything together. Sometimes a recipe or the ingredients look too daunting, and we give up and opt for beans on toast.

The second level of play: achieving competence

The second level is about acquiring new skills. Now the all-important question has progressed from 'What is it?' to 'How does it work? How can I control it?' Children practise new skills over and over again. For instance, how many hundreds of times has Freddie pointed urgently across the street or at a book, and said 'Lorry!' (And this is probably two sorts of practice, one about using language to tell us what he has seen, and the other to check his lorry-identification skills). Children use their discoveries about people and things as the starting point for coming to terms with their world and what they can do to control it. This is why play is so important in the development of children's sense of agency.

Here is Freddie again, still 20 months. He is working very hard indeed at slides. Getting up the steps, sliding down, ways that are allowed and ways that are not (never backwards head first), taking turns (learning 'mine' or 'ours') – these have been just a few of the issues for him. They have a little plastic slide on the grass outside at the back; and now he is outside, with Kathy and Ellie sitting on the rug at the side, carrying on the good work.

> Freddie loves this slide. Unlike in the park, he can manage on it all by himself, and he doesn't have to wait for other children and take turns. Sometimes in the park he just watches the bigger children running and climbing, sliding and running.
>
> They have been outside for 10 minutes or so, and Freddie hasn't stopped yet. He clambers quickly up the steps, sits straight away at the top of the slide, and down he goes. A long time ago Kathy stopped saying 'Wheeeeeee!' encouragingly every time. At the bottom he jumps up and without a pause, runs around again to the bottom of the steps, and up again. Round and round and round he goes ...

Freddie shows us many of the characteristics of this stage of play: energy, intention, determination, persistence. Soon he'll be able to join the bigger ones in the park. For us, the second stage with cooking is actually to make the dish as you're supposed to. This is about as far as many of us get – what Athey called 'mere competence'. Some would say (though this is surely open to question) that closely following a recipe only needs 'mere competence' too.

The third level of play: imagination and creativity

The third level is about playing – real playing. Now children can use their skills to re-present their experiences in their own way, putting their own unique perceptions into their play, bringing together their skills and their experiences. Their question now is 'How can I use my skills and knowledge to play *my* way?' Here, children are using a combination of two parts of themselves: the rich texture of their ideas, feelings and relationships, combined with the application of their competence and technical prowess. They have worked at something long enough to know it so well that they can play with it. It might be said that play at this level is 'real' play, whereas the previous stages are preliminaries. Even the very youngest children often play at this level with certain people and things that they have come to know very well.

Slides may be fairly new to Freddie, but the swimming pool is not. His parents have taken him swimming regularly from the age that babies are allowed to start, and swimming is one of his all-time-favourite expeditions. Here is Freddie playing in the bath in the same week as the slide day. Kathy is in charge, and Freddie's gran is sitting in the doorway of the bathroom with Ellie on her knee.

Freddie has decided that he would like a few little play people with him in the bath, and Kathy has spotted a couple on the bathroom shelf. She reaches them down and sits them one each end of the blue boat.

While Freddie is giving them a ride in the boat, Kathy tells Gran about swimming that morning. 'He loves jumping in now, but I have to hold his hand' she said.

'Why's that?' asks Gran.

'I don't want him to slip and hurt himself' answers Kathy. 'I don't mind if he's sitting down and just leans forward into the water, but seeing him jumping freaks me out!'

'Mmmm' says Gran … and then 'What are you up to, Freddie?'

Freddie is standing up in the bath, play person in each hand, trying to sit them on the edge – but he hasn't quite got the knack, and they keep falling into the water.

'Sit down Freddie' says Kathy, 'shall I help you?'

Freddie nods and sits down, handing her the little people.

'It might be easier with them standing up' she says. 'Shall I make them do that?'

Freddie nods again, grinning. Kathy puts them side by side on the edge of the bath, facing the water. 'OK?' she asks.

Freddie carries on grinning. Reaching carefully round behind them, and with half an eye on his mother's face, he very deliberately knocks them into the water.

Kathy gets it. 'Oh naughty people' she says. 'They jumped without holding hands!'

Freddie laughs delightedly.

Freddie wants this game again and again. Eventually he has to be dragged screaming from the bath because the water has cooled down too much – and anyway it's bedtime.

The third stage for us with cooking means we can be creative, thinking up our own recipes, and being clever with left-overs in original ways that are unique to us. It is about combining skills with creativity – at this level making delicious inventions of our own.

Thinking Patterns in Play

The idea of thinking patterns

Athey, who wrote about progression in play, has also taken us into a world based on schemas, or patterns, in children's thinking and play. Subsequently this world has been 'played with' by others.[9] Children's favourite ways of playing are based on these schemas, and they need to do things again and again. Here is part of Peers Early Education Partnership (PEEP)'s explanation:

> How a child is thinking can show in many ways – how he moves, the marks and patterns he uses in drawings, his choices and enthusiasms. Patterns come and go over time, and develop into more complex combinations. In some children one or more of these patterns can seem very strong – and in other children they are harder to notice. Children can understand with their whole bodies what 'round and round', 'inside' and 'outside' or 'over' and 'under' mean, and this helps their thinking and their language to develop, along with their confidence.[10]

We can use our awareness of these patterns of repeating behaviour to support and extend children's play. All of them are part and parcel of children's everyday life experiences: things that connect (e.g. holding hands), that enclose or envelop (e.g. key holes), that rotate (e.g. the washing machine drum), that fly through the air (e.g. balls), and that transport (e.g. shopping bags).

All the 'classic' toys – for instance Lego, posting boxes, spinning tops, footballs, dolls' buggies – are redolent of these patterns. Athey describes many other schemas, too. Although we often observe particular patterns in children's play, not all children appear especially schematic. Some children display one pattern particularly strongly; in others we can observe all these patterns at once. Sometimes one pattern that has been particularly strong will seem to fade, possibly to be replaced by another.

Making the most of thinking patterns

These patterns are so familiar to children in their everyday experiences that they are, inevitably, part of children's play about those experiences. Observing children's patterns in their play offers a key to understanding the kinds of materials in which particular children would be especially interested. Figure 6.1 'Children's thinking patterns in play' shows these easily identifiable patterns, together with a few of children's many likely play preferences.

Thinking patterns	Children's likely play preferences
Connecting (joining things)	Building blocks Train track Construction sets String and Sellotape Holding hands Cooking – following a recipe
Enveloping, enclosing (covering up, putting inside)	Dolls' blankets Peek-a-boo games Cardboard boxes Dens Wrapping 'presents' Cooking – mince pies
Rotation (round and round)	Wheels Roundabouts Running in circles Repetitive stories Circle games Cooking – stirring
Trajectory (e.g. jumping, running, throwing)	Throwing games Football Hose play Swings Drumming Cooking – tossing pancakes
Transporting (moving things from one place to another)	Shopping trolley Playing postman Laying the table Cars, tractors, lorries Doll's pram Cooking – going on a picnic

Figure 6.1 Children's thinking patterns in play

Many young children's all-time-favourite activities can encompass most or all of these pattern categories, for instance:

- Cooking: fetching ingredients, putting them into the bowl, stirring, beating, rolling, covering, putting in the oven.
- Book sharing, especially with the range of books designed for the youngest children: repetitive stories, flap books, books with Velcro, books about rockets, books with holes, books about cars, trucks and lorries …
- Fixing something using glue, paint, a screwdriver, a saw, a tool box

- Taking a doll to the playground – the climbing frame, the playhouse, the roundabout, the slide and the swings.

We retain these patterns into adulthood. Thinking about the characteristics of the game of golf in this light, do these patterns perhaps go some way to explaining its popularity?

What Children Need for Wellbeing Play

The purpose of the rest of this chapter is to make a case for the centrality of wellbeing play in the development of everyday wellbeing; explaining how we can support play, and how it relates to children's wellbeing.

In Chapter 5 'Children's Wellbeing', the four 'A's of everyday wellbeing gave us a structure within which to consider children's wellbeing needs. Here is the same now familiar structure, used to identify children's play needs.

Anchoring

In the same way that children thrive on 'anchoring' in everyday life, when they are playing they need the security of companions they can rely on to be there if they need them. They need to know that their companions will help them with their play, that they will be 'midwives' to their play.[11] This approach to supporting children's play can operate, in the psychological sense, as a kind of containing function. It means that a companion respects and accepts a child's feelings and ideas. If needed, companions can 'hold' these feelings and ideas initially, making them available again for the child to explore in manageable 'play-packaged' ways.

Children need their play to be anchored in another sense, too. Sensitive companions understand that the starting points for children's play need to be anchored in children's own interests and experiences.

Authority (their own)

There are two aspects of authority relating to wellbeing play. First, children themselves need to be the ones in authority. This is about them being able to use what they know, in the ways that they choose. Their authority is rooted in their knowledge. (When we use play with the intention of teaching them things they don't know, we hi-jack that authority.)

Second, children need us to give our authorisation for them to decide how they want to play, so that they can play their way. They need to know that they have our permission – that we have given them the authority to make their own play decisions. This is not to say that we should abdicate all responsibility for what happens though. It is not a general abdication of authority that children need, but a specific one in relation to their play. And even then, they cannot play safely unless they know they are still within the usual boundaries. The dictum 'OK if it's safe, and not upsetting anyone' is a useful way of delineating the boundaries of authority.

Play that has been planned in detail by adult companions is less likely to be spontaneous and relating to children's intentions, and this 'authority' factor in wellbeing play really rules out play that could be called structured. This, as Fisher explains, implies more than adult intervention, and borders on adult interference.[12] The lines in Shakespeare's sonnet 116, 'Love is not love, which alters when it alteration finds' might be re-phrased as 'Play is not play, which alters when it interference finds'.

Apprenticeship materials

Apprenticeship materials are the particular kinds of things that children need for their wellbeing play. They need to play about things they know, e.g. everyday events and activities that feature in their lives, and so they need things they know – or objects they can use to represent what they know. Settings that make 'real-life' objects and natural materials available for wellbeing play will be richer and more satisfying for children than those that are stocked entirely with brightly coloured plastic toys.

When children play together, a 'companionable learning' apprenticeship model is often observable between them, as they share with each other what they know. Children who are used to companionable apprenticeship at home are especially comfortable with this.

Allowed time and space

We tend to use our knowledge of children to plan situations, activities and experiences for them, usually filling their time. Supporting wellbeing play means giving children more time – lots of it – and rather fewer plans.

Inevitably the time will be boundaried by everyday routines, but it will be none the worse for that. Space, physical or mental, needs containing in some way, for children to feel secure. Yet within these boundaries children need to be given enough space to be creative, playing with people and things in their own unique ways.

Companions Supporting Wellbeing Play

Children play wherever they are; at home, in the park, at friends' and relatives', in settings. Children's play at home is often different from when they are out: different companions, different things to play with, different places and time-scales, different issues of choice and control. In spite of this, the same supporting principles apply. In Figure 6.2 we see what it means to be a companion supporting children's wellbeing play; both at home and when they are out, including in settings.

The four 'A's of play ...	Children need their companions ...
ANCHORING IN PLAY	... to be around, companionably attentive and available ... to listen out for and support children's own ideas, so their play is anchored in their own experience ... to plan for child-initiated play, and try not to initiate or 'push' their own ideas
AUTHORITY (THEIR OWN) IN PLAY	... to arrange things so that children feel 'authorised' to play *their* way ... to be available to *their* play; not to make it ours ... to respect children's play intentions ... to provide resources that feed play patterns
APPRENTICESHIP MATERIALS FOR PLAY	... to provide materlals for children to play with, that will ... satisfy them ... to provide natural materials and real-life objects to provide toys with many possibilities (e.g. cardboard boxes or wooden bricks) rather than only one (e.g. computer programs that progress through a series of right answers)
ALLOWED TIME AND SPACE FOR PLAY	... to plan time for uninterrupted play ... to think about and plan for the freedom children need for ... their play where possible, to allow children spacial freedom, as ... well as 'free' time to consider the possibilities of the four 'A's outdoors (NB most young children long to be outside and don't want to come in)

Figure 6.2 Companions supporting wellbeing play

All to Play For

In this chapter about play we have explored the situations and experiences on which children thrive. Many of these are so familiar that we probably take them for granted. Here we have looked at some possible reasons for their importance to children. Now, using real-life examples of children playing, we briefly re-visit the four 'A's, highlighting as we go the connections between these glimpses of early childhood and the ABC of wellbeing.

Anchored play for wellbeing

We have seen how important 'anchoring' is for young children, in their play and in everyday life in general. Here is Dylan, aged 24 months, anchored securely with his mother Mya as they play an 'earring' game.

It is mid-summer, a blazing hot afternoon. Mya and Dylan have retreated to the house, and Dylan has found a curling, dangly piece of black sticky tape on the floor. He holds up his arms for Mya to pick him up. Once he is settled on her hip he tries to make the tape stick to her ear, as if it was an earring.

At first it falls off, he catches it, and they both laugh.

'Ooooh' says Mya, gazing into his eyes at very close quarters. Dylan shrieks excitedly.

He tries again – I have the strong impression that this is a familiar game, and he knows how it will go. Leaning round to the side and using both hands, by concentrating on her ear he manages to make the tape stay put. Then he leans back again and they look at each other – exactly the way that after you have turned your head sideways in front of the mirror to put in an earring, you straighten and lean back slightly to check how it looks. This time it is Dylan checking how Mya looks – really, it seems, checking how loving she looks.

All is well. Out of an instant of seriousness a special smile of love and satisfaction grows between them, the 'mirroring' development process of his self concept. Her special smile says to him 'I love you', and so he knows 'I am lovable'. (And unconsciously in the reciprocated smile, Mya hears *his* 'I love you' and knows 'I am a lovable mother').

'Aaaah' says Mya now, still smiling and eyebrows raised, swaying slightly to and fro with Dylan hanging on tight. He giggles, watching her adoringly and waiting for her to tickle him. She does, gently. Off drops the 'earring' again.

'Oooh, it's on the floor' she sings. 'You dropped it!' She reaches down to get it, then settles him back on her hip.

On the surface this was a game about the 'earring' – but really, it was Dylan's way into a loving cuddle with Mya. The sticky tape 'earring' game dictates her holding him very close so that he can reach her ear, and so he is satisfyingly 'anchored'.

Dylan has been playing these kinds of intimate little games with his mother all his life. He has learned that when he invents a game that requires her to hold him securely close, he will be satisfied. On a more mundane level he has learned about sticky tape: that it sticks to things, even ears, so it can be used for joining things together – in this case joining him and his mother together. In this tiny playful anchoring experience (40 seconds from start to finish) we can see all the wellbeing constructs. Figure 6.3 illustrates this.

	Dylan's 'earring' game developing agency, belonging-and-boundaries, communication and physical wellbeing
A	There is pride in the moment when Dylan manages to achieve what he was trying to do, make the earring stick; and more importantly, behind that pride in his skill is the knowledge that it was him that had invented this satisfying game and made it happen.
B&B	Mya's smiles, cuddles, laughter, rocking and soft singing voice all give a very clear message to Dylan: 'You belong with me'; while at the same time he knows he has to be gentle with her.
C	Dylan and Mya are communicating with each other throughout the game, sometimes using body language, sometimes spoken language.
P	Dylan's efforts to get the tape to stick require considerable motor control.

Figure 6.3 Dylan's 'earring' game

Authority in play for wellbeing

It is because of the boundaries that children can make with their own authority in wellbeing play that they experience the security and the freedom to play and to stop playing, as and when they need to. This is why it is safe for children to explore dangerous situations in their fantasy play – as Paley argued – because they are wholly in control.

Of course children are not in control of the experiences that they and their companions bring to their play. For a very small minority of children, the freedom of this kind of play opens the door to re-enactments and fantasies that may be unsuitable, painful or shocking to their companions. While being able to process their experiences in this way may be a vital lifeline for such children, at the same time other children may need protecting. These very vulnerable and sometimes damaged children have even more to play for, but more appropriately and safely in the company of attentive, understanding adults, rather than with child companions.

The real-life balance of authority which children experience, and indeed need to experience with us, their adult companions, is very much weighted on our side. But they are the ones who need total authority in their wellbeing play, and so this authority must be 'granted' to them (within the boundaries mentioned above) by us, their adult companions. Without it they cannot have the freedom genuinely to explore, to discover, to practice their learning often beyond reason, to consolidate concepts to add to their collection of 'toys in the mind'.

Here is Hamza, aged three years two months, playing alone in the lounge. Although I am sitting at the other side of the room watching, my presence does not appear to be a factor in his play. Occasionally he tells me what is going on, or asks me the questions he is in reality asking himself.

For some time Hamza has been playing with his cars on the settee. Sometimes Hamza and his father go out for expeditions in his father's car, which is clearly the starting point of this play. He has four little metal cars, and most of the time he has been 'driving' them by pushing them along carefully with one hand while he kneels up and balances himself with the other. The cars have been in and out of the 'petrol station' – the gap between the cushions at the far end of the settee – several times.

Now he is taking them to another gap, this time in the middle of the sofa.

'That's a petrol station' he tells me.

'Oh ... another one?'

He points to the previous petrol station, saying rather agitatedly

'They can't go ... they're stuck down ... that's a bit older'.

Then turning back to the new gap he says

'This is the *good* one, this is'.

He carefully drives the yellow car into the supposedly good petrol station, and then peers down after it. There is a pause – then he drives the car out again and points back to the gap.

'There's no petrol in this' he says, and again 'There's no petrol in this … the man have looked'. He drives the car away across the flat cushions of the settee.

With enormous concentration he lines the four cars up into a queue across the cushion. Then 'Why are they waiting – why are they waiting?' he asks.

'Why are they waiting?' I echo.

Taking the last one in the queue he pushes it backwards, saying

'This one's driving backwards'. He makes it go behind him to the end of the sofa and into the gap beneath the blue cushion.

'Why is the BMW going in there?' he asks rhetorically.

He brings the car back out of the gap and carefully positions it alongside the piping on the edge of the cushion.

'It's park[ed] up' he says briskly.

He takes another car – the one now at the end of the queue – and drives it off, saying 'Now this car'.

After a little more driving the cars around he suddenly gets off the settee with the BMW in his hand and heads for the door, informing me as he whizzes urgently by

'I want to go to … fix the car … not working'.

Hamza is definitely an authority on cars, and his drives with his father combine two of his passions: cars and dad. Safely strapped into his seat he is happy but helpless. He takes it all in, saving it up to process later in his play. Then he was anchored; and now, in his play, it is Hamza who is in the driving seat. See Figure 6.4.

Apprenticeship play for wellbeing

The processes of apprenticeship are full of satisfying possibilities for young children, both in real life with their adult companions and in their play with real and imaginary friends. Apprenticeship play is especially satisfying in a well set up home corner, as it will be full of 'props' reflecting children's lives at home. Having appropriate materials helps to stimulate this kind of play – although once the play is underway (and it doesn't take much), children are happy for more or less anything to represent what they need.

Here is Alena at nursery, aged two years two months, playing with her three-year-old friend Ava. Clearly Alena and Ava have been watching the doctor closely – and their mothers.

	Hamza's cars developing agency, belonging-and-boundaries, communication and physical wellbeing
A	Hamza's baby brother is now 16 months, and he is definitely making his mark in the family. Hamza's confidence has taken a knock, and his sense of being able to make things happen is often in a precarious state. Consequently this kind of play is extremely important for him, because it gives him healing interludes in which he is once again completely and confidently in control.
B&B	In his play Hamza is revisiting his passionate interest in 'car behaviour' and – the context of this play – his attachment to his father. Here we see him exploring some of the boundaries that dictate 'car behaviour' – having to get fuel, parking neatly, queueing.
C	Using speech with another person to formulate the pressing questions in our minds is an accepted way of exploring important issues. It helps us to understand our world and the people in it. 'Why are they waiting?' Hamza is able to ask – and in doing so, to re-visit something that had intrigued him. Here is a virtuous circle – language helps play, and play helps language.
P	Hamza takes great care to place his cars exactly as he wants them. Although he has developed the fine coordination required to do this because he needs it for his play, now it will stand him in good stead in most other areas of his life.

Figure 6.4 Hamza's cars

Alena looks thoughtfully across the room to the home corner where Ava is still 'doctoring' her doll. Then she walks over to them and deliberately sits down on the bed. Picking up the bottle she lies back with it in her mouth, looking expectantly at Ava. Janet, who is standing nearby watching, says 'It looks like you've got real baby in your hospital Ava – is she ill?' Readily picking up the idea, Ava seizes the stethoscope and thermometer and 'doctors' Alena for a while, then tucks her up with the blanket.

But Alena doesn't want to stay put. She gets up and moves away, although still watching Ava and holding the bottle.

Ava comes over with a new little bottle in her hand. Alena stands still while Ava holds it to her mouth, saying it is her medicine, and will make her better. When Ava stands back (apparently to watch the effect of the medicine!) Alena becomes very animated, waving her arms and jigging up and down and blowing raspberries.

Ava steps forward again with the bottle and says 'It's lipstick'. While Alena stands very still Ava performs a round-the-lips gesture, nearly touching Alena's lips but not quite. Alena seems very happy to stand completely still for this. Ava returns to Alena several times during the afternoon to touch up the lipstick!

	Alena and Ava playing 'doctors' and 'mummies' developing agency, belonging-and-boundaries, communication and physical wellbeing
A	Alena has the confidence to ask to join in Ava's game, and is confirmed by Ava's acceptance of her. Her sense of agency is further supported by her experiment as to whether, if she moves the location of the game, Ava will follow her – and Ava does.
B&B	Alena speculates that she will be allowed to belong in Ava's game, and finds she is right. But she has to know the conventions of this kind of game, and 'play by the rules' – e.g. lie down to be doctored, respond to medicine, keep still for lipstick.
C	Although we don't hear Alena say anything, we see a great deal of communication – both expressive ('I want to be in your doctor game Ava' body language) and inductive (she understands when Ava tells her she is being given medicine).
P	Playing like this requires a certain level of dexterity if it is to be properly satisfying and not frustrating.

Figure 6.5 Alena and Ava playing 'doctors' and 'mummies'

Time and space to play for wellbeing

Allowing time and space for children's wellbeing play is perhaps the most challenging of all the four 'A's. So much militates against this in our modern society – the pressures of 'too much' are everywhere: too much to do, too much to think about, too many things, too much expected of us, too much to worry about, too much exhaustion. Children need an antidote to all this – the antidote of time and space to play. Some are fortunate enough to get it, in unhurried families and carefully planned Centres. Jayden, aged 11 months, is one of them. Here he is in the Centre, playing alone and unhurriedly in a quiet-ish corner, but every now and then looking across to check on his key person and his mum, who are chatting together.

There is a semi-circular nursery table with a semi-circular cut-out in the middle of the straight edge. The straight edge is pushed against a safety-glass wall mirror, and Jayden is standing inside the cut-out with his back to the room, looking into the mirror. The only thing behind him on the table is a small solid yellow cylindrical brick, from the wooden posting box. The table top is the height of Jayden's waist.

Jayden bumps his head very gently a few times against the mirror. Then he stops bumping, and turns around to seize the yellow brick, which he throws rather randomly across the table. It rolls to the outer edge, and falls to the floor.

Jayden watches it go, then carefully slides to the floor between the table and the mirror, and crawls over to pick up the brick.

He stands up with it, now at the outer edge of the table, and rolls it back across the table towards the cut-out and the mirror. He watches it go, smiling with satisfaction to himself as it falls down the hole between the two and back onto the floor. Now he crawls back under the table, retrieving the brick from the floor as he goes, and standing up again in the space where he started.

He throws the brick again, this time more deliberately. It rolls smoothly, drops, he retrieves it, and rolls it back again into the hole. Another gratified smile ... surely this is a golf player in the making?

	Jayden's brick game developing agency, belonging-and-boundaries, communication and physical wellbeing
A	Jayden's sense of achievement is evident in the smiles of gratification. He is completely in charge, allowed to decide for himself how the game should go, and experiencing the satisfaction of making his own decisions.
B&B	His glances across to his mother and his key person indicate his attachment to them – a degree of belonging and reassurance that contains the time and space he needs to play like this.
C	Children communicate about things that matter to them, and these kinds of playful experiences give them important questions to ask. In a very short time Jayden will be able to say words like 'where' and 'down', as in 'Where has it gone?' and 'Will it fall down the hole?'
P	Negotiating the space between table and mirror requires considerable coordination, and Jayden's skill rolling the brick at 11 months shows an impressive degree of motor control.

Figure 6.6 Jayden's brick game

We began this chapter with the question, 'Why is wellbeing play so important?' The answer, 'Because wellbeing play is rich in "ABC of wellbeing" experiences', is illustrated by these examples. Children's agency, especially, develops in their wellbeing play, and agency is the 'peak' of wellbeing. When children are engaged in wellbeing play, they do indeed have all to play for.

Key messages

- Wellbeing play is child-initiated, open-ended, un-rushed; adaptable, available, intense, intentional; leisurely, creative, free – and profoundly satisfying.
- Freedom to play in this way is vital for children, a principle to be defended.
- Progression towards play moves from exploration and struggle, through competence, to imagination and creativity.
- Knowing about children's thinking patterns can help us to understand and to satisfy children by making play provision that provides for their most compelling interests.
- In their play, children's needs include anchored situations, authority, apprenticeship materials, and time and space to play.
- Children need their companions to take supporting roles in relation to their wellbeing play.
- Children have all to play for: their agency (especially), their sense of belonging-and-boundaries, their developing communication and their physical wellbeing.

Questions to think about and discuss

1. Record some observations of children playing. Can you see different levels of progression in their play? What do these observations tell you about how you might enrich the play of particular children?
2. Make an observation of a child engrossed in 'wellbeing play'. How does what you see relate to the child's four constructs of wellbeing?
3. How do your own schemas impact on the way you approach your work?

Further reading

BRUCE, T. *Learning Through Play: Babies, Toddlers and the Foundation Years*. London: Hodder and Stoughton, 2001.

With her feet firmly on the ground (and indeed, firmly in the early years setting) Bruce examines the role of play in children's learning, from traditional views to modern research. Set in a perspective of children's rights and diverse cultural contexts, Bruce explores how play underpins children's learning, and offers principled and practical ways of observing, supporting and extending babies' and young children's play.

FEATHERSTONE, S. (ed.) *Again! Again! Understanding Schemas in Young Children*. London: A&C Black, 2008.

This meticulous and extremely readable book introduces young children's schema play. It covers the theory of schemas, the development of schemas in play and learning, supporting schema play, observation and planning. Linking with England's Early Years Foundation Stage, it is full of vivid examples from experienced practitioners, and wonderful photographs. Practitioners will find it extremely useful.

HOBAN, R. *How Tom beat Captain Najork and his Hired Sportsmen*. Boston: David R. Godine, 1974/2006.

Tom, our hero, knows all about fooling around. Aunt Fidget Wonkham-Strong (who wears an iron hat and takes no nonsense from anyone) has definitely forgotten all about playing – if she ever knew. She considers Tom is having too much fun, so she summons Captain Najork and his hired sportsmen to sort him out. But who needs sorting ...? Superlative Quentin Blake illustrations, too.

References

1 BRUCE, T. *Time to Play in Early Childhood*. London: Hodder and Stoughton, 1991; BRUCE, T. *Learning Through Play: Babies, Toddlers and the Foundation Years*. London: Hodder and Stoughton, 2001; FEATHERSTONE, S. (ed.) *Again! Again! Understanding Schemas in Young Children*. London: A&C Black, 2008; FISHER, J. *Starting from the Child*, 3rd edn. Maidenhead: Open University Press, 2008; GOLDSCHMIED, E. & JACKSON, S. *People Under Three*, 2nd edn. London: Routledge, 2004.

2 FISHER, J. *Starting from the Child*, 3rd edn. Maidenhead: Open University Press, 2008: 129–131.

3 PALEY, V.G. *A Child's Work: The Importance of Fantasy Play*. London: Heinemann, 2004: 8.

4 ISAACS, S. *The Educational Value of the Nursery School*. London: The British Association for Early Childhood Education, 1954: 23.

5 LINDON, J. *Understanding Child Development: Linking Theory and Practice*. London: Hodder Arnold, 2005: 115–138.

6 DEPARTMENT for EDUCATION AND SKILLS (DfES), *The Early Years Foundation Stage: Setting the Standards for Learning, Development and Care for Children from Birth to Five*. London: DfES, 2007: 7.

7 CHUKOVSKY, K. *From Two to Five*. Berkeley, CA: University of California Press 1966: 103 (first published in the Soviet Union in 1925); KOESTLER, A., *The Act of Creation*. New York: Dell, 1964; HUIZINGA, J. *Homo Ludens: A Study of the Play Elements in Culture*. London: Routledge and Kegan Paul, 1949.

8 ATHEY, C. *Extending Thought in Young Children*, 2nd edn. London: Paul Chapman Publishing, 2007: 192–193.

9 FEATHERSTONE, S. (ed.) *Again! Again! Understanding Schemas in Young Children*. London: A&C Black, 2008; NUTBROWN, C. *Threads of Thinking: Young Children Learning and the Role of Early Education*, 2nd edn. London: Paul Chapman Publishing, 1999; PEEP *The Learning Together Series: Learning Together with Ones: Play Patterns, and Learning Together with Threes: Making the Most of Play Patterns*. Oxford: Peers Early Education Partnership, 2000: 26 (www.peep.org.uk).

10 PEEP *The Learning Together Series: Learning Together with Threes: Making the Most of Play Patterns*. Oxford: Peers Early Education Partnership, 2000: 26 (www.peep.org.uk).

11 PALEY, V.G. *Mrs. Tully's Room: A Childcare Portrait*. Cambridge, MA: Harvard University Press, 2001.

12 FISHER, J. *Starting from the Child*, 3rd edn. Maidenhead: Open University Press, 2008: 132.

Part 4

INVESTING IN WELLBEING

Observation, Assessment and Planning

Observation for Wellbeing

Observation is about watching and listening – and other things, too. As with so many other aspects of living and working with young children, there is no one right way to do it. The observation, assessment and planning cycle described here relates especially to children's wellbeing. This model has its own particular characteristics. It is different in some ways from other methods – yet in some ways similar. It may be useful to incorporate aspects of it into existing models. It is a set of strategies that practitioners may want to use exactly as described here, or – perhaps more interestingly – to play with in the context of what they do already.

The best models of observation, assessment and planning are those that are most nearly fit for purpose – whatever that purpose is. In this model, the purpose of observation relates to children's developing wellbeing as well as to other requirements. The process of observation is essentially one of communication, using all of our senses.

For early years practitioners, observation is a basic element of our work. It is often best achieved by using not just our eyes and ears and other senses, but also our heads and hearts. This kind of observation is the most likely kind to help us to think about 'what is going on in the heads of these children – if only we could see inside'. It is very far, for instance, from the kind of observation schedules that are designed to be essentially objective, quantifiable and comparable. These are important too, but have been designed to answer different questions.

Chapter 4 described the concept of 'companionable attention'. When we are giving children the companionable attention they need, we will – if we are being properly companionable and attentive – be observing them as part of that process. Observation, recording and assessment are different processes, although the term 'observation' is often used interchangeably for all three. The quality of our observation depends primarily on the quality of attention that we give to the children we are observing. Our skills in recording and assessing those observations are different, subsequent issues.

When observation is an interactive process of companionable attention, it not only gives us the material that we need, for purposes such as planning, or reporting, or accountability – it actually *is* the work of companionable learning. Companionable attention is how we make relationships with children, so that we know what support they need in order to learn. It is an important factor in how young children's wellbeing thrives. In curriculum terms, the processes of companionable attention and companionable learning are central to the areas of personal, social and emotional development, and to the development of communication and language.

Observing children is how we come to know them; and the better we know them, the better we shall be able to provide for them and support their wellbeing. Vygotsky says that the best way to support children's learning is to find out about the things that they want to do on their own and can nearly do, and help them to achieve those things them-selves.[1] This question of what children want to do on their own and can nearly do is immeasurably more useful for supporting their learning, than 'ticking off' what they can already do on their own. Many early years practitioners who possess a high degree of professionalism have, over time, developed ways to observe children with companionable attention as an integral part of their practice.

Purposes of observation

In general there are two main purposes of this kind of interactive obser-vation. The first is directly to benefit children through their experience of the companionable attention that it involves. Their agency, their sense of belonging and boundaries, and their communication, are all supported by this kind of sensitive observation. These observations are sometimes recorded, sometimes not – except mentally. Skilled practi-tioners are likely to sustain this observation technique throughout the day, but could not possibly write down everything.

Much of the rest of this book is about that kind of companionable atten-tion. This chapter focuses on the second main purpose of observing children, which is directly to benefit practitioners through collecting, recording and organising information that they are required to provide. This may be done for a variety of possible purposes, most but not all of which benefit children too – but indirectly. Because the information needs to be retrievable in order to be used, observations for these purposes need to be regularly, reliably and systematically recorded.

Possible uses for recorded observations include:

- To create opportunities for practitioners' own reflective practice.
- To collect information in order to assess and plan more appropriately for children's individual and collective needs and interests.
- To focus on particular children (invisible/vulnerable/challenging) whom practitioners would like to understand better, or about whom they have concerns.
- To audit provision in a setting in relation to wellbeing.
- To collect information as a starting point for discussions with parents and/or colleagues.
- To acknowledge every child's right to express his or her views.[2]
- To fulfil statutory requirements.
- Above all, to learn about how children learn.

A single rich observation may be used for more than one of these purposes, for instance both for reflection about how this child learns, and as a starting point for talking to parents; and/or to feed into planning, as well as to fulfill statutory requirements.

Principles for observation

The overarching principle for observing, recording and assessing children is that the purpose should be of benefit to them in some way, directly or indirectly.

In addition, children are entitled to:

- observation that is attentive, sensitive, honest and respectful
- a positive approach that starts with what they can do, or can nearly do, and which protects the child's positive sense of self
- a relationship with the observer based on mutual trust.

Practitioners should:

- ensure children's entitlements are met (see above)
- make observation an integral part of their everyday practice
- ask themselves reflective questions about the observations they record
- appropriately involve parents and colleagues
- base their planning on what they have observed.

Doing observations

If observation is seen as a separate activity in addition to the rest of the working day with children, time may well be a major problem. Very many practitioners acknowledge that it is a struggle to find time to do such observations. But we are watching and listening to children throughout our day with them, and observing is essentially a watching and listening process. Paying companionable attention to the children with whom we are working does not need dedicated time. It is a particular kind of approach, involving companionship, collaboration, and 'leading from behind'.

Practitioners whose approach is to impart or transmit knowledge, skills and understanding may be too involved in 'leading from the front' for this kind of approach. But the side-by-side companionable learning described in Chapter 4 will be rich with opportunities to observe children as part of normal daily interactions. As well as being at the heart of the educator's job – learning how children learn – this is surely one of the greatest pleasures of living and working with young children. When we let them know that they have our attention – and when they trust us – they are very likely to want to tell us about what is important to them. That is their response when we let them know that we are deeply interested in them.

Here is Mrs Weston, a teacher in a foundation stage setting, wanting to learn more about Freddie, now nearly 3 years.

It is Tuesday morning, about an hour into the session. The room is busy, most of the hum coming from the big table where the children are mixing paints with Jim, ready for the big brushes and rolled out lining paper outside. Mrs Weston knows they will be busy for a while yet, and everyone else seems settled. Groping in her pocket for notebook and pencil she writes the date on a clean page, and looks around for Freddie. For once he does not seem to be hovering on the edge of the action, watching the others. Then she sees him, playing on his own in the home corner and completely absorbed in his own 'mixing' with plastic saucepan and spoon. She goes over and sits down unobtrusively on a nearby chair. He glances up and sees her watching him, stops with spoon in midair and looks at her uncertainly. She smiles at him gently and affectionately, but says nothing. Reassured, he turns back to his mixing. Without taking her eyes off Freddie, Mrs Weston writes 'Freddie', 'Cooking' and 'Just checking' on a fresh page in her notebook.

After a few minutes Lisa wanders into the home corner too, watches Freddie for a moment or two and then, having seized a bowl and a spoon, she starts 'mixing' too. She seems unaware of Mrs Weston, who scribbles 'Lisa' while still watching, not wanting to miss what happens next. Freddie puts the saucepan into the little 'microwave' cupboard over the pretend cooker. He slams the door shut with a flourish, and presses the buttons exactly the way his mum would. He turns away looking pleased, and Lisa, who by now is standing right next to him, tries to put her bowl into the microwave too. As she reaches up Freddie realises what she is doing, and firmly pushes her aside. She tries again, looking determined, and they struggle. But Freddie is taller and heavier than Lisa, and in the end she gives up. First looking reproachfully at him she turns away and wanders off, looking solemn. Freddie watches her go, a strangely adult look of guilt and regret on his face, as if to say 'Please come back, you can play, I'm sorry'; and after a moment also reaches out a hand after her. But it is too late, she has forgotten about cooking and with her back to him is bending over to pick up a doll.

Mrs Weston has watched attentively through the whole episode. Now she scribbles down 'pushing' and 'regret', then returns the notebook to her pocket. Freddie looks past her towards the big table and she smiles at him sympathetically, but doesn't know if he sees. Suddenly the paint mixing has come to an end, and Mrs Weston goes to help Jim and the children take it outside.

Recording observations

At the time of an observation, we do not necessarily know what we will use it for. We are simply absorbing, as accurately and appropriately as possible, everything that is going on. Consequently we are often on the receiving end of a huge amount of information – especially when working in this way with two or more children at the same time. While this 'companionable' perspective may make the initial process of observation more manageable, it does not ease the problem of the time needed to record what we have seen. A problem is that our memories can get overloaded, and with so many layers of episodes the earlier ones may tend to get lost.

Word notes

One solution is 'word notes', with which events can be brought back to mind very easily (provided it is the same day) by the trigger of a single word or two. These words act as 'hooks' on which to hang our memories until the end of the day. This strategy can work well if word notes are sorted at the end of each day and just some of them written up. But with the best will in the world this is not always possible, and the strategy works less well if left overnight. Inevitably, many rich observations will not make it on to record. Yet they will not have been wasted, because the process of companionable attention that generated them will have directly benefited the child.

A pencil and scrap of paper in the pocket is all that is needed for word notes. Alternatively, short observations are often written on Post-its, scraps of paper, in a small notebook, and so on. They all need collecting together regularly – somewhere safe, and using some sort of system. Usually they are slotted into a folder or stapled into a larger notebook, and given identifying details of name and age of child, and a title such as 'Dylan + watering can', or 'Sasha's ice-cream'. A really rich observation may justify a much more detailed record, and the greater breadth and depth of such records always pays off when it comes to assessment.

Organising observations

A degree of careful organisation can be very helpful. There are a few essentials to bear in mind at this recording stage:

- At the time of observing, make sure that every single observation carries: (a) the date of the observation; and (b) the name(s) of the child(ren). The age of the child is essential too, but assuming that the dates of birth of all the children being observed are on record, that can be worked out later.

- Use a small memory trigger (word notes) at the time of each episode, in order to recall it in more detail later.

- Use a confidential system that keeps all observations together, and that ensures they can be retrieved easily to assess and use them. This means page numbers or labelled pockets.

- Be careful not to let speculations or assessments leak into the record of what actually happened.

- Remember that parents have the right to share records of their children. Using a positive approach that starts with what children *can* do, is very helpful in this respect. We still identify children's needs, but in the context of achievements.

Mrs Weston puts the kettle on. The staffroom is quiet for the moment, but soon they'll all be through with clearing up and ready for the team meeting, so she hasn't got long. While the kettle comes to the boil she fishes the notebook out of her pocket, and flicks through it thoughtfully. Coming to the page headed 'Freddie', she stops. She is puzzled by Freddie … he is so often on the edge of things, never any trouble. But she feels she knows almost nothing about him, in spite of him being in the nursery for several months now. She has been so taken up by the usual little lot lately that she hasn't really noticed him. Freddie is brought to nursery and collected by his mum, but Mrs Weston sees very little of her – she always needs to go quickly because of little Ellie's feed. 'Perhaps a home visit would help' thinks Mrs Weston. 'It would give me a chance for a chat with Freddie's mum'.

The kettle boils, and Mrs Weston decides. Quickly she pours tea into the pot, puts the mugs ready, and then takes her work diary from her bag. Sitting at the table over in the corner, she checks the page number and starts to write rapidly, recording her observation of Freddie that morning in enough detail for her to think about it. This takes her about five minutes. 'Maybe just enough time to assess it', she thinks. Just then the door opens and in comes Joanne, her student, carrying the video camera. With a small sigh she closes her diary. 'In the cupboard over there' she points for Joanne; and 'Did it work alright?' Then 'Tea's ready, would you like some?'

There are many ways to record what we have observed, and no best way – our choice of method or methods will be the ones that are practical in our own particular circumstances, and that work best for us in relation to what our observations are going to be used for. A helpful strategy is to build into the end of each day a little time to select and write up some of our observations. This becomes a great deal quicker and easier as it settles down into a routine.

Inevitably, though, some days are better than others in terms of getting this part of the job done. But building up a collection of observations can be immensely satisfying and reassuring. There is always information when it is needed, and it certainly will be needed – for some, or possibly all, of the purposes identified above.

Using still and video cameras

One way to help the memory at the end of the day is to have a digital camera always accessible for taking still photographs. Discreetly use it a lot. Photographs can replace word notes, as well as becoming part of the record itself. 'A picture is worth a thousand words' as the saying goes.

Another great strategy is using a video camera. Filming an observation can save the time needed to write it. More importantly, video gives more vivid, detailed and accurate pictures than written observations. A digital camera with a basic editing facility works best, as then anything unwanted can be deleted straightaway.

This way of recording sometimes requires a different approach to written observations. If the observation is to capture an episode of companionable learning between a key person and child, a third person will be needed. This may be possible, as for instance when Mrs Weston's student does the filming (see below). But often it requires planning in advance, so video observations are less likely to be a spontaneous part of a key person's day.

Joanne has just asked if she can film something special for her project next week. The video camera battery is fine, and Mrs Weston thinks the best idea would be something outside. So when Jim says it is a lovely calm day and why don't they do giant painting outside, Joanne says eagerly 'How about that, today?'

Now they are nearly all outside, and Joanne is ready with the camera. Mrs Weston stands watchfully by the door as the children carry out the paints. She has put on her apron and now she notices Freddie is standing watching too, so she hands him an apron and says 'You'll need that I expect' and when he seems happy with the idea she helps him get it on. He steps carefully over the ledge into the garden and she follows.

Mrs Weston has asked Joanne if she has filmed children before, for college? Joanne says no, only her cousins. Mrs Weston explains about needing permission from parents, and that in this nursery parents are always asked to sign the permission form when they start, and that if they are OK about it they get to see the films any time, which they love. She says Joanne will need to make absolutely sure that Alex is not filmed because his mum has asked them not to; and that to be sure, she will keep an eye on him. Mrs Weston has also explained to Joanne that as they will want to watch and discuss what she films, the clips musn't be longer

(Continued)

than two or three minutes. Short clips are also a good thing if you need to delete anything straightaway, as you have to delete the whole clip, so you don't lose too much. Mrs Weston says that it's amazing how often observing and filming seems to fall into quite short episodes anyway, so it works; and that you only have to press 'pause' to separate the clips.

Out in the sunshine, the children are clamouring for the big brushes. Luckily Jim has gone overboard with stretches of paper, so there is plenty of space. He gathers them all together first though, and they crouch around him talking about what they are planning to do. Freddie stands on the edge, just watching and listening. Mrs Weston says to Joanne that she has been observing Freddie this morning, and it would be great to have a bit of film of him to think about too – please could she catch him on film if she gets the chance? She explains that focusing the film on individual children engaged in an activity often tells you more about both the children and that activity, than if you focus on the activity itself. Joanne says she will do her best, and Mrs Weston goes off to look for Alex.

This method of recording observations can pay huge dividends. It enables practitioners to identify and reflect on their own and each others' good practice, and areas for professional development. And watching a video clip together with parents makes a wonderful basis for discussion, especially about their child's wellbeing.

Very young children can be amazingly communicative on video film. Even babies often very deliberately 'speak' to the camera. Sometimes people comment on this, worrying that the observation is somehow 'contaminated' by the direct voice of the child. Whether this is a valid concern depends on the purpose of the observation, and is usually connected with a desire for objectivity. But in addition to the advantages outlined above, the camera can strengthen the value of an observation by capturing the voices of babies and young children themselves.

Video clips can be easily and instantly viewed by using a connecting cable to a television monitor, deleting them from the camera when no longer needed. If they are to be saved, they can be transferred to a hard drive. It is essential to have an external one for the computer though, because the size of video files would overload most computers. Each saved clip needs to be systematically labelled so that it can easily be retrieved. Enter the label into the observation diary together with minimum information: child's name and age, and an explanatory title.

Video observations are a powerful tool because:

- They are vivid, detailed and accurate.
- They give babies and very young children a recorded 'voice'.

- They facilitate the kind of very fine-grain observations that are especially important when supporting children with additional needs: for instance noticing with parents of a child who is 'not communicating' the sounds and body language made by the child which were communicative.

- They facilitate discussion with parents – watching a clip together is a more level playing field than practitioners describing to parents what they have seen.

- They give opportunities for colleagues to reflect together – again a more level playing field than one describing to another what they saw.

- The play-back button provides unique opportunities for reflection and discussion.

- Using video with children, parents and colleagues can be fun.

And here are some of the challenges:

- The time it takes to become familiar with the camera.

- The expense of the camera and external hard drive (although this is becoming considerably more manageable).

- Ethical issues about what happens to the material.

- Great care must be exercised in seeking permissions properly, especially if the material is to be retained.

Assessment and Planning for Wellbeing

Assessing observations

The term 'observation' is often followed by 'assessment' and then 'planning'. Observations provide the material for assessment (the thinking and the decisions we make about children's needs, based on our observations); and assessment feeds into planning. The process of assessment is about looking at the evidence and asking ourselves: 'What does this tell me?'

An important aspect of assessment is that it involves reflection. As we saw in relation to children's need for their own time and space (Chapter 5) reflection is an essential part of any learning process. Assessment is how we learn from our observations. Unfortunately in the rush of daily tasks with young children it is all too easy for reflection to be lost. We need time to think – at least briefly – about what we have seen, to try to make sense of it.

The need for conceptual structure

It can be helpful to use some sort of conceptual structure to think about observations. Whatever our purpose, when we study an observation it is helpful to have some points of reference to help answer the following questions:

• What was happening, when and with whom?

• What were the child's interests?

• What was the child learning?

• What else does the observation tell us about the child's wellbeing?

• What do we need to do next?

Unless we use a conceptual structure to scaffold these questions, inevitably our assessments will be based on our own temperaments and experiences (which is always a danger in any case). This may or may not be appropriate. Such a basis is likely to be largely unconscious and random. But if we do use a conceptual structure it needs to be valid, accessible and relevant if it is to be helpful. The familiar child development framework of emotional, social, cognitive and physical development has been one such structure. Alternatively a curriculum structure such as the areas of learning and development in the UK's Early Years Foundation Stage is often used; as are a range of 'principles' frameworks.

Whatever we use, we should be aware that the assessments we make are heavily influenced by the frameworks within which they are made. An advantage of using the Wellbeing Framework for assessment is that it focuses on the fundamental needs of children. As one child-minder put it: 'I'll go on using the (wellbeing) framework for thinking about my observations. It works because it's about what really matters'.

Introducing wellbeing codes

How can we ascertain whether children's wellbeing is developing? Which aspects are thriving? In what areas do they need more support, and why? These are the 'million-dollar questions' of assessment and planning.

Originating from the four wellbeing constructs, the components and coded elements in Figure 7.1 give us a structure to think about what is going on for the children we have observed. They have been used and refined by parents and practitioners over a four-year period, and are one way to break down the wellbeing constructs. A few of the coded elements may need some explanation, for instance A2.1 Positive learning dispositions, or B2.5

Self regulation. Brief explanations of their meanings can be found in the Glossary; with more detail in Chapter 3 The ABC of wellbeing.

Wellbeing constructs and components	Wellbeing elements and codes
AGENCY INFLUENCING	A1.1 Caring disposition (for self and others) A1.2 Sense of empowerment: making things happen A1.3 Internal decision-making
AGENCY LEARNING	A2.1 Positive learning dispositions A2.2 Sense of pride and achievement
AGENCY POSITIVE SENSE OF SELF	A3.1 Self esteem A3.2 Confidence
BELONGING-&- BOUNDARIES BELONGING	B1.1 Sense of identity (in relation to others) B1.2 'Attached' to companion(s) B1.3 Sense of belonging to place
BELONGING-&- BOUNDARIES BOUNDARIES	B2.1 Respect for people and places B2.2 Awareness of expectations B2.3 Familiarity with routines and rules B2.4 Understanding reasons for boundaries B2.5 Self regulation
COMMUNICATION RECEIVED	C1.1 Listening C1.2 Looking C1.3 Touching C1.4 Smelling and tasting
COMMUNICATION EXPRESSED	C2.1 Talking C2.2 Body language C2.3 Visual representing C2.4 Stories C2.5 Music and moving
PHYSICAL HEALTH & DEVELOPMENT	P1.1 Eating P1.2 Sleeping P1.3 Motor control P1.4 Health routines P1.5 Managing ill health
PHYSICAL ENVIRONMENT	P2.1 Income P2.2 Housing P2.3 Environment

Figure 7.1 Wellbeing codes

Returning to Mrs Weston we find her taking 10 minutes to think about Freddie. The assessments she makes here, and again at the end of the day with Joanne, are based on the wellbeing codes in Figure 7.1.

On Wednesday morning, Mrs Weston is in a bit early. She likes this time of day, when the phone is switched through to the office and the others are not in yet for setting up. She makes a cup of coffee and collects the codes list and Freddie's assessment sheet from the folder. Taking the diary, a pen and a high-lighter from her bag, she goes and sits at the table by the window in the sun. She enters the date and his age on the sheet, and opens the diary at yesterday's record. Quickly she reads through it again, and enters the diary page number on the sheet.

Now she pauses, looking vacantly out of the window, her mind's eye on Freddie reaching out to Lisa yesterday as she moved away from him. Then she looks back at the sheet and starts ticking the codes: A1.1 (Caring disposition), A1.3 (Internal decision-making), A2.1 (Positive learning dispositions), A2.2 (Sense of pride and achievement), B2.2 (Awareness of expectations), B2.3 (Familiarity with routines and rules), C1.2 (Looking), C2.2 (Body language), P1.3 (Motor control).

She pauses, then codes again but this time with rings: A3.2 (Confidence), B1.1 (Sense of identity in relation to others), C2.1 (Talking). 'Mmmmm, that makes sense' she mutters. 'Does he need to be doing things specially with particular other children? ' And then, 'Mmm, I was going to the shop on Friday, wasn't I? Could take him with Lisa and give the two of them a special job to do'. She writes in the final column on the sheet 'Playing well on own, but !belonging!, needs to be making friends. Take him and L. to shop on Friday with list they have made together & both to do cooking?'

She pauses again, then as she highlights this last sentence she hears the sound of arrivals in the corridor. 'Good timing' she says, and replacing the assessment sheet in the folder she goes off to start the day.

Often we need the opportunity to talk about observations reflectively, too; with parents or carers, colleagues or children. Even the very youngest children respond to conversations reflecting on and dis-cussing recent events in which they have taken part.

It is later on Wednesday, and Mrs Weston and Joanne are meeting in the staff-room after nursery to review Joanne's week so far and make sure she is doing what she needs for her project in College next week. Mrs Weston asks Joanne how she got on filming Freddie and the giant painting in the garden this morn-ing. Joanne says she thinks OK, although most of the time Freddie was just watching the others. 'What happened then?' asks Mrs Weston. Joanne describes how there was a moment when the other children were getting on with it and Jim went and stood next to Freddie and watched them too for a bit – so she pointed the camera that way at both of them. Jim was holding a paint pot with a giant brush in each hand, but they were just standing there. Joanne says she was nearly going to point the camera back at the others but then Jim looked down at Freddie and smiled at him, and Freddie saw. So then Jim gave him a pot, still smiling, and said 'Come on mate'. Joanne says then she filmed the next bit too – there was a clear bit of paper right near them, and they did a bit together and Jim and Freddie made each other laugh by pretending their brushes were excited, so Freddie was having a great time. But then some other children came and joined in, and Freddie just dropped his brush on the grass and went away. Joanne says she thought she had better not follow him with the camera as he might get upset, so she stayed with the others.

'Yes – good' Mrs Weston says, and 'Well, that might be a help'; and Joanne asks 'Why – how do you know that?' Mrs Weston says that this is probably a good time to show Joanne about assessment in the nursery – how they think about things they have observed. She says that if they watch the bit of film about Freddie together, that would be a good way to explain it. So Joanne fetches the camera from the cupboard and plugs it into the monitor in the corner; and Mrs Weston takes the codes list and Freddie's assessment sheet from the folder again.

'OK' says Mrs Weston, 'Let's just watch it first. How long is it?' Joanne says she thinks it's only about three minutes, because the other children came over soon after Freddie and Jim started laughing. 'Perfect' says Mrs Weston as they sit down. 'I hope it tells us something useful. He's been here several months and I really feel I don't know anything about him at all – and he always looks so solemn'.

Joanne finds the clip easily, and there is Freddie in the garden with Jim. It's just as she remembered it, and she says it's nice to see Freddie laughing for a change, but she can't really see that it tells them anything, does it? Mrs Weston smiles thoughtfully and says 'Let's look at it this way'. She shows the codes sheet to Joanne, explaining about the ABC constructs and how the constructs are made up of components and then the coded elements. Then she shows Joanne the assessment she did that morning about Freddie, and Joanne begins to see how it works. In the next row of the assessment sheet Mrs Weston puts the video clip number in the reference column and says 'OK, all ready, let's just watch him again, and we can pause it as we go along.'

As they watch, Joanne is getting drawn into the 'story' again, but Mrs Weston stops it now and then and asks her what she thinks about the codes. They do ticks first: C1.1 (Listening), and C1.2 (Looking), for the first bit; then something about the way they see Freddie's awareness of Jim standing next to him and smiling at him makes them put B1.1 (Sense of identity in relation to others). The laughing bit is different, and they decide to add several other codes: A3.2 (Confidence) –

(Continued)

the way Freddie paints – A1.2 (Sense of being able to make things happen) – making Jim laugh – B1.2 ('Attached' to companions) – for a while his almost tangible trust in Jim. Then as well they add C1.3 (Touching) – Freddie used his fingers as well as the brush – C2.2 (Body language) – his evident enjoyment of being with Jim – and P1.3 (Motor control) – his skill with the brush and how he coordinates with Jim. 'Mm' says Mrs Weston, 'We've seen his motor control before – and now we know it's not that he minds getting in a mess, either'.

Soon they are near the end, where the other children arrive and Freddie goes away. 'Ah!' says Mrs Weston. 'I think this is the bit. Look at Freddie's face'. Watching it again, Joanne sees for the first time Freddie's frustration and disappointment as Jim includes the others in the game; the unobtrusive way Freddie puts down his brush so that Jim doesn't even notice; and the miserable hunch of his shoulders as he walks away. At the end they sit in silence for a moment. 'What d'you think?' asks Mrs Weston. 'Well' says Joanne, now thoroughly hooked, 'Surely it's about B1.2 isn't it? He felt attached to Jim, but suddenly the others had Jim instead and he's on his own again'. 'Yes' agrees Mrs Weston. 'That makes sense'.

They continue talking it over for a few more minutes, then Mrs Weston says 'Now we need to plan what we can do to help him. That's what the last column is for'. They are quiet again for a moment, thinking, and then Mrs Weston brightens up. 'Tell you what!' she says. 'Instead of us doing it now, how about if you think it over for the case study part of your project?'

'Oh yes!' says Joanne enthusiastically. 'And then if it's OK, working with Freddie can be part of what I do after next week, can't it?'

A reductive process

Moving from observation to recording to assessment is essentially a reductive process: out of all the things that we observe happening we are only able to record some of them. And then we need to decide which of those recorded observations we are going to assess, and for what purpose.

At this point we need to be able to answer the question: 'What am I doing this assessment for?' Maybe we simply want to reflect in more breadth and depth about a particular child. Or perhaps our purpose is to contribute to a child's formative assessment – in which the observations, photographs, video clips and things children have made are being used to inform or guide everyday planning. Eventually, too, some assessments are likely to be needed for a summative assessment such as a child's profile. Or perhaps we need something positive and vivid to start a conversation with parents, or with colleagues in other services.

Connecting observation and assessment with planning for individual children

Having explored some reasons and processes for observation and assessment, this section is about a system for using the Wellbeing Framework. The system takes us from a work diary of observations of children and provision, through recording and assessment, to planning that meets the needs of those individual children. It introduces and gives examples of assessment sheets and 'Pebbles Records'. This system is just one way of putting into practice the Wellbeing Framework of constructs and companionable learning – a kind of wellbeing 'toolbox'. Once practitioners understand the framework well enough to play with it, they come up with many variations and uses. This is a description of just one way, based on a particular assessment sheet format.

There are three versions of these assessment sheets, for three different purposes: standard, for each child; diagnostic one-week special; and provision assessment.

The Pebbles Records are for capturing a selection of assessments from the sheets. These are especially useful for sharing information with parents and colleagues, as the design makes them arresting, memorable and easy to use.

The 'what to do' sections aim to provide enough guidance to get people started. There can be no substitute for learning how to use something by actually using it ... and by using it, coming to know it so well that you can play with it.

Wellbeing Assessment Sheets: What to do

Version 1: 'Child wellbeing' assessment

The 'standard' wellbeing assessment sheet can be used for each child. The assessment sheets are a format for 'processing' observations in three stages:

1. Enter details and note location (in your collection of observations) of recorded observations (written/video/photos) you want to assess.

2. By using the wellbeing codes, assess those observations in relation to the child's wellbeing, and (for practitioners in England) their relevance to the EYFS.

3. Note resulting thoughts, and ideas for planning.

It helps to bear in mind that there is no 'right' way for constructs, components and elements to be allocated during coding. The purpose of this kind of coding is not to 'get it right', but to use it as a process for reflection, assessment and planning. This is just one way of thinking about the complex processes of child development in relation to resilient wellbeing. Rather than asking ourselves 'Is this right?', we can ask 'Is this useful?' In a pragmatic sense, a theory – in this case of wellbeing – can be said to be just as good as it is useful.

The observations on a standard child wellbeing assessment sheet will have been collected and analysed for planning over a period of months. Figure 7.2 shows the child wellbeing assessment sheet that Mrs Weston was using for Freddie on that Wednesday morning.

What to do

1. Each child that you are using this system for will need their own assessment sheet (and Pebbles Record, see below).

2. The process starts by selecting the most interesting/revealing/ challenging/rich/puzzling, etc. observations of the child (written, photographic or filmed) from your notebook – i.e. the ones you want to analyse and think about, use for planning, and may want to share with others.

3. Focus on the positive – what children can do, and especially the things children are struggling to do independently.

4. If so far there are only 'word notes', write an account of what happened, or if it is a video observation, watch it through.

5. Enter identifying details for this observation on the assessment sheet, i.e. practitioner name and date; child's name, d. of b. and age; diary reference; memory trigger.

6. Read (or watch) again, stopping on the way to identify and enter wellbeing codes in the columns. (At first, you may need a list of the codes to hand.) Which codes come up often? Are some conspicuous by their absence? What do the codes tell you about the child's wellbeing?

7. Some codes might indicate the need for particular support and planning. These 'downside' ones can be circled.

8. Enter comments and planning ideas into the final column.

9. Amend existing planning as appropriate in the light of these ideas.

It is worth noting that this apparently lengthy procedure becomes

CHILD WELLBEING ASSESSMENT

Child: Freddie A.

d of b:

Obser ver & date	Child's age	Diary / video ref	Memory trigger	AGENCY			B & B		COMM		PHYSICAL		EYFS refs	Notes and planning
				A/1	A/2	A/3	B/1	B/2	C/1	C/2	P/1	P/2		
1 RW 09/12/08	2.5	3/ p.11	Sofa + boots, with Grace + me (11.30)	NEW	2.1			2.2 2.3 2.4 TRUS	1.1 1.2	2.1			PSE CLL KUW	F. interested but on edge of conversation — except for the Digger book. Talk to Mum re favourite books?
2 RW 27/01/09	2.8	4/ p.21	F. arriving (8.30) + Mum & Ellie				1.1 1.2	2.2 2.3 2.4 2.5		2.2			PSE	F. hanging on to Mum but toddler sister had all her attention. Ask Mum re F at home? How comes play?
3 RW 03/04/09	2.11	5/ p.17	Microwave (10.00) bottle with Lisa	(1.2)	2.1 2.2	3.1 3.3	(1.1)	2.2 2.3	1.2	(2.1) 2.1 2.2	1.3		PSE CLL	Friday shopping — make list with F + L first? special job for both — locating? (no hurry to bring)
4														
5														
6														
7														
8														

Figure 7.2 Freddie's 'Child wellbeing assessment' sheet

fluent and fast with very little practice. It is like the difference between a drive to a new destination following step-by-step directions, and the same drive later when it has become so completely familiar that the car almost seems to drive itself.

Version 2: 'One-week special' assessment

Version 2 is the 'one-week special' sheet. Although using the same format, this 'diagnostic' version allows a more in-depth perspective. It is designed to capture and analyse more frequently what is going on for a particular child over a short period of a few days.

For more vulnerable children with especially complex needs, the rigour of careful recording and assessment is especially important. For these children a helpful strategy can be to by-pass the routine child observation sheet for the time being. Instead, use the 'One-week' sheet, together with a Pebbles record (see below). It is important to continue to focus on the positive. First, concentrate on what the child can do, and especially things the child is passionately interested in and struggling to master. As well as recording these efforts and achievements, it may also be helpful to record particular challenges that need reflection and planning.

This can be a useful format for 'key person' reception teachers who may not have time to use the assessment sheet for all children, but may find the 'one-week special' very helpful and appropriate for those occasional children that they find especially challenging. This version can be a lifeline in relation to supporting children who may have additional needs, too, about whom there are worries or puzzlement, and also for children who might be called 'invisible'. These are the few who are always occupied and compliant and never ask for anything, so do not get their share of companionable attention.

When Mrs Weston is sitting on the bus, sometimes she mentally lists her key children, and about a third of them instantly come crowding into her mind: the very conversational ones, the challenging ones, and the ones with complex developmental needs – those for whom this diagnostic version can obviously be so useful. Then she easily recalls nearly all the others – she feels she knows them well, and is unlikely to need this sheet for them. But the last two or three usually escape her, sometimes so completely that she has to look up their names. She is uncomfortably aware that they have not been getting their share of companionable attention.

It is Monday morning, and Mrs Weston and Joanne are setting up the room. Mrs Weston has been away for a few days with the 'flu, and Joanne is telling her about how they managed in her absence. Mrs Weston asks what happened about the idea for Freddie to go shopping and do cooking with Lisa. Joanne says that although the shopping and cooking had happened, Freddie and Lisa hadn't made the shopping list together first; and in fact Freddie had refused to go, and got seriously upset. 'The supply teacher had to call his mum and she took him home early'.

'Why was he so upset?' asks Mrs Weston.

'Well ... I think it started because he didn't want to hold anyone's hand. But then he started really crying and couldn't stop'.

'Mm ...' Mrs Weston puts a big bowl of earth down on the table and looks around for the box of magnifiers. She adds 'And you haven't seen your tutor about your project yet, have you, so we can't really get on with anything for him just yet. For Freddie's sake I really don't think we should do nothing just now though, do you?'

'No' agrees Joanne. 'And I wonder how he'll be today'.

'I know what we could do' says Mrs Weston. 'If he comes today, would you like to have a go at one of the one-week assessments I told you about the other day? Then we'll sort of be doing something, because there's something very reassuring for children like Freddie when someone is really interested in them for a while – and it will help you plan for him too, won't it?'

The one-week assessment form completed by Joanne is shown in Figure 7.3.

Use this version as an occasional one-off 'in-depth' strategy to help assess and plan for children in your setting about whom you are puzzled, or who have additional health needs, language delay, challenging behaviour, precarious confidence, and so on.

What to do

1. Over a period of a few days, record brief written observations directly onto this sheet.

2. Carry out steps 5–9 as for the standard version (see above).

3. Write further notes/discussions on the back of sheet.

Version 3: 'Wellbeing provision' assessment

This third version differs from the other two. Rather than focusing on the child, it is about auditing and assessing provision for wellbeing in settings. Capturing the main situations and experiences for children through the day and analysing them for wellbeing reveals a great deal

ONE-WEEK SPECIAL
Child: Freddie A.

Place in family: 1/2

d. of b. 21.05.06

age: 2 yrs 11 months

Background notes: e.g. medical, separations & greetings, special events, companions, food, sleep, nappies/toileting, etc.

Busy weekend, F. quite tired on Monday. Mum having to push this week as Ellie (12 months) is just starting with the childminder & Mum is settling her there before she goes back to work. She says F. still quite clingy at home. Nothing special at Nursery this week.

Obser ver & date	Time, place, people	Observation	AGENCY →			B & B →		COMM →		PHYSICAL →		EYFS refs	Notes and planning
			A/1	A/2	A/3	B/1	B/2	C/1	C/2	P/1	P/2		
1 JF 10/04/09	10.00 Workshop M & F.	I persuaded F. first difficult about using a Book Box. He was v. competent with scissors etc. & quiet about it being in Book Box – lots of chat about them.	1.2	2.1 2.2	3.1 3.2	1.2		1.1 1.2	2.1 2.4	1.3		PSE CLL KUW PD	F. seemed quite attached to me. Followed me around for rest of morning. Great F. to explain his box to the group?
2 JT 11/04/09	11.30 Garden F. on his own	Water play. F. had doll, was washing her hair over & over, then wrapped her up & put her in the towel & put her into the Book Box, lid on.	1.2		3.1 3.2 3.3	1.1 1.2	2.3 2.5		2.2 2.3	1.3 1.4		PSE CD	Try home corner play, especially cot, blankets, dolls etc?
3 JT 12/04/09	10.00 Cooking in kitchen with 2 children & RW.	Making sandwiches for snack time. Happy but with F. RW gave him "important jobs" – keen to be in charge of plate & hand round sandwiches.	1.1 1.2	2.2 2.3	3.2 3.3	1.2	2.3	1.1 1.2 1.3 1.4	2.1 2.2	1.1 1.3		PSE CLL	More cooking!
4 JT 13/04/09	11.30 Circle time on carpet, widespread + RW?	RW telling story. F. right at back, not engaged or watching. Riding at edge of carpet; seemed to be just watching. (Others loved it)	loved it)				2.3		2.2			?	Did he realise he was missing something? Sit him at front? Hearing test?
5													

Figure 7.3 'One-week special' for Freddie

WELLBEING PROVISION ASSESSMENT

(Teacher supervising students' provision)

Observer & date	Provision	Who	AGENCY A/1	A/2	B & B A/3	COMM B/1	B/2	PHYSICAL C/1	C/2	P/1	P/2	Notes and planning for wellbeing
1 RW 02/02/09	Snack time (Prep. & s'vision by J)	Sofia Bhavna Hamza				1.1 1.3	2.3	1.1 1.2 1.4	2.1 2.2	1.1		Used children waiting, the chatting. ?Others ?— feels like a wasted opportunity. Involve children in prep, serving, clearing away?
2 RW 03/02/09	Circle time (J's college task)	All						1.1 1.2	2.2			Formal & rather boring phonics game. Need to re-think this re wellbeing.
3 RW 05/02/09	Going to corner shop – Mrs J + 4 children	RW JT + Richard ...	1.1 1.2	2.1 2.2	3.2 3.3	1.1 1.2	2.1 2.2 2.4 2.5	1.1 1.2 1.3 1.4	2.1 2.2	1.3		Wonderful. V. well done by J. Explore midwife children in planning to follow through. Make a list of possible tiny expeditions.
4 RW 06/02/09	Tidy up time	All		(2.2)			2.2 2.3 2.4	1.2 1.3		1.3		Could be much richer — needs more doing together + done it (A2.2)
5 09/02/09	Puzzles		1.2	2.2				1.1 1.3		1.3		Only 2 children, both could do them easily already. Monitor which children come ... Why?
6	Construction											
7	Home corner											
8												

© 2010 Rosemary Roberts

Figure 7.4 'Wellbeing provision assessment' example

about the richest and most important times of day for children's development – and about those times, sometimes rather lengthy, that do little to contribute to children's wellbeing. It offers opportunities to think about certain times of day – for instance dinner time, or going home time – in terms of maximising possibilities for wellbeing development. The example in Figure 7.4 reveals a critical appreciation of some of the daily situations that are often taken for granted and not perceived as opportunities for wellbeing.

What to do

Use this sheet for identifying and making the most of those situations and experiences in the children's day that are likely to be richest in terms of wellbeing development. Auditing all the main situations may stretch over a period of a few weeks. It is important actually to observe them, rather than just list them.

1. Observe and briefly describe children's frequent situations and experiences through the day, e.g. water play outside, doing puzzles, play in the home corner, story time, circle time, etc. Give each description a new line.

2. As soon as possible, code each one.

3. What does this process tell you? Which situations and experiences are rich for wellbeing? Perhaps children are spending time regularly in situations and experiences with little or no wellbeing richness – does this need to continue?

4. Enter questions, ideas and planning possibilities into the final column. What might be done differently, to make the day richer?

5. Discuss with colleagues.

Pebbles Records and Charts: What to do

Pebbles records

The Pebbles record is the 'summarising and reporting' sheet for each child. The 'reminding' pebbles across the centre of the sheet represent the ABC constructs of Agency, Belonging-and-Boundaries, and Communication. The circles are interlinked, emphasising the interdependence of the four constructs. The spaces inside the pebbles are places for photographs and observations of the child. These can be placed near to the most relevant of the 'reminding' pebbles in the middle, and/or colour-coded, often with more than one colour: red agency, yellow belonging-and-boundaries, blue communication and green physical wellbeing. 'Companionable learning' runs along the foot of the records, highlighting the fundamental process through which well-being develops. When the first page is full, the record can be continued indefinitely on subsequent sheets of blank pebbles.

Figure 7.5 is an example of what a Pebbles record can look like when completed. This particular one was used as a starting point for the 'set-tling in' meeting after a few weeks in the nursery, between the child's parents and her key person.

These records are especially useful for involving parents in discussing and planning for their children's wellbeing. Rich/interesting/revealing obser-vations from assessment sheets can be entered into the pebbles here, and colour coded using highlighters. Photographs make a compelling addi-tion. Pebbles records have been found to work well as starting points for discussions with parents; for feeding into planning with colleagues; and as the cover sheet in a child's Early Years Foundation Stage profile. They are especially useful, in combination with 'one-week specials', for children that tend to be the focus of many discussions both with parents and with colleagues, often from other services. Positive Pebbles records can be an ideal starting point for such discussions.

What to do

1. Start a Pebbles record for each child (name and date of birth at top left).

2. Enter a brief description of the observation with codes into a pebble, together with the diary/video reference (this enables you to locate the details if you need them for a more detailed discussion).

3. Colour-coding each pebble round the edge tells you at a glance which constructs were identified. Agency is red; Belonging-and-boundaries is yellow; Communication is blue; and Physical wellbeing is green. The most interesting in terms of wellbeing will be the most colourful observations.

4. When the front is full, continue on the back. (The 'reminding' peb-bles need only feature on the front of the first sheet). Further Pebbles sheets can be added, as observations build up.

A Pebbles short-cut ...

This short-cut involves missing out the assessment sheets and going straight to the Pebbles record. Bear in mind that using Pebbles records in this way therefore involves cutting down on your reflection time, and that it cuts out the connection to the English EYFS, and to your planning. But it can still work very well for sharing information and generating discussions with parents and colleagues. So while it has the undeniable advantage of saving time, inevitably the observations will be less detailed, and the assessments and coding not quite so reflective and reliable.

1. You can record brief observations straight onto the Pebbles record sheet and then code them, thereby cutting out the assessment sheet. Especially for hard-pressed reception teachers seeking strategies for the key person approach, using the Pebbles records as a single-stage process can be a very useful tool. We visit this idea in more detail in Chapter 6.

2. For early years practitioners who incorporate the Wellbeing Framework into their whole approach and become extremely fluent with it, this again can work very well as a one-stage process, for most children.

Pebbles wall charts

An enlarged, laminated version of the Pebbles record can be used for auditing wellbeing provision in a setting; as a basis for planning and displaying provision; for discussions with parents about the curriculum; and as a tool for staff development (see Chapter 10).

Purpose and Value

Using these wellbeing formats provides us with assessments and plans – but assessments and plans for what? They do not quantify progress, nor 'test' children's knowledge, skills and understanding in an objective or comprehensive way. Other 'tools' are designed for such purposes. These wellbeing formats can, however, tell us about children's interests, their companions and their experiences, structured in a way that informs our thinking and helps us plan appropriately for each individual child. And they can, if we choose to use them for the purpose, provide a rich source of evidence about children's experiences and abilities in relation to early learning goals or other summative assessments.

The quality of our practice depends on how well we know and understand children. Broadly, we obtain this knowledge and understanding in two ways: firstly through our professional study of child development (which is why the study of child development is of such primary importance); and

Figure 7.5 'Pebbles record' example

secondly, through our knowledge and understanding of individual children. This need to know and understand is the purpose of observation and assessment. It is why, all being well enough, parents are known to be the best people to care for their children, because they know them better than anyone else. And it is why 'key people' can also do a good job. They bring a knowledge of child development that parents often do not have (now supported in England by the Early Years Foundation Stage guidance); together with a detailed knowledge of their individual key children. These wellbeing formats are a 'tool' for filling in the second half of the picture: knowing and understanding the needs, interests, efforts and achievements of individual children.

So the real purpose and value of these formats is that they provide an accessible tool to support key people's understanding and consequent planning for children's holistic, everyday development. The starting point here is not a particular curriculum or a prescribed set of learning goals, relevant and appropriate though such things may sometimes be. They offer a tool for key people to base their planning on what matters to children, by starting with what children tell them, and what they know of their lives and their holistic, integrated development.

Key messages 🔑

- The processes of observation, recording and assessment for planning are essentially circular ones.
- Wellbeing observation is about communication: not just looking and listening with eyes and ears and other senses, but also with heads and hearts.
- Wellbeing observations need not be 'something extra'. They can be an integral part of everyday good practice with young children, using the process of companionable attention.
- Video observations are detailed and accurate, and can be extremely useful.
- Observations need to be underpinned by principles and systems.
- Assessments are the reflective thinking we do and the decisions we make, based on our observations.
- Our assessments are fundamentally influenced by whatever structures we choose for 'scaffolding' them, and by the purposes for which they are made.
- Wellbeing constructs, components, elements and codes form the basis of this system for assessing and planning for children's wellbeing. The system involves observation and assessment sheets, and Pebbles records for summarising and reporting.
- These assessments of children's wellbeing can feed into planning for individual children, into overall planning, and into summative assessments (such as the Foundation Stage Profile in England).

Questions to think about and discuss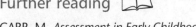

1. What principles and methods for observing children do you use? What are your observations for?
2. Using the wellbeing codes in Figure 7.1, draw up a 'Child Wellbeing Assessment Sheet' along the lines of the example in Figure 7.2. Try it out by using it to analyse one of your recent observations – or one in this book. With a colleague or fellow student, exchange explanations of what you have done, and your planning ideas for the child.
3. How could you use the Wellbeing Framework and ideas in this chapter in your current work?

Further reading

CARR, M. *Assessment in Early Childhood Settings: Learning Stories.* London: Paul Chapman Publishing, 2001.

This influential book elegantly combines theory and practice. It shows practitioners how to record and assess the things that matter to children, focusing especially on children's learning dispositions. With many illuminating examples, it builds a story around four 'D's: describing, discussing, documenting and deciding. Two more 'D's – difficulties and dilemmas – are addressed. The book is about 'a journey towards assessing the complex and the uncertain'.

DRUMMOND, M.J. *Assessing Children's Learning.* London: David Fulton, 1993 (2nd edn. 2003).

Like Carr, Drummond approaches assessment in a spirit of trust in children and their learning. The book addresses three central questions about assessing children's learning: what is there to see; how best can we understand what we see; and how can we put our understanding to good use? Drummond's answers to these questions, which resonate with the themes in this chapter, are illuminating and thought-provoking. The book is rich with the wisdom of past educators; and its reflective treatment of vital assessment issues makes it an extremely important book for early childhood practitioners.

FISHER, J. *Starting from the Child*, 3rd edn. London: Open University Press, 2008.

Starting from the Child, another important book for all practitioners, is a clear and practical description of what good practice in early childhood from three to five years means. Fisher's approach has much in common with Carr and Drummond, emphasising the competence of young children's thinking and learning. This is a meticulously researched and principled book that explains the vital role of assessment within the central themes of teaching and learning.

References

1 VYGOTSKY, L.S. *Mind in Society: The Development of Higher Psychological Processes.* Cambridge, MA: Harvard University Press, 1978.
2 CHILDREN'S RIGHTS ALLIANCE FOR ENGLAND *Children's Human Rights: What They Are and Why They Matter.* London: CRAE 2006.

Being Key Companions

This chapter looks at key people in settings, through a wellbeing lens. The key person approach, a requirement of the Early Years Foundation Stage in England, is:

> a way of working in nurseries in which the whole focus and organisation is aimed at enabling and supporting close attachments between individual children and individual nursery staff. The key person approach is an involvement, an individual and reciprocal commitment between a member of staff and a family.[1]

These key relationships are triangular, involving child, family and key person. Being a key person for the youngest children and their families is partly about relationships in the setting; and also, because of the impact on the child, about being aware of families in relation to their wellbeing at home.

As the Early Years Foundation Stage extends until age six, the key person role extends beyond nursery provision to involve teachers in the reception year in Primary Schools. From the child development point of view this is wholly appropriate, especially as it will be a time of transition for children – although it is a particularly challenging requirement for the teachers themselves. This chapter seeks to offer ideas and support to key people throughout the Foundation Stage.

Being Key Companions in Settings

The impact of companions' wellbeing on each other

In the triangle of child, family and key person relationships, a key person's own wellbeing underpins the quality of companionable attention that is available to the children and families with whom they work. When parents' wellbeing is low, we know that children are affected, from inevitable 'off days' to evidence of the impact of psychiatric disorder and physical illness.[2] The impact that young children's low wellbeing makes on their key people, and especially their mothers, is deeply familiar.

This 'impact factor' is a fundamental issue for mothers. A frequent comment by mothers is 'When my children are happy, so am I'. So although this chapter is about key adult companions – key staff and primary carers – it also includes children's wellbeing from the perspective of those companions.

The issue of damaged wellbeing both for adults and for children is the subject of Chapter 9 When Things Go Wrong.

Being a child's key person

What does it mean to be a key person? We know that for babies and young children, having a key person offers a sense of belonging, companionable attention, acceptance and inclusion, someone with whom to talk and listen and share ideas, and who provides consistency of care and expectations. All these things are of prime importance in relation to the child's wellbeing. But what about the wellbeing of the key person? Let us consider for a moment what is involved.

A key person's role is about getting to know certain families, and making close companionable relationships with those children; as distinct from making less close relationships with all children. It includes managing the daily hellos and goodbyes for those children; being the person who does most of their intimate physical care such as nappy-changing, sleep times, cuddles; taking the lead on observation, assessment and planning for those children; being responsible for organisational aspects of caring for the children; and liaising with other staff.

The complexities of being a key person for several children at once are highlighted in these accounts of moments in Dylan's nursery day with his key person Sally. We see the skilful way in which Sally 'holds' children simultaneously while responding appropriately to Dylan. First, we see them 'anchored' together as he wakes up; then she is there to encourage him down the slide, and be there for him at the bottom.

A few children are still asleep, others are awake but dozy, and Dylan has just woken up. He is cuddled up on one side of Sally, who is sitting on the floor with her back to the wall. Another child is waking up on her other side. There is gentle 'waking up' kind of music playing. It is very peaceful.

After a few moments Dylan slides down so that he is lying on the floor, looking up at Sally and smiling, inviting her to play; but the child on her other side needs her attention. After a while he gets up and wanders into the middle of the room. Sally takes the other child for a nappy-change, and Dylan follows them so that he can watch her through the gate.

Sally has finished the nappy-change and now she is sitting on the floor at the bottom of the slide. She looks up at Dylan who, by now, is sitting at the top ready to slide down – but hesitating. She smiles at him encouragingly and asks if he is coming down? He slides down on his bottom, shouts with excitement as he gets up, and goes straight back to do it again. This time he comes down head first on his tummy. His arms are reaching out in front of him, and as he picks himself up he puts his arms affectionately round Sally's neck and hugs her. Then, smiling to himself, he goes back for another slide, repeating the whole sequence including the cuddle – although by this time Sally has another child beside her as well. Sally sits Dylan on her knee while she goes on talking to the child beside her.

Here are two more glimpses of Sally in her key person role; first, picking up and responding to Dylan's wish for music but unable to dance with him, and second, noticing and calming to his frustration with 'going out' delays.

Later, Dylan is standing in the middle of the room and making some dancing movements. Sally notices immediately and says 'Shall we put the music on?' She goes over to the player on the shelf. Dylan runs after her, very excited and dancing in anticipation as she finds a CD and puts it on. When it starts he holds up his arms to Sally in an eloquent 'let's dance together' gesture … but another child is waiting for her and she isn't able to respond.

Now they have decided to go outside, and the staff begin to get the children ready. Dylan, quick off the mark, immediately seizes a pair of wellingtons placed nearby on the floor by Sally – but they are not his, and anyway it is his shoes that he needs. When it is his turn to have his shoes put on, he becomes very animated as soon as one shoe is on, and has to be patient ('hold on, one more to go' says Sally) while the other is put on too. Dylan runs over to the door, and after a moment picks up a basket that looked as though it has been put there in readiness for going out. But another member of staff relieves him of the basket, saying they are not ready to go yet. Discouraged, he goes off to the far side of the room where the play kitchen is, and with his back to the room begins to play determinedly with the pans. But Sally has noticed his frustration, and she goes over and holds out her hand, saying 'Let's go?' Dylan instantly drops the lid he had picked up and takes hold of her finger ... and off they go.

These observations of a key person in action tell us a great deal about Dylan's needs, and about Sally's professional skill, but nothing about Sally's own needs. What does this role mean for a key person's own wellbeing? How do these responsibilities sit with the four 'A's of wellbeing, those elements that children and adults need in order to function effectively? Which elements of wellbeing are likely to be fed by the key person role, and which are likely to be undermined? Here are some of the pluses and the minuses of the key person role in terms of his or her own professional wellbeing.

What about the first 'A', 'feeling anchored' in your job? Surely this is a plus, because of close relationships with children and families; so plenty of belonging. The second 'A', living with 'companionable authority', both on the giving and the receiving end? This is a plus, for boundaries. The third 'A', 'apprenticeship' – companionably learning together? When your practice is underpinned by companionable learning with both children and colleagues, this is definitely a plus. These three 'A's all apply to the children too, so it becomes a virtuous wellbeing circle.

But the fourth 'A', allowing 'time and space' to do a good job? Sometimes a plus and sometimes not, depending on the staffing levels in a setting; and unfortunately often a resounding minus in reception classes. Here is a comment from one reception teacher who had helped to develop the Pebbles sheets and wanted to continue exploring how she could use them.

> We had an OFSTED inspection so it was difficult to find time to continue evaluating observations for the wellbeing project using the Pebble sheets. I guess that emphasises the biggest downside for teachers with large class sizes – finding enough time to spend evaluating any observations.

> The wellbeing of the children certainly has much more emphasis in the new curriculum framework for Early Years; and the Pebble sheets certainly help to support this and would provide quality assurance to settings using them. I feel to give them justice they would be best used in smaller settings, or where there are more key workers who are able to give more attention to smaller numbers of children.

This honest reflection from an excellent teacher highlights the challenge. Thousands of reception teachers with large classes in England are now – appropriately for children's wellbeing – faced with the additional responsibility of the key person role. This teacher's words are a serious indictment of staffing levels and pressure at the top end of the Foundation Stage. Her children are not yet six years old, and yet in spite of her commitment to them, her job as it stands creates barriers against allowing her the physical time and the mental space to think reflectively about the children with whom she works.

Yet in spite of the difficulties, many teachers have managed to make adjustments to their day to support the key person requirement. These include: creating 'soft starts' to the day which give time for parents to exchange information and settle their children before register; planning key person group times into their day which are not focused or pressured, but allow a gentle exchange of information and ideas between the children and their key person; and organising their breaks so they can share lunch with their children. Ways of supporting reception teachers' key person role will develop – this can be done, and with committed and enthusiastic teachers leading the way it will be an on-going process.

In England, having a key person is an entitlement for children. Schools need to develop a shared vision between all the players – staff, parents, governors – to provide this continuous entitlement throughout the Foundation Stage. Individual teachers – especially reception teachers – cannot effect this change alone; but schools that support reception teachers in their key person role are investing in wellbeing and learning throughout the school.

There are other undeniable challenges of being a key person. What of the complexities of emotional involvement, the increased responsibility, the inevitable loss when child and family move on? Managing these things – rather than avoiding them – is not unrelated to positive wellbeing. The 'belonging' of emotional involvement and the 'agency' of increased responsibility are powerful things. As for having to learn how to manage loss with some degree of equanimity, can that be such a bad thing?

This account of being a key person may be less practical than the reader expects. It is more about why, in terms of the wellbeing of both children and key people, the key person approach is such a good one; provided it is properly understood and appropriately supported. Practical activities relating to children's everyday wellbeing and play are to be found in Part 3. Support in observing, assessment and planning for wellbeing is the focus of Chapter 7. Another very important aspect of being a key person is the organisational side of the role – the requirement to be the holder of information and the coordinating person in relation to other professionals. Strategies to integrate this aspect within the wider key person role are proposed in Chapter 10.

Supporting Companions at Home

The main players

An important part of the key person role is to be aware of children's lives at home, and to support families in relation to their children's wellbeing. Companions at home can come in many shapes and sizes – old and young, human and animal, real and imaginary. This section is about supporting the usual players: children, their parents, and other carers – often grandparents. Again using the structure of the four 'A's to scaffold our thinking, we look at some of the key messages for practitioners in this 'family focused' aspect of their work.

One factor from the wellbeing research referred to in the introduction to this book is relevant here. From analyses made of observations of the youngest children at home, an intriguing story emerged about the different 'agendas' of children and their parents in their everyday interactions. Parents were considerably more focused on their children's sense of belonging-and-boundaries than on the other wellbeing constructs; and this is hardly surprising, given parents' universal wish for their children's happiness on the one hand, and the need for boundaries that is brought home vividly by the many challenges and tantrums of this period of childhood.

Meanwhile, for the children themselves, their struggle for agency and their need and determination to communicate were the over-riding concerns. These two different agendas are reflected in many of the narratives in this book. It may be useful for practitioners supporting families to be aware of likely different priorities in their families, of belonging-and-boundaries for adult companions; and of agency and communication for the children. Home visiting can be an extraordinarily valuable strategy.[3]

So what are the main messages for key people supporting families' wellbeing in homes? While many answers to this question in relation to children are to be found in Part 3 about everyday wellbeing and play, here are some four 'A's headlines, together with some illustrative examples of developing wellbeing at home.

For children's anchored wellbeing at home, children need companionable attention and a sense of belonging. Here is Hamza aged two years six months with his mother Nyah, completely engrossed in a board book they found in the library a few days earlier.

Hamza and Nyah are side by side on the settee. Hamza is sitting with his feet tucked under him, the book open on the cushion in front of him. Beside him Nyah is quietly telling him the names of the various vehicles, leaning over and pointing things out. Hamza is passionately interested and very animated; but the combination of his interest and Nyah's close proximity and gentle voice 'anchors' him. Across the floor at her feet is a snaking line of Hamza's toy cars and trucks that he lined up earlier – all 19 of them. Nyah turns a page.

'Look, diggers' she says.

He exclaims 'Dig … ' and impetuously grasps her shoulder. 'Diggers!'

'Where's your one?' asks Nyah, still looking at the page. 'Can you see your one somewhere?'

'O deh' [over there] he points at the floor, dragging his eyes away from the book only for a moment to glance down.

'Yes' she says, pointing at the page. 'But where is it here, in the book?'

'Deh!' [There] he says, pointing too.

'Yes' she agrees. 'It's just like yours – yours over there, look.'

And so the conversation goes on, from loaders to giant excavators, and concrete crushers to recovery trucks.

'Ooooh, what are these?' They gaze at a new page together …

This anecdote shows how companionable book sharing can do so much to support wellbeing at home.

In Ivan's family, the 'A's of anchoring, apprenticeship and allowing time and space are all experienced within the authority of routines. Here is Ivan's mother Kathleen, explaining why routines are so important for their wellbeing.

'I think knowing what's going on, and being able to predict what's going on, is absolutely fundamental. So I think that's the first thing, that there are no surprises, and then he has some sense of control over what's going on and when it's going on … routine key people can come and go, so Daddy goes off every morning, but he comes back at a predictable time. Having predictable routines where the person always says goodbye … '

'The reason why they [routines] are important are because I think it's the foundation of stability for Ivan … it means he doesn't have a sense of helplessness or "I've no idea what the world is going to throw at me". So some things are in place, and they *are* going to happen. That leaves space, then – it leaves emotional space to explore the world. Because the foundations are stable, you can go off and do other things. He is able to be adventurous because he's not worrying about basics'

Sometimes when Ivan and Kathleen have had a busy day and now it's a quiet moment, they look back together on what has been happening. As she tends to involve him in her usual tasks of shopping and so on, this has an 'apprenticeship' ring to it. And yet it also feels like giving Ivan time, and mental space, to think back over what has happened – a way of 'processing' his experiences. Here they are coming downstairs after Ivan's afternoon nap.

Kathleen is bringing Ivan downstairs and he is crying, sounding like he doesn't really want to be awake. She is sympathetic but firm – she needs him to wake up. They sit on the settee while she gives him his afternoon bottle. Soon he settles down and seems entirely relaxed. While he drinks, Kathleen talks to him about his morning, going through the things that happened. She mentions Tracey [child-minder], the fish, the settees and the fireguard … and a dog! This is all in a very quiet, gentle, conversational voice. Ivan finally finishes the bottle, at the end holding his hands together and banging it in a rhythmical sort of a way, as if to get the last drops out. Kathleen sits him up and he looks around expectantly …

Back with apprenticeship, this time in relation to siblings' wellbeing, Lara explains how she had helped her son Zeb, now four years and 10 months, to come to terms with the birth of his new sister Sasha, now aged 12 months – which she had managed so effectively that now they are good friends. She says:

'I didn't actually do anything, he is a caring person anyway. My eldest one is more of a "leave me alone I'll be quite happy if there isn't anybody else" sort of child. But Zeb is much more caring. He did acquire a dolly, we had a dolly that we actually bought for my eldest while I was expecting Zeb, and quite soon he [Zeb] was quite happy to play with the dolly too. So once she [Sasha] was born we encouraged him to, like, help do her nappies and that sort of thing, so he was quite happy – yeah.'

Although prefacing her explanation with the statement that she hadn't actually done anything, Lara then describes here a companionable 'apprenticeship' kind of process in which there would have been many opportunities for Zeb's wellbeing – and everyone else's – to develop.

Time and space are important at home for everyone, especially in a busy family. Even the youngest children are able to find this when they need it; or maybe the youngest children are especially good at it, before they become susceptible to the rapidly increasing pressures of advancing childhood and young adulthood. They have an ability simply to 'switch off' when they need to. Here is Freddie aged two years and 11 months, switching off for a while after a particularly busy and hot afternoon.

The friends have just gone, and Kathy is rather wearily tidying up. Ellie started off 'helping' (this involves her sitting on the floor by her bottom shelf so she can put things back onto it – and take them off again of course) but then she starts throwing wooden blocks across the floor, so now she is 'captured' in the sling on Kathy's back.

The back door is open, Kathy has locked the gate, and for the moment their shared space outside is quiet. Freddie wanders outside, and Kathy is about to call him back because he usually has to have someone with him in the garden. But then she thinks of the weekend last month that they spent mending the fences, ready for the moment when Freddie would be old enough to be outside on his own. 'Perhaps this is the moment' she thinks, and 'I can watch him through the window'.

Some washing hangs on the drying green lines, and walking past it down the path towards the wall at the bottom is Cat, waving his tail in the air. Freddie follows, not chasing him as he sometimes does, especially when no one is looking, but just watching him. Cat jumps up onto the top of the wall and disappears over the other side into the parking lot beyond. Freddie stands for a while looking at the spot where Cat has vanished. Then he wanders slowly to and fro, sometimes bending down to examine things, and sometimes just standing apparently deep in thought or daydream.

After a while Kathy hears the sound of small urgent feet on the path outside the door, and suddenly he's back in the kitchen – looking around for the biscuit tin.

Examples of wellbeing will vary across cultures, ethnic groups, social class and family structures, of children and their companions at home experiencing the four 'A's of wellbeing; but beneath the various visible examples, the same familiar structure is there. These examples show how parents can help wellbeing to develop. Key people can enable families to realise that much of what they do at home is exactly what children need for their wellbeing.

Key messages for wellbeing at home

Figure 8.1 helps to identify 'helpful' everyday experiences for family wellbeing. Here are some key messages for supporting the wellbeing of companions – children, parents, and others, mainly grandparents – at home.

At home ...		... Key messages for ...
ANCHORING	Children	... Plenty of companionable attention ... A sense of belonging in the family
	Parents	... Share books with children, every day ... Be available every (not all) day to have fun and play with children if they want you
	Others	... Enjoy the children
AUTHORITY	Children	... Opportunities to play in their own way ... Clear family routines and boundaries for security
	Parents	... Decide on routines and rules that are good for the children and for you, and stick to them
	Others	... Follow the parents' rules and routines
APPRENTICESHIP	Children	... Involvement in everyday tasks ... Learning self-help skills ... Included in important experiences and decisions
	Parents	... Know about healthy food: what it is, where to get it, ways to cook it Share problems and make the most of useful advice
	Others	... Talk about the children with the people who know them best – their parents
ALLOWED TIME AND SPACE	Children	... Sometimes an unhurried pace – time to wander and ponder, and 'process' experiences ... Opportunities to play and run outside
	Parents	... Make time for yourself Try to find ways to get more sleep Have some child-free zones Make family time
	Others	... Be clear about how much you can and can't manage

Figure 8.1 Key messages for wellbeing at home

Wellbeing words

We think a lot about 'important' words that children say – or that we want them to say. To conclude this section on supporting companions' wellbeing at home, in Figure 8.2 are a few words that children, and possibly their companions too, need to hear – rather than say – often, for their wellbeing.

Figure 8.2 Wellbeing words for children's ears

Key Companions' Professional Development

Key people's own professional wellbeing

As with everyone, key people need a sense of their belonging-and-boundaries, the ability to communicate, and good enough physical wellbeing in order for their learning – part of their agency – to thrive. So, in relation to professional development, what are the main messages for key people's own professional wellbeing? In Figure 8.3 we see how the four 'A's work for them too. This table about practitioners' professional wellbeing is central to the messages of the book.

Key companions work best when they ...	Key people need the four 'A's to ...
... feel anchored	... experience a sense of belonging in the staff team and to the setting ... have an attentive line manager with whom to share communications about their work
... work with companionable authority	... feel secure in their work ... feel good about their professionalism ... develop an understanding of the need to respect colleagues and physical surroundings ... be aware of professional expectations, be familiar with the setting's routines and rules, and understand the reasons for boundaries in their work
... experience everyday apprenticeship with colleagues	... learn useful professional skills and feel proud of their achievements ... become familiar with routine required tasks ... collaborate in making decisions and making things happen ... learn about their own professional wellbeing, and the wellbeing of others around them ... understand about the need for 'a right way' to do certain things, and to distinguish those from the ones requiring their own professional judgement ... improve observation, assessment and planning skills
... are allowed time and space to work well	... observe, assess and plan their work with children ... think reflectively about their work with children and colleagues

Figure 8.3 Key people's own professional wellbeing

Further sources of professional development material

In a sense, the whole of this book is a source of professional development. However, some sections of it are especially relevant in this respect, focusing particularly on areas that are often professional development priorities in early years. Here are those main areas, and where to find them in this book, together with key references to other authors and organisations:

- For supporting children's play, see Part 3 Chapter 6.[4]

- For observation, assessment and planning, see Part 4 Chapter 7.[5]

- For developing the key person approach, see Part 4 Chapter 8.[6]

- For supporting wellbeing in families, see Part 4 Chapter 8.[7]

- Organisations for further support.[8]

In addition to the Early Years Foundation Stage Guidance (for practitioners in England, but including a great deal of generally helpful material), the 'Further reading' below points the way to other excellent sources of useful practical material. This includes approaches, ideas, information and suggestions to support the professional development of people working with the youngest children and their families. It is offered as a starting point for exploration, to be added to in whatever ways will be most useful for particular readers.

This book is about thinking positively – building resilient wellbeing 'from the bottom up'. In making the most of the earliest years, the focus is on preventive work. From birth and throughout early childhood, prevention makes sense. However there is no getting away from the reality that most of us spend a great deal of our time struggling with situations where, in one way or another, things have gone wrong. When the approaches and processes described here are part of the lives of young children and their families, perhaps things go wrong less often. But there will always be ups and downs, and the question 'What about when things go wrong?' is an important one. This is the subject of the next chapter.

Key messages

- Key relationships are triangular, involving the child, the family and the key person.
- Wellbeing in families – or lack of it – can be catching.
- A key person's job can be emotionally draining, physically tiring, intellectually challenging, complex, responsible and deeply satisfying – all at once.
- The four 'A's structure that can underpin work in settings can also help in family work.
- Key people need professional wellbeing too: to feel 'anchored'; to work with companionable authority; to experience everyday apprenticeship with colleagues; and to be allowed time and space to work well.

Questions to think about and discuss

1. Mothers say that having a key person makes a big difference. Putting yourself in a mother's shoes, can you explain why?
2. What do you think are the most enjoyable aspects of being a key person? And what are the hardest?
3. What do the 'Words for children's ears' have to do with wellbeing and the four 'A's? Can you come up with some 'Words for practitioners' ears'?

Further reading

ELFER, P., GOLDSCHMIED, E. & SELLECK, D. *Key Persons in the Nursery.* London: David Fulton, 2003.

This small book is a wonderfully wise distillation of what it means to be a key person, and what it means to have one. With a focus on quality in early childhood, it very accessibly explains what the key person approach is about, in theory and in practice. It outlines why it is so important, and also includes much good practical advice about how to make it work.

GOLDSCHMIED, E. & JACKSON, S. *People Under Three: Young Children in Daycare.* London: Routledge, 1994 (2nd edn. 2004).

People Under Three is organised chronologically from birth to the end of the third year, with sound and authoritative information and practical advice on organising provision, the key person approach, treasure baskets and mealtimes, amongst many other aspects of daycare. There is an extremely helpful chapter entitled 'Children in Difficulties', which includes sections on such challenges as children's reactions to stressful events, and handling difficult behaviour such as temper tantrums, aggression against other children, biting, over-activity, non-compliance and many others. This book is full of solid, reliable wisdom.

WHEELER, H. & CONNER, J. *Parents, Early Years and Learning: Parents as Partners in the Early Years Foundation Stage – Principles into Practice.* London: National Children's Bureau, 2009.

Arising from the work of the UK government-funded PEAL project (Parents, Early Years and Learning) this book underpins a National Children's Bureau training programme. It is about working with parents as partners in their young children's development and learning, and contains much invaluable support for key people about forging partnerships with parents.

References

1 ELFER. P., GOLDSCHMIED, E. & SELLECK, D. *Key Persons in the Nursery: Building Relationships for Quality Provision.* London: NEYN, 2002.

2 STEIN, A., RAMCHANDANI, P. & MURRAY, L. 'Impact of Parental Psychiatric Disorder and Physical Illness', in M. Rutter et al. (eds) *Rutter's Child and Adolescent Psychiatry* 5th edn. Oxford: Blackwell Publishing, 2008.

3 WHEELER, H. & CONNER, J. *Parents, Early Years and Learning: Parents as Partners in the Early Years Foundation Stage – Principles into Practice.* London: National Children's Bureau, 2009: 108.

4 **For Play:** FISHER, J. *Starting from the Child*, 3rd edn. Maidenhead: Open University Press, 2008; FEATHERSTONE, S. (ed.) *Again! Again! Understanding Schemas in Young Children.* London: A&C Black Publishers Limited, 2008.

5 **For Observation, Assessment and Planning:** CARR, M. *Assessment in Early Childhood Settings: Learning Stories.* London: Paul Chapman, 2001; DRUMMOND, M.J. *Assessing Children's Learning*, 2nd edn. London: David Fulton, 2003.

6 **For Key Person Approach:** ELFER, P., GOLDSCHMIED, E. & SELLECK, D. *Key Persons in the Nursery.* London: David Fulton, 2003; EDWARDS, A.G. *Relationships and Learning: Caring for Children from Birth to Three.* London: National Children's Bureau, 2002.

7 **For Wellbeing in Families:** PEAL *Parents, Early Years and Learning.* London: National Children's Bureau, 2009; PEEP *Learning Together,* folders and videos. Oxford: Peers Early Education Partnership, 2000: 26 (www.peep.org.uk).

8 **Organisations:** Early Education at: www.early-education.org.uk ; National Children's Bureau at: www.earlychildhood.org.uk

When Things Go Wrong

What about when things go wrong? On a spectrum stretching from inevitable and essentially transitory problems (for instance teething or tantrums) to life-long states of mental or physical disability, all children (and consequently their companions) will experience things going wrong. How, in these situations, can we help them to retain as much wellbeing – agency, belonging-and-boundaries, communication and physical wellbeing – as possible?

The ideas that have formed the basis for the positive, preventive approach in previous chapters – for building wellbeing from birth – may stand us in good stead here too, as a guide to considering possible remedial approaches. Here, as before, we consider the theory (agency, belonging-and boundaries and communication – the ABC of wellbeing); the processes (of play, companionable attention and learning); and the practices (anchoring, authority, apprenticeship, allowed time and space – the four 'A's of wellbeing) to scaffold our thinking.

One way to think about all 'gone wrong' situations is as problems of loss. We are familiar with the idea of death as loss – but what about other problems such as high levels of stress, worry or fear; family breakdown; a terminal illness? These kinds of situations – usually resulting in multiple problems – can be perceived as losses too – losses of wellbeing. For some adults, being fearful about loss of wellbeing – for example loss of freedom, of happiness, of financial viability – can be as bad or worse than the event itself. While, mercifully, young children are usually firmly rooted in the present, their behaviour when a new 'supplanting' sibling is imminent tells us that they too sometimes worry, albeit on a subconscious level, about their lives going wrong.

A great deal of information is available – and easily accessed now on the Web – about almost any problem, great or small, known to man and woman. This chapter is not about adding to that 'what to do' knowledge. It is about a way of thinking about when things go wrong, in terms of loss of wellbeing. It is about recognising that while the gravity of a situation or diagnosis may be intractable, nonetheless it need not dictate the extent of wellbeing loss.

When things go wrong, wellbeing is liable to plummet; and in this chapter the 'P' of wellbeing that so far has stood for 'physical wellbeing' extends also to 'P' for 'pain' – both physical and mental pain. But even while the situation itself continues, understanding the nature and processes of wellbeing can help with beginning to restore it. This applies to children – the ups and downs of toddler lives, for example, are well documented[1] – and to their companions too. In situations where the problem itself is 'a given', the way it is processed by all concerned need not be. We can all instance children or adults in terrible situations, whose wellbeing, against all the odds, seems to be thriving. Conversely, children or adults for whom life seems basically trouble-free sometimes seem to have very low wellbeing. Here we look at some of the reasons for this variable 'coping ability', and how we might use this understanding to support children and their companions in difficulties.

Whose Problem?

When something goes wrong, whose wellbeing problem is it? Clearly the child or adult concerned; but also – and sometimes extremely significantly – that person's companions. Living and working with other children and adults who are 'processing' their own loss of wellbeing is emotionally as well as physically draining.

Remedial services understandably focus primarily on the person for whom things have gone wrong – the child presenting developmental delay or behavioural difficulties, the mother suffering from post-natal depression, and so on. But other family members' wellbeing will also be implicated. For example, a mother caring for her paralysed husband, with two young children also, is fit and well herself and doing a superb job. However, she has four people's wellbeing to consider and support: her husband's, her elder child's, her younger child's, and her own. This is a huge and seemingly never-ending challenge. In the five years since the elder child was born the husband himself has been able to access a range of services relating to his condition. Yet in all that time, no one asked him how his role as father of his two sons had been affected. Neither were the issues of the boys' wellbeing, or her own, raised with the mother.

Siblings can be especially affected by living with others' problems, often invisibly. In another family, the elder child of two was born with a hearing impairment. Over time the impairment caused enormous tensions between that challenging child and everyone else in the family. While the parents constantly struggled with the usual parenting issues writ unmanageably large, the younger sibling says she learned, from being an observer, how to win love by compliance and cheerful self-effacement.

In both these families a more holistic, integrated service approach would have been wholly appropriate. When someone in a family needs special support, the chances are that, to a greater or lesser extent, so does everyone else.

A crisis in baby or child development can impact powerfully on a mother's wellbeing, creating tensions for services in trying to meet the wellbeing needs of both mother and child. We can see this happening in 18-year-old Bianca's account of giving birth prematurely to her twins.

'It was at 33 weeks. When I found out my waters had broken, it was the same sort of shockedness as when I found out I was pregnant. I was, like, smiling, oh my god; but I wasn't scared, I was just, like, worried. I didn't want to be, like, too worried or, like, scared anyway because I didn't want them to get, like, shock inside me, and I wanted them to think it was a happy thing, like 'oooooh, we're going to be born!'. … and straight after the birth they were whisked off to special care … and I was, like, 'I want to see my babies, how long do I have to wait [shouting] I can't wait two hours'. I was really – oh I'm going to cry again – really intent on *never* leaving them for, like, months [B. is really crying now] and then I had to leave them straightaway. I'm sorry … '

The babies needed to be in intensive care. But meanwhile, Bianca swings from wanting the best for the babies and feeling confident that she can provide it, to profound distress and frustration at her feeling of total absence of agency. While babies' and young children's wellbeing must always be the priority, there needs to be an awareness of their companions, too.

The question of identifying who has the problem is an important one also in relation to children's proximity to each other. Carefully observing one child can lead us to the realisation that we are watching the wrong one. In a setting, a child who seems often to be aggressive with other children may simply be responding to persistent provocation, in the only way that remains. Sometimes the provocation is quite unintentional, and we learn most about the needs of the provoked child; but this is often how bullying becomes apparent – and perhaps we sometimes jump to conclusions too readily as to the identity of the culprit. At home, sibling rivalry can work the same way, with one sibling getting into trouble for something the other has initiated.

Mothers' feelings of depletion in the first year are frequent and pervasive features of a child's early months. Again, the central problem – in this case the mother's 'unwellness' – cannot help but profoundly affect the wellbeing of the rest of the family. While her efforts to contain her depletion only add to the burden of it, other companions can play a vital compensatory role. Here is Kathleen's account, when Ivan is nine months, of how the early months felt.

> 'It was living hell [horrified laughter]. And it was just relentless, absolutely relentless. It was like … it was like having … suddenly having no time for yourself. Three months of on-going jet lag. And just a vertical learning curve. There are big adjustments to make and I think at nine months … well, in some ways you're only just working out which way is up.

Many of the problems are so familiar, often because they have become part and parcel of our working lives. We need strategies that will help us to deal with the frequent challenges when things go wrong – working through them so that all concerned can have opportunities for re-building wellbeing.

Towards What Works

What's the problem? The missing link

When something goes wrong, our first thought is usually about what needs doing to fix it – or maybe to manage it. We probably see the symptoms of the problem very clearly, and when solutions are urgently needed our inclination is to swing into action as soon as possible. But to do so is to miss out a stage in the wellbeing process. Moving towards what works involves filling in this missing link. Instead of jumping from symptoms straight to solutions, we need to address the issue of causes. In this context, losses of wellbeing – for children and adults – are the causes. We need strategies for analysing how this is happening, and for linking up relevant solutions to those causes.

Stages of knowledge, understanding and creativity

Our first strategy is to re-visit, in this new context, the levels of play which were described in Chapter 6 All to Play For. This is because the apex of wellbeing is a sense of agency, and we saw, in Chapter 6, how children develop agency in their play. Ultimately, although linked with the associated sense of belonging-and-boundaries, it is a sense of agency that generates the resilient wellbeing that is needed when things go wrong. Here are those levels again, this time related to loss of wellbeing. And we meet Mrs Weston again as she finds out all she can about David.

The first level: exploration and struggle

This is about when we first observe or are presented with the symptoms of the problem. It will be a process of observing and assessing, so that eventually we can carry those assessments through into appropriate planning. A 'tool' for recording these observations and assessments can be the 'one-week' record described in Chapter 7 Observation, Assessment and Planning. The record gives us the evidence that we will need to move on to the next stage.

This week there is a new child in the nursery called David, and Mrs Weston knows there is something wrong. His mother hasn't said anything's the matter, except she told Mrs Weston that David sometimes squeezes other children too hard, and please will they keep an eye on him as she wouldn't like him to hurt anyone. She always looks tired and tense though.

When they come in in the morning David always heads straight for the sand tray. He doesn't look at the other children or at Mrs Weston, even when she crouches down beside the sand tray to talk to him. Sometimes he pulls very strange faces, and often he stares up at the corner of the ceiling instead of looking at her.

Mrs Weston has decided the first thing to do is to get to know him as quickly as possible – she needs to find out if there are other things he likes doing, besides playing with the sand. She decides to get everyone to help her with a 'one-week special' record sheet; and also to see if David's mother would let her pop in for a home visit after nursery one day soon.

The second level: achieving competence

In children's play, this is about finding out how things work and practising skills. When things go wrong, once we have identified the problem we need to find out as much as we can about it – what it really is, and the various options for dealing with it. Access to the internet makes this so much easier than it used to be. It can help to think about the difficulty in terms of loss of wellbeing. While this can be a useful strategy across the whole spectrum, from 'normal' transitory problems to terminal complex conditions, it can complement more specialist perspectives but in no way replace them. This is the stage at which, at the more extreme end of the spectrum, specialist help will be needed. And we need to find out all we can, often from the most obvious source of information, the family.

Here we see Mrs Weston again, finding out all she can about David's condition.

It is several months later, and David has something of a reputation with the other children since the day he bit Madison and squeezed Kelly (they were going out to the park) – and he can't seem to play with anyone. The home visit had been a long session. Just as Mrs Weston had been about to leave, David's mum started telling her how worried she was about him and all about the things he does at home that seem to be so different from other children. Mrs Weston tells her about David in the nursery. In the end they decide on a referral.

This week David's family has been told that he has Asperger's syndrome, and that he will need a special assistant in the nursery. Mrs Weston – who likes David a lot and has become friends with his mum – is thankful that there can be some extra help for him. And now that they know what it is, she's finding out all she can about Asperger's, and is beginning to think that they might be able to understand him better.

The third level: using imagination and creativity

As for children in their play, this is the stage we want to get to, where we know the problem well enough to think creatively about it in relation to a particular child or companion. At this level we know the problem well enough to play with managing it. Here is Mrs Weston with David on a difficult day.

A year has passed in the nursery and David is still there, although soon he will be going to another school. He loves Mrs Weston, and often needs a quiet time on her lap – although he is happy with his assistant Claire, too. Mrs Weston knows David very well by now, and has learned to anticipate most of the times that are going to be difficult and painful for him. Today he suddenly squeezes her hand much too tight, and she knows he'll be hurting someone else next if she doesn't do something. Perhaps he needs some music in his little quiet corner where they keep all his favourite books – about stars and planets – so she gently takes him over there and puts it on.

Taking Action

The four 'A's

Now we come to the question of taking action. We have, we hope, some knowledge and understanding with which to match our solutions to the problem. We already have the 'tool' of the one-week record to hand, and planning action is the purpose of the final column. Our planning may be helped by another familiar strategy, using the four 'A's of wellbeing: anchoring; authority; apprenticeship; and allowing time and space. The four 'A's, introduced in the first section of Chapter 5 Children's Wellbeing, have been used as a framework in subsequent chapters: in Chapter 6 for thinking about how companions can support their children's play; and in Chapter 8, for thinking about supporting wellbeing in the home, and about key people's own wellbeing needs.

In these explorations of the four 'A's framework for supporting wellbeing development, the 'A's were framed as a tool for identifying positive wellbeing experiences. The process of identifying and analysing experiences to feed into the final 'notes and planning' column on the one-week records, can also be used in relation to when things go wrong; although in complex and fraught situations any 'tool', including this one, needs the underpinning of practitioners' deep understanding and experience if it is to work well.

Out of balance

In this chapter the focus is on when things go wrong, rather than when they are working well. This means that, using the two frameworks of the ABC & P of wellbeing and the four 'A's, we are on the look-out for different kinds of evidence, of what is actually going wrong. When things are going wrong with wellbeing, it will be because there is too little – or sometimes possibly too much – of these elements: too little or maybe too much agency, belonging or boundaries, or communication. Pinning down the causes of problems in this way helps us to plan more effectively for resilient wellbeing – whatever the 'given' situation.

A major dilemma facing services to support the most vulnerable children and families is about if, and when, to move from support to intervention. What evidence is there that a child is 'keeping safe'? What is the 'at risk' threshold? Fundamentally, it is disastrously low wellbeing that constitutes risk. These strategies can help generate evidence of too little, or too much of the 'A's of wellbeing. Very little or no anchoring, authority, apprenticeship and time and space – or too much of these things – can be abusive. This kind of evidence, in the hands of people with knowledge and understanding about wellbeing, may help to assess levels of risk.

When, in 2007, UNICEF reported dramatically low wellbeing in the UK's children,[2] the general response – while taking many forms – was basically 'Why?' One way of looking at this question might be as a widespread loss or absence for UK children of experiences of anchoring, authority, apprenticeship and allowed time and space.

Quick Fixes

Are there any? It may be that you have just picked up this book, and this section is the first one that catches your eye. The bad news is that unfortunately there are few, if any, quick fixes for things that have gone wrong in early childhood. Possibly a behavioural technique for breaking a habit might be useful, if used very judiciously. But while the ideas, frameworks and practical suggestions throughout this book are about supporting development to go well, they shed light on both sides of the development coin: when things go well and when things go wrong. So the good news is that while you may have been drawn to this section on a false premise of finding instant solutions, the book does indeed contain a great deal of material that may be of help.

Keeping going

As a postscript to the main messages of this chapter, here are three general principles that can sometimes be useful when things go wrong:

• Break the problem down into manageable chunks. Make a plan to tackle one aspect of it at a time, and not starting with the hardest – that way you begin to feel you are making progress and are less likely to feel totally overwhelmed. Remember that success generates success.

• If you feel you are on a treadmill to nowhere, there is a three-stage strategy you could try involving giving the problem 'a rest'. First, make sure that you have the facts – note your observations of the problem, with dates; second, decide an appropriate period of time you will allow to elapse (not too ambitious) before you return to it; third (if you can manage it), return to the problem only after the allotted time. It is amazing how often you will find that by then it has been resolved; and if not, at least you will have evidence of the nature and duration of it to help with the next stage. (NB This is not of course appropriate in urgent situations, or if child protection is your concern.)

• Get help sooner rather than later.

On a more mundane level, remember to look after yourself. Here are a few things that might help you to keep going. These are mostly about your physical wellbeing – empirical evidence, if they work, of the connection between physical and mental wellbeing.

1. Review your diet. As we are often told, 'you are what you eat', and your physical wellbeing is profoundly affected by what goes in your mouth.

2. Take some exercise.

3. Give yourself time and space by taking a long bath.

4. Find a way to get one good night's sleep.

5. Learn something – anything – unrelated to the problem.

Key messages 🔑

- When things go wrong for someone's wellbeing, the impact extends to that person's companions as well.
- It is possible to be mistaken about the source of a problem.
- Moving towards what works involves identifying the causes of lost wellbeing, before moving to solutions or strategies.
- The three levels of progress in play (see Chapter 6) can also be used to think about the way we process problems.
- The 'one-week record' (see Chapter 7) can be used as a wellbeing tool for assessing what is happening when things go wrong.
- We can use the structure of the four 'A's (see Chapter 5) to help make plans when things go wrong.
- There are probably no quick fixes in early childhood; but a few strategies might help.

Questions to think about and discuss

1. When things go wrong for children, how do you usually respond – towards the child, towards the family, with your colleagues, within yourself? Given that we cannot get everything right all the time, what might you want to adjust, add, or do instead?

2. Can you give a specific example of how you could use the ideas in this chapter to support your work with a family? (In your discussions, be aware of the need for confidentiality.)

3. How do you usually respond when your own professional wellbeing is undermined? On reflection, would you want to change in any way how you usually respond?

Further reading

For further reading and support, see the links in the Appendix to Chapters 9 and 10.

References

[1] LEACH, P. *Your Baby and Child.* London: Dorling Kindersley, 2003; SUNDERLAND, M. *The Science of Parenting.* London: Dorling Kindersley, 2006; BRAZELTON, B. *Touchpoints – Birth to 3: Your Child's Emotional and Behavioral Development,* 2nd edn. Cambridge, MA: Lifelong Books, 2006.

[2] INNOCENTI REPORT CARD 7 *Child Poverty in Perspective: An Overview of Child Well-being in Rich Countries.* Florence: UNICEF, 2007.

10

Wellbeing and Integration

This chapter is based on outcomes from three consecutive wellbeing projects in England, starting in 2007. It tells a story of linked groups of practitioners exploring the usefulness of the Wellbeing Framework and its related processes. The material in this chapter relates especially to developing more integrated services. In particular it describes on-going developments in one Children's Centre where the staff decided to work towards integration by embedding the framework in their practice across all their centre services.

An Integrating Model

Aspects of integration

Integration is about bringing separate elements together into a whole. This chapter explores a range of aspects of integration in relation to wellbeing in early childhood. First, this model of wellbeing is itself an example of integration, both in the way that it brings together the affective and cognitive elements of child development (described in Chapter 3); and in the integration, within one of the four main constructs, of 'belonging' with 'boundaries'. Integration involving people is essentially about collaboration; and the companionable collaboration of practitioners described below is an integrating process for them. In relation to the schemas that we still harbour as adults, integration is so much easier for connectors who tend to collaborate easily, than it is for 'enclosers', whose intrinsic inclination is to put boundaries around things, including aspects of their work.

The ways in which the Wellbeing Framework can be used contain the potential for a variety of 'connecting' processes. The Framework supports the way we integrate our understanding of child development with the experiences we offer; it enables key companions to integrate their thinking together; it integrates with curriculum guidance that has been based on research and consultation with practitioners, for instance with Te Whariki in New Zealand, and the Early Years Foundation Stage in England; and it is a way of integrating services for children and families in settings and outside them.[1]

The Three Projects

Wellbeing Project 1: action research by groups of practitioners

In this first project, practitioners doing their own action research investigated the optimal conditions for supporting the development of wellbeing, both for the youngest children, and for the people who live and work with them. The groups of practitioners involved were childminders and Children's Centre staff.

Working collaboratively, the teams used the Wellbeing Framework to analyse the observations they made of children and of their own professional experiences. Video cameras were used to observe and record children's situations and experiences. Many of the video observations illustrated the very early development of resilient wellbeing.

Wellbeing Project 2: exploring uses for the Wellbeing Framework

The rationale for this second project was to build on Project 1 by investigating possibilities for the use of the Framework in various services. The core project group consisted of pairs of practitioners from a range of services, generating perspectives from advisory teachers, early years special educational needs teachers, health visitors, child-minder network co-ordinators, and a head of centre. In addition to exploring future patterns of use, the project was tasked with considering implications for wellbeing training, and with mapping the model to ensure that it was consistent with, and complementary to, any other current frameworks.

Wellbeing Project 3: piloting Pebbles training packs

Project 3 provided a pilot of training materials including the wellbeing assessment sheets and Pebbles records, undertaken by various practitioners who had been involved in the previous projects and who wanted to continue their involvement.

What We Found

About the Wellbeing Framework itself

One of the most frequent comments was about the value of using a positive approach. Practitioners agreed that in wellbeing work it was crucially important to avoid a deficit model, and that the positive Wellbeing Framework facilitated collaboration with families. The special needs teachers commented that 'because it is not a rating scale but a subjective qualitative tool it was not perceived as judgemental'.

The following comments from the three project reports summed up people's main responses to using the Framework.

From the advisory teachers: 'The process generated a very particular focus on the quality of interactions between child and adult, and practitioners' need for time to reflect'.

- The Framework helps with analysis of observation.

- It raises the confidence of practitioners and adds more insight into their practice.

- It helps unpick what is essentially good practice in the Early Years.

- It is useful for peer mentoring.

From the special educational needs teachers working with parents: 'Working on the project crucially encouraged and validated our process of critical observation'. Using the camera with this Framework they were able to:

- 'hear' the child with no speech

- appreciate and respect the child's agenda

- improve parents' awareness of positives of their SEN child.

It also worked well as a tool for parents, supporting them to become more confident and 'positive'. It was viewed by them as companionable – emphasising strengths, showing the breadth of their child's wellbeing and helping them to realise that what they do, when playing with or caring for their child, is essentially worthwhile.

> This framework supports, extends and values our relationship with parents. It provides a tool for talking about the things that matter. Sometimes parents ask big questions like 'Will he ever fall in love?' While no research tool can answer such a question, this [framework] does show that the building blocks of wellbeing are becoming firmly placed by the parents' high quality interactions.

From the health visitors, who also felt that the project had been good for the wellbeing of the parents: 'We concluded that the wellbeing of the mums was very important, and we used the framework informally to get a sense of this'.

The health visitors reported some difficulties with using the camera, including the following:

- managing to film in a situation where there is a great deal going on (comings and goings, barking dogs, needy children, etc.)

- cancelled visits

- unfamiliarity with equipment, leading to a realisation of how very important it is to master filming and associated techniques before the visits

- noisy and/or chaotic environments.

They added the following comments:

- The Framework is very useful in breaking down observations and being able to explain explicitly to parents why something is good.

- It could be useful in training, to enable health visitors and support workers to give informed feedback from informed assessment.

- It fits in with the five key outcomes in Every Child Matters:[2]
  - being healthy
  - staying safe
  - enjoying and achieving
  - making a positive contribution

- economic well-being
- It is useful for specific short term interventions with vulnerable families.

The practitioners on these projects concluded that working with the Framework had brought them together, and given them a shared language and a common understanding. As one child-minder put it, 'This is great for working together'. But they also emphasised the need to remember that the Framework itself consists of two equally important and inter-dependent elements: on the one hand the ABC model of wellbeing; and on the other, the processes of companionable attention and learning that can become a 'mindset' for practitioners engaged in wellbeing support. It was the integration of these two elements, both consciously and uncon-sciously, that had proved new and useful to them.

About using the Framework

Some useful comments were made about having used the video camera in Wellbeing Project 2 for recording observations and then analysing them using the wellbeing codes. During a group discussion about using video material the following observations were made.

> The difference between this and [another method of observation] is in the depth of the analysis. This is more powerful because you have *so* much information in the video clip; together with a way of analysing it, using the Framework.

> Videoing helps pick up on what is essentially important.

> It's a way of 'drilling down'.

> It gives a purpose to observation – a real relevance.

> Coded video clips could be used in case conferences, not as part of an assessment or to make a judgement, but to demonstrate the child's wellbeing and, after the assessment, to support the mother's wellbeing.

The point was made that during filming children were very aware of the camera, and that the children sometimes 'performed', rather than act-ing 'naturally'. This concern was echoed by other practitioners. Yet they also wanted to stress how important they felt it was for parents and practitioners to understand that 'it's OK to see a "once-off" best'. While they agreed to having a sense of 'if it's not typical it's not valid', nonetheless they felt that sense to be wrong.

It is this very aspect of filming the youngest children – the way that they often 'play to the camera' – that is one of the great strengths and potentially liberating aspects of using the video camera for recording observations. This is one way in which these very young children's feel-ings and views can be heard and acknowledged to be as important as anyone else's – child or adult. It is a moving and effective way of promoting 'the voice of the child'.

A fundamental discovery was about the need for practitioners to understand the Wellbeing Framework, before building it into their practice in a setting. This was seen to be especially important in relation to very vulnerable children and complex situations. Essentially, exploring ways of using it is a process of playing with it – and practitioners and others need to be given the necessary opportunities to hear about it, read about it, discuss it and to try using it – getting to know it so well that they can play with it.

The basic question for these projects was 'Is this Wellbeing Framework fit for purpose?' And the follow-on question has to be 'Fit for what purpose?' The comments and discussions of all these groups of practitioners ultimately distilled into six main uses for the Wellbeing Framework, relating to particular purposes. The six main uses that were identified can all contribute to processes of integration in early years settings.

1. For observation, assessment and planning.

2. For delivering the Early Years Foundation Stage (in England) and key person relationships.

3. For multi-agency training and working towards integrated teams in localities.

4. For working with parents.

5. For supporting transitions.

6. For staff wellbeing and performance management.

Comments relating to job satisfaction were heard again and again throughout the three projects. Here is a small selection.

- 'The model highlights the importance of the key person approach'.

- 'It's enabled staff in the early stages of relationships with families to have different kinds of conversations from before – about the things we really want to talk about'.

- 'Looking back over my observation sheets I had written proof that I was supporting wellbeing in all the daily activities, social events and free play that I was offering'.

- 'Before doing this project I felt as if parents didn't know what their children were getting out of their time with me. I was amazed to discover just how much children can get out of things we do on a daily basis. Now I can tell the parents'.

- 'We've got a collective sense of agency from doing this'.

- 'A lot of these words echo throughout life'.

In relation to staff wellbeing and performance management, here is a message from a head of centre about the ways in which she and her staff are playing with a laminated wall-chart-sized version of the Pebbles sheet.

> We are still using the large sheet up in the staffroom; and everyone can comment about anything, good or bad, in relation to their wellbeing or indeed that of others. The idea is they put the comment in an envelope under the area it relates to. This is working OK for us in that it gives staff the opportunity to say whatever they feel or think about something which they may not want to say out loud. We are still working out how and when I can best acknowledge their comments. Not everyone wants them universally shared, so some have to be signed so I can deal with them individually. It is things like this that we are finding our way with.
>
> The comments don't always relate to the area they are under and I think some staff find this difficult to work out. However I think that it is important we have the Pebbles as the backdrop for everyone to be able to express themselves. Because it is the wellbeing of staff which is the starting point, the more we have to explain and discuss the four areas, the better.
>
> We are also still working on encouraging everyone in the centre to use it. The interesting thing the staff wanted to share, is that this was not just a complaining opportunity about things like leadership; but that we are all responsible for each others' wellbeing, so we can all make a difference to the points expressed. Some staff have used it to share compliments for the larger group.
>
> We still have lots to do with it, but I think it will grow and become an integral part of the setting'.

Investors in Wellbeing

One Children's Centre's journey to integration: first steps

This analogy of a journey towards integration brings to mind the Greek poet Cavafy's poem 'Ithaka', the opening words of which seem particularly appropriate here.

> As you set out for Ithaka
> hope your road is a long one,
> full of adventure, full of discovery.[3]

This section is about the journey of one Children's Centre as the staff began to explore how they could use the Framework with its associated tools for observing, assessing and planning, in becoming more integrated across their services.

Two years earlier the head of Centre and three pairs of staff had been involved in Wellbeing Project 1, with staff from the day care setting, the

Nursery School, and the Family Centre-run 'drop in' provision for families. One of their final comments had been 'We're going to embed this into the Centre'; and a long and fascinating journey is probably what that will take. The head of Centre has remained involved in the wellbeing development work, and now the original group has decided to try working together with all the staff across the Centre.

The first step was to induct all the staff in the Wellbeing Framework, and ideas for its use so far. In the morning of a training day for all the staff, including a parent-governor, the sessions covered the Wellbeing Framework and companionable learning, and using Pebbles training packs. In two afternoon sessions, the different Children's Centre teams discussed ways in which they might use wellbeing in their work, and then shared these ideas with each other. Figure 10.1 shows the range of ideas at the end of the day.

Exploring new paths

In the months following the training day, the Centre staff began to explore some first paths. The task of matching purposes with strategies that fit those purposes is on-going. The wall chart version of the Pebbles record has generated much thinking, especially in relation to sharing planning for wellbeing with parents in the Family Centre. The team there are experimenting with different ways of using it.

Figure 10.2, Pebbles wall chart planning, shows how they are using it for weekly planning, relating it to the Early Years Foundation Stage principles of 'unique child', 'positive relationships', 'enabling environments' and 'learning and development'.

Their 'big' ideas are inspirational – for instance a central Pebbles record 'bank'; a Pebbles record that can work as a wellbeing 'cover sheet' for the Early Years Foundation Stage profile; and key person teams across the Centre. They recognise that these transforming strategies will take years rather than months to embed.

Meanwhile, when the staff used the wall chart to analyse the wellbeing provision in the Centre, they realised that such an analysis was not especially revealing for them; it was too easy to say that every provision contributes to all aspects of wellbeing. This realisation led them to ask a different and much more challenging question. Here is the head of Centre's account of what happened.

> We see that we must identify the key messages that we can all 'buy into'. We used the model to think about those elements of our ethos and our practice that we need to provide consistently, throughout all of the services that a child and their family may use throughout their time in the Children's Centre. These are the

things that we strive for, and that we emphasise to new staff. Achieving these with consistency is a constant challenge.

This is the first time that I have ever been able to connect these messages (that I'm constantly explaining and reminding about) onto one model or framework and show how they all, in their different ways, impact on the child. So here is our current fundamentally challenging question:

'Now that we are using the wellbeing model to bring all our services across the Centre together, what can we do *across the Centre* to promote the development of agency, belonging-and-boundaries, communication, and physical wellbeing?'

This is the 'bottom line' question for all of us. We need to articulate the importance of these elements of *consistent practice and continuous provision* throughout the Centre; so that staff provide consistently for all children, wherever and whenever they are in the Centre.

Centre team		Ideas
FAMILY CENTRE	... ...	Planning on Pebbles wall chart – ethos of wellbeing. Use photos of children in the setting, at planned activities; change weekly. WB model as strand which runs through all our work.
OUTREACH	... ...	Taking model to map families' strengths. Use it to look at how work is planned. Use as a planning tool with individual families. Focus groups, especially post-natal and young mums; use lots of photos. Use for the staff six-month review.
HEALTH VISITORS	... ...	Use Pebbles to highlight issues for vulnerable children. One language/framework when sharing information re children and families. For complex/hard-to-reach families: a useful visual tool to aid planning with the family.
CHILD-MINDERS	... ...	Pebbles sheet for each child. Develop role of the Centre in introducing the model to new families. Use Centre as a venue for training local child-minders in the model.
LUNCH CLUB AFTER SCHOOL CLUB STAY & PLAY	... ...	Tracking children, for long-term record, and for planning and supporting – for each child a Pebbles sheet in each setting attended, regularly combined in a central file, linking children's different experiences. A central 'bank' of Pebbles records, to track the history of each child, and as an aid to transitions. Pulling together views of the same child, in different services. The Pebbles record could (should?) start with mothers. After-school club – use it with children, to reflect on their day. In After School Club, possibly a tool for older children to reflect on their day.
NURSERY SCHOOL	... ...	Settling-In Reports – already working well, used at parent consultations. Carry on after settling-in period – select a number of observations to discuss with parents at termly meetings. Useful as a way into a discussion (doesn't have to encompass everything to be said). Use photos: valued highly by parents, can be included in profiles. For rigour, still need written observations and analyses with the WB model. Use the Pebbles to review routines/experiences.
GEMS DAYCARE	... ...	Use for identifying the rich experiences, situations, routines. Can improve our work with parents. Introduce Pebbles at Parents Evenings, using to open discussions. Aid to parents valuing professionalism of staff. Basis for planning – close links with Early Years Foundation Stage. Establish teams of Key People in the Centre – continuity as they move. A 'buddying' system for key people. Parents' perspective: comforting to hear same message/model running through Centre Services.

Figure 10.1 Children's Centre teams' ideas

Figure 10.2 Pebbles wall chart planning

Recurring integration themes

Both in this particular Centre and in others that have been involved in this wellbeing development work, three very familiar themes have been central to thinking and discussions about the challenges of integration. They are firstly, observation, assessment and planning for continuous provision; secondly, 'sustained shared thinking' with children, parents and colleagues (in which parents can use the language of the Wellbeing Framework to talk with key people about their children's lives at home); and thirdly, integration with services and the community beyond the Centre. While already well-known but separate theoretical entities, these three themes seem likely to become the 'main roads' of wellbeing integration in the early years. The Epilogue picks up on these themes, putting them in the wider context of collective wellbeing and making a practical call to action.

Key messages 🔑

- The Wellbeing Framework contains potential for various aspects of integration.
- Using the Wellbeing Framework opens up a wide range of possible strategies for integrating the work of practitioners with each other, and with families.
- Using the Wellbeing Framework tends to generate job satisfaction.
- The Wellbeing Framework can be used to support staff wellbeing and performance management.
- The Framework provides many opportunities for integrating services across a Centre.
- Three recurring themes that underpin integration are: observation, assessment and planning; sustained shared thinking; and integration beyond settings and Centres.

Questions to think about and discuss

1. What do you understand by the term 'integration' in the early years context? Why is it thought to be so important to integrate services for children and families?
2. Looking at Figure 10.1 and identifying with one of the teams on the left, what ideas can you contribute?
3. Imagine you are given the task of setting up a central bank of wellbeing records across all of a Centre's services. Bearing in mind the possibilities of using new technology, and the challenges of maintaining appropriate confidentiality, how would you do it?

Further reading 📖

For further reading and support, see references and links in the Appendix.

References

1   MINISTRY OF EDUCATION *Te Whariki Early Childhood Curriculum*. Wellington NZ: Learning Media, 1996; DEPARTMENT for EDU-CATION AND SKILLS (DfES) *The Early Years Foundation Stage: Setting the Standards for Learning, Development and Care for Children from Birth to Five*. London: DfES, 2007.
2   DEPARTMENT FOR EDUCATION AND SKILLS (DfES) *Every Child Matters*. London: The Stationery Office, 2003.
3   CAVAFY, C. P. *Collected Poems*. London: The Hogarth Press, 1984: 29.

Epilogue

The Prologue began with a story about having been unable, only a few decades ago, to work with a child because he was too young. Now all that has changed, and today we have many opportunities to support the development of children's resilient wellbeing from birth. This book offers some ideas and strategies for making the most of those opportunities.

The concept of 'collective' wellbeing, in families, communities and society, is a powerful one. Agency, belonging-and-boundaries, communication and physical wellbeing applies not only in relation to an individual child or adult; but also collectively, in families, in communities, in society.

The element of caring comes to the fore in collective wellbeing. In the context of racial justice, Lane describes the concept like this:

> It is about re-orientating our thinking and learning to care about and understand each other across cultural backgrounds and boundaries, listening to people's experiences and perspectives and building up trust. Something of this concept is included in the southern African term *'Ubuntu'*, meaning largeness of spirit and humanity to others. This was defined by Archbishop Desmond Tutu in 1999 as:
>
> > 'A person with *ubuntu* is open and available to others, affirming of others, does not feel threatened that others are able and good, for he or she has a proper self-assurance that comes from knowing that he or she belongs in a greater whole and is diminished when others are humiliated or diminished, when others are tortured or oppressed.'[1]

Rich wellbeing experiences in early childhood are the foundations for later wellbeing; yet sometimes things go wrong. Our collective response as a society to loss of a sense of wellbeing as evidenced in, for instance, mental and physical illness, criminality or infirmity, is deeply concerning. These symptoms are, to a greater or lesser extent, found in people who have lost some or all of their sense of wellbeing. In our society the 'prescription' for such loss is usually a period in an institution, in order to recover enough wellbeing to return to 'normal' life – or at least to make the most of the remainder of life. For some, a safe place with undeniable boundaries can be an absolutely essential first step away from the chaos and destruction in which they have become entangled. For them, as for others, this means institutions such as hospitals, detention centres or prisons, and care homes for the elderly; where opportunities for agency, belonging-and-boundaries, communication and physical wellbeing will usually be greatly curtailed. Yet the original problems are a consequence of loss of wellbeing, and restoring that lost wellbeing or minimising that loss is fundamentally what is needed. That, surely, should be the prime purpose of such institutions. From this perspective, we have a long way to go.

In describing his bioecological model, Bronfenbrenner asks 'What is the prospect for the future development of our species?' His answer, too, is about the central importance of caring for others. Arguing for developmental scientists to communicate 'in words that can still find an echo', he writes:

> In the United States it is now possible for a youth, female as well as male, to graduate from high school, or a university, without ever caring for a baby; without ever looking after someone who was ill, old, or lonely; and without comforting or assisting another human being who really needed help. The developmental consequences of such a deprivation of human experience have not as yet been scientifically researched. But the possible social implications are obvious, for – sooner or later, and usually sooner – all of us suffer illness, loneliness, and the need for help, comfort and companionship. No society can long sustain itself unless its members have learned the sensitivities, motivations, and skills involved in assisting and caring for other human beings.[2]

This statement is a call to action, to education for citizenship, to collective wellbeing. But what do these words mean, in practice, in the early years? Here are five practical questions and advices in relation to wellbeing in the early years.

1. How can we make our settings into communities in which each person is accepted and nurtured, and strangers are welcome?

   Take time to learn about children's, and other people's experiences.

2. Do we cherish our friendships with children so that they grow in depth and understanding and mutual respect? Do we recognise the needs and gifts of each person we work with, not forgetting our own?

   Work adventurously.

3. Are we alert to practices which discriminate against people on the basis of who or what they are, or because of their beliefs?

   Stand up for the humanity of all people.

4. If pressure is brought upon us to lower our standards of professional integrity, are we prepared to resist?

   Our responsibilities to children may involve us in taking unpopular stands.

5. Do we remember our responsibilities in educating children for citizenship?

We do not own the world, and its riches are not ours to dispose of at will. Help children to show a loving consideration for all creatures, and seek to maintain the beauty and variety of the world.[3]

The youngest children need experiences of individual and collective wellbeing, in their families and their communities. The foundations of resilient wellbeing are laid very early, in each child's sense of individual and collective agency and belonging-and-boundaries; and through their communication with their companions, from birth. These are the vital first steps of many individual journeys towards building a society in which 'they all lived happily ever after'.

References

[1] LANE, J. *Young Children and Social Justice: Taking Action for Racial Equality in the Early Years – Understanding the Past, Thinking about the Present, Planning for the Future.* London: National Children's Bureau, 2008.

[2] BRONFENBRENNER, U. (ed.) *Making Human Beings Human: Bioecological Perspectives on Human Development.* Thousand Oaks, CA: SAGE Publications, 2005: 14.

[3] THE YEARLY MEETING OF THE RELIGIOUS SOCIETY OF FRIENDS *Quaker Faith and Practice.* London: Religious Society of Friends (Quakers),1994; based, with permission, on the spirit of Advices and Queries 1.02. 5, 18, 21, 24, 26, 27, 33, 34, 38, 42.

Appendix to Chapters 9 and 10

Links for Chapter 9: When Things Go Wrong

BBC Parenting
Information for parents across an extensive range of topics, by age group.
www.bbc.co.uk/parenting

Child Poverty Action Group
Acts on behalf of all poor and distressed families. Has over 60 branches.
www.cpag.org.uk

Contact a Family
Brings together families who have a disabled child. Has information on hundreds of support groups associated with disabilities and conditions, including rare and unusual ones. Website includes downloadable Factsheets on a range of special needs issues, CAF also runs a national helpline for parents.
www.cafamily.org.uk

Homestart
Offers support, friendship and practical help to parents with young children in local communities who are finding it hard to cope, through-out the UK and with British Forces abroad.
www.home-start.org.uk

National Family and Parenting Institute
An independent charity whose role is to bring together organisations, knowledge and know-how to enhance the value and quality of family life, to make sure that parents are supported in bringing up their children and in finding the help and information they need. Maintains the on-line Parenting Services Directory.
www.e-parents.org

National Society for the Prevention of Cruelty to Children
A UK children's charity specialising in child protection.
www.nspcc.org.uk/

Parentline Plus
A charity offering support to anyone parenting a child.
www.parentlineplus.org.uk

References and Links for Chapter 10: Wellbeing and Integration

BROADHEAD, P., MELEADY, C. & DELGADO, M. *Children, Families and Communities: Creating and Sustaining Integrated Services.* Maidenhead: Open University Press, 2008 (120 pp).

Provides an account of how Sheffield Children's Centre grew from its beginnings as a small community project to becoming a multiagency and international network of services for children and families. Details the centre's work with families, and describes the centre's approach to service development and delivery as a community co-operative.

Early Childhood Forum
The Early Childhood Forum (ECF) is a coalition of 50 professional associations, voluntary organisations and interest groups united in their concern about the care and education of young children from birth to eight. It aims to bring together partners in the early childhood sector, promoting inclusion and challenging inequalities. See www.ncb.uk/ecf for more information.

National Children's Bureau (NCB)
The National Children's Bureau promotes the voices, interests and wellbeing of all children and young people across every aspect of their lives. An umbrella body for the children's sector in England and Northern Ireland, it provides essential information on policy, research and best practice. Within the NCB is the Early Childhood Unit, which aims to ensure that all who work with young children and their families can access the best information and support to improve their policies and practice. See www.ncb.org.uk

TUNSTILL, J., ALDGATE, J. & HUGHES, M. *Improving Children's Services Networks: Lessons from Family Centres.* London: Jessica Kingsley, 2007 (158 pp).

Examines and evaluates research into the developing role of family centres in light of current political and social trends, including the Every Child Matters legislation. Outlines the different user groups served by family centres, the range and combination of services provided, and the contribution of these services to positive outcomes for children. The authors also examine the challenges facing family centres in optimising services and managing partnerships across social care, health and education.

WARIN, J. 'Joined-Up Services for Young Children and their Families: Papering Over the Cracks or Re-Constructing the Foundations?', *Children & Society*, 2007, 21(2): 87–97.

Explores competing goals for children and families; for example, helping a parent towards employment by providing accredited courses accords with the goal of lifting families out of poverty but it can also topple the delicate work–life balance of a family in a way that impacts negatively on the quality of parent–child relations. Argues that a conception of the 'child-in-family' must be at the heart of children's services if these contradictions are to be overcome.

Glossary

Definitions refer to meanings of these terms *as they are used in the context of this book.*

achievement: having a sense of 'I did it!'

affect: emotion

agency: feeling that you can make a difference to your own life, and to the lives of other people.

anchored: guaranteed companionable attention (e.g. book sharing, bath time)

apprenticeship: children's active companionable involvement in everyday tasks; 'helping'.

ascertaining: finding out for certain about something.

assessment: the reflective thinking we do and the decisions we make, based on our observations.

attachment theory: a theory that describes and explains enduring patterns of relationships from birth to death; an affectional tie that binds people together over time. In this study the focus is on attachment in the earliest years.

bioecological theory: the dynamic, developmental relations between an active individual and his or her complex, integrated and changing ecology.

caring for others: actively empathising with others.

child observation: attentive watching and listening.

cognition: knowledge, knowing.

cognitive science: the interdisciplinary study of the cognitive processes underlying the acquisition and use of knowledge.

collective wellbeing: a communal sense of wellbeing in families, in communities, in society.

companionable attention: 'mindfulness'.

companionable learning: child and companion mutually engaged in learning.

companions: those people a child/person sees often, knows well, and to whom he/she is bound by love or affection.

confidence: positive self reliance.

construct: a structural component.

cortisol: a hormone produced by the adrenal cortex that influences the response to stress; it increases blood pressure, blood sugar levels, may cause infertility in women, and suppresses the immune system.

curiosity: the disposition to wonder 'what, 'how' 'why', 'where', and 'who'.

determinant: what makes something develop or happen.

diagogy: child and companion mutually engaged in learning.

dispositions: habits of mind, tendencies to respond to situations in certain ways. Curiosity can be a disposition.

dummy: 'comforter'.

early childhood: birth to six years.

ecology: the observation of behaviour in natural settings; the study of people and institutions, in relation to the environment.

ecology of early childhood: the child in the family, family in the community, community in society.

empowerment: a sense of purpose in action.

holistic wellbeing: wellbeing that encompasses all aspects of child development – and subsequently, adult life.

inclusion: including minority groups in the mainstream.

integration: bringing separate things together into one whole.

interaction: active connection

internal locus of control: internal decision-making.

intersubjectivity: the development of active 'self-and-other' awareness in infancy.

job satisfaction: when work generates a sense of wellbeing.

key person approach: a way of working in early years settings in which each child and family is attached to a key person; an emotional relationship as well as an organisational strategy.

learning dispositions: attitudes to learning, e.g. exploring, experimenting, persisting, learning from mistakes; situated learning strategies + motivation (see 'positive learning dispositions'); learning dispositions can also be negative, e.g. disinterest, over-compliance.

motor control: bodily control ranging from gross motor skills such as running and climbing, to fine motor skills such as picking up a small object with two fingers, or using a spoon.

neuroscience: scientific study of the nervous system.

paradigm: the overall conception and way of working shared by workers within a particular discipline or research area.

pathologise: to interpret in terms of disease.

personal time and space: mental and physical freedom; time and space to reflect.

play (free-flow): an intrinsically motivated active process (solitary or companionable) about possible alternative worlds; a child's work.

play for wellbeing: see 'wellbeing play'.

positive learning dispositions: wanting to learn, as evidenced by consistent tendencies such as exploring, experimenting, persisting.

pride: internal pleasure at the knowledge of having done well.

professional wellbeing: wellbeing (agency, belonging-and-boundaries, communication and physical health) as it relates to work.

progression in play: exploration and struggle, through competence, to imagination and creativity.

quick fix: instant relief (which is often short-term).

resilience: the ability to bounce back from life's difficulties.

resilient wellbeing: wellbeing that survives through challenging circumstances.

risks: threats to wellbeing.

schemas: patterns in children's thinking and play, e.g. connection, enclosure, rotation, transporting, trajectory.

self-esteem: estimation of your own worth.

self-regulation: involves the ability to control impulses and expressions of emotion.

sustained shared thinking: extended companionable learning.

visual representing: describing or explaining experience (re-presenting it) with drawings, paintings, drama, dance.

wellbeing: feeling alright in yourself and with other people, and reasonably 'coping'; the extent to which your agency, belonging-and-boundaries, communication and physical health are both well enough developed, and in balance.

wellbeing play: child-initiated, open-ended, un-rushed, adaptable, available, intense, intentional, leisurely, creative, free – and profoundly satisfying.

References

ABBOTT, L. & LANGSTON, A. (eds) *Birth to Three Matters: Supporting the Framework of Effective Practice.* Maidenhead: Open University Press, 2005.

AHLBERG, J. & AHLBERG, A. *The Baby's Catalogue.* London: Puffin Books 1982.

AINSWORTH, M. *Patterns of Attachment: A Psychological Study of the Strange Situation.* Hillsdale, NJ: Erlbaum, 1978.

ALBON, A. & MUKHERJI, P. *Food and Health in Early Childhood.* London: SAGE, 2008.

AMERICAN SOCIETY OF PEDIATRICS *Children, Adolescents, and Television, Pediatrics,* 107, 2001.

ATHEY, C. *Extending Thought in Young Children,* 2nd edn. London: Paul Chapman Publishing, 2007.

BALL, C. *Start Right: The Importance of Early Learning.* London: RSA, 1994.

BERNARD VAN LEER FOUNDATION (ed.) *Early Childhood Matters: Enhancing a Sense of Belonging in the Early Years.* The Hague, Netherlands: Bernard van Leer Foundation, 2008.

BERRY, D., FAZILI, A., FARHAD, S., NASIRY, F., HASHEMI, S. & HAKIMI, M. *The Children of Kabul: Discussions with Afghan Families.* Kabul: Save the Children UNICEF, 2003.

BLAKEMORE, S-J. *Early Years Learning,* Parliamentary Office of Science and Technology (POST) Report, 2000.

BLAKEMORE, S.-J. & FRITH, U. *The Learning Brain: Lessons for Education.* Oxford: Blackwell Publishing, 2005.

BOWLBY, J. *Attachment.* London: Penguin Books, 1969.

BRAZELTON, B. *Touchpoints: Birth to 3 – Your Child's Emotional and Behavioral Development,* 2nd edn. Cambridge, MA: Lifelong Books, 2006.

BRETHERTON, I. 'The Origins of Attachment Theory', *Developmental Psychology,* 1992, 28: 759–775.

BROADHEAD, P., MELEADY, C. & DELGADO, M. *Children, Families and Communities: Creating and Sustaining Integrated Services.* Maidenhead: Open University Press, 2008.

BRONFENBRENNER, U. *The Ecology of Human Development: Experiments by Nature and Design.* Cambridge, MA: Harvard University Press, 1979.

BRONFENBRENNER, U. (ed.) *Making Human Beings Human: Bioecological Perspectives on Human Development.* Thousand Oaks, CA: SAGE Publications, 2005.

BRUCE, T. *Time to Play in Early Childhood.* London: Hodder and Stoughton, 1991.

BRUCE, T. *Learning Through Play: Babies, Toddlers and the Foundation Years.* London: Hodder and Stoughton, 2001.

BUCHANAN, A. & HUDSON, B. *Promoting Children's Emotional Well-Being.* Oxford: Oxford University Press, 2000.

CALLAN, S. (ed.) *Breakdown Britain: The Next Generation.* London: Centre for Social Justice, 2008.

CARR, M. *Assessment in Early Childhood Settings: Learning Stories.* London, Paul Chapman, 2001.

CAVAFY, C.P. *Collected Poems.* London: The Hogarth Press, 1984.

CHILDREN'S RIGHTS ALLIANCE FOR ENGLAND *Children's Human Rights: What They Are and Why They Matter.* London: CRAE, 2006.

CHUKOVSKY, K. *From Two to Five.* Berkeley, CA: University of California Press, 1966 (first published in the Soviet Union in 1925).

CROCKENBERG, S. & LEERKES, E. 'Infant Social and Emotional Development in the Family Context', in C.H. Zeanah (ed.) *Handbook of Infant Mental Health*. London: The Guilford Press, 2000.

CSIKSZENTMIHALYI, M. *Flow: The Psychology of Happiness*. London: Rider, 1992.

DAVID, T., GOOUCH, K., POWELL, S. & ABBOTT, L. *Birth to Three Matters: Literature Review Research Report 444*. London: DfES, 2003.

DEPARTMENT for CHILDREN, SCHOOLS AND FAMILIES (DCSF) *The Children's Plan: Building Brighter Futures*. Norwich: The Stationery Office, 2008.

DEPARTMENT for EDUCATION AND SKILLS (DfES) *Starting with Quality*, London: HMSO, 1990.

DEPARTMENT for EDUCATION AND SKILLS (DfES) *The Early Years Foundation Stage: Setting the Standards for Learning, Development and Care for Children from Birth to Five*. Nottingham: DfES, 2007.

DEPARTMENT for EDUCATION AND SKILLS (DfES) *Birth to Three Matters: A Framework to Support Children in their Earliest Years*. London: DfES, 2003.

DEPARTMENT for EDUCATION AND SKILLS (DfES) *Every Child Matters*. London: The Stationery Office, 2003.

DEPARTMENT for EDUCATION AND SKILLS (DfES) *A Sure Start Children's Centre for Every Community: Phase 2 Planning Guidance (2006–08)*. London: Sure Start, 2005.

DEWEY, J. *Democracy and Education*. New York: The Free Press, 1966.

DOWLING, M. *Young Children's Personal, Social and Emotional Development*, 2nd edn. London, Paul Chapman Publishing, 2005.

DRUMMOND, M.J. *Assessing Children's Learning*, 2nd edn. London: David Fulton, 2003.

DUNN, J. *Young Children's Close Relationships: Beyond Attachment*. London: SAGE, 1993.

DUNN, J. *Children's Friendships: The Beginnings of Intimacy*. Oxford: Blackwell Publishing, 2004.

EARLY EDUCATION at: www.early-education.org.uk

EDWARDS, A.G. *Relationships and Learning: Caring for Children from Birth to Three*. London: National Children's Bureau, 2002.

ELFER, P., GOLDSCHMIED, E. & SELLECK, D. *Key Persons in the Nursery: Building Relationships for Quality Provision*. London: David Fulton, 2003.

FEATHERSTONE, S. (ed.) *Again! Again! Understanding Schemas in Young Children*. London: A&C Black, 2008.

FEINSTEIN, L. *The Relative Importance of Academic, Psychological and Behavioural Attributes Developed in Childhood*. London: Centre for Economic Performance, LSE, 2000.

FISHER, D.C. 'A Montessori Mother', London: Constable, 1913: 22–24 in D. Rich, M.J. Drummond & C. Myer *Learning: What Matters to Children*. Clopton: Rich Learning Opportunities, 2008.

FISHER, J. *Starting from the Child*, 3rd edn. Maidenhead: Open University Press, 2008.

FONAGY, P., STEELE, M., STEELE, H., HIGGIT, A. & TARGET, M. 'The Emanuel Miller Memorial Lecture 1992: The Theory and Practice of Resilience', *Journal of Child Psychology and Psychiatry*, 1992: 35(2).

GADSBY, G. & HARROP, B. (eds) *Flying a Round*, London: A&C Black, 1982.

GAMMAGE, P. *Well-Being: The Generic Perspective: Power and Protection*. Adelaide, S.A.: Department for Early Childhood Services, 2004.

GAMMAGE, P. & KRIEG, S. *REFLECT: An Observation System for Teachers of Young Children*. Adelaide, S.A.: Department of Education and Training, 2001.

GERHARDT, S. *Why Love Matters: How Affection Shapes a Baby's Brain*. Hove: Routledge, 2004.

GOLDSCHMIED, E. & JACKSON, S. *People Under Three*, 2nd edn. London: Routledge, 2004.

GOPNIK, A., MELTZOFF, A. & KUHL, P. *How Babies Think*. London: Phoenix, 1999.

GROARK, C. & McCALL, R. 'Community-Based Interventions and Services', in M. Rutter et al. *Rutter's Child and Adolescent Psychiatry*, 5th edn. Oxford: Blackwell Publishing, 2008.

GROTBERG, E. 'A Guide to Promoting Resilience in Children: Strengthening the Human Spirit', *Early Childhood Development: Practice and Reflections 8*, Bernard van Leer Foundation, 1995.

HALSEY, A.H., LAUDER, H., BROWN, P. & STUART WELLS, A. (eds) *Education: Culture, Economy, and Society*. Oxford: Oxford University Press, 1997.

HANNON, P. 'Developmental Neuroscience: Implications for Early Childhood Intervention and Education', *Current Paediatrics*, 2003 (13).

HEANEY, S. (2009) In conversation with Mark Lawson on Front Row, BBC Radio 4, 13 April 2009.

HOBAN, R. *The Mouse and his Child*. London: Faber and Faber, 1967/2005.

HOBAN, R. *How Tom Beat Captain Najork and his Hired Sportsmen*. Boston, MA: David R. Godine, 1974/2006.

HOBSON, P. *The Cradle of Thought: Exploring the Origins of Thinking*. London: Pan Books, 2002.

HOLMES, J. *John Bowlby and Attachment Theory*. London: Routledge, 1993.

HOWE, D. *Attachment Theory for Child and Family Social Work*. London: Macmillan Press, 1999.

HUGHES, S. *Giving*. London: Walker Books, 1993.

HUIZINGA, J. *Homo Ludens: A Study of the Play Elements in Culture*. London: Routledge and Kegan Paul, 1949.

INNOCENTI REPORT CARD 7 *Child Poverty in Perspective: An Overview of Child Well-Being in Rich Countries*. Florence: UNICEF, 2007.

ISAACS, S. *Intellectual Growth in Young Children*. London: Routledge, 1930.

ISAACS, S. *The Children We Teach*. London: University of London Press, 1932.

ISAACS, S. *Social Development of Young Children*. London: Routledge, 1933.

ISAACS, S. *The Educational Value of the Nursery School*. London: The British Association for Early Childhood Education, 1954.

JOHNSON, B. & HOWARD, S. 'Resilience – a Slippery Concept', *AEU (SA Branch) Journal*, May, 1999.

KOESTLER, A. *The Act of Creation*. New York: Dell 1964.

LAEVERS, F. *Wellbeing and Involvement in Care: A Process-Oriented Self-Evaluation Instrument for Care Settings*. Leuven, Belgium: Kind & Gezin and Leuven University Research Centre for Experiental Education, 2005.

LAEVERS, F., DEBRUYCKERE, G., SILKENS, K. & SNOECK, G. *Observation of Wellbeing and Involvement in Babies and Toddlers*. Leuven, Belgium: CEGO Publishers, 2005.

LANE, J. *Young Children and Social Justice: Taking Action for Racial Equality in the Early Years – Understanding the Past, Thinking about the Present, Planning for the Future*. London: National Children's Bureau, 2008.

LEACH, P. *Your Baby & Child*. London: Dorling Kindersley, 2003.

LINDON, J. *Understanding Child Development: Linking Theory and Practice*. London: Hodder Arnold, 2005.

MACDONALD, G. *Castle Warlock*. London: Samson Low, 1982.

MALAGUZZI, L. *The Hundred Languages of Children*. Municipality of Reggio Emilia: Reggio Children, 1996.

MARTY, A., READDICK, C. & WALTERS, C. 'Supporting Secure Parent–Child Attachments: The Role of the Non-Parental Caregiver', *Early Child Development and Care*, 2005: 175(3).

MASLOW, A.H. *Motivation and Personality*. New York: Harper, 1954.

MASTEN, A.S. & GEWIRTZ, A. 'Resilience in Development: The Importance of Early Childhood', *Encyclopedia on Early Childhood Development*, www.childencyclopedia. com/documents/Masten-GewirtzANGxp.pdf , March 15, 2006.

MEADE, A. *The Brain Debate*. Washington: Fulbright Lecture, 2000.

MURRAY, L. & ANDREWS, L. *The Social Baby*. Richmond, UK: CP Publishing, 2000.

NATIONAL AUDIT OFFICE *Sure Start Children's Centres: Report by the Comptroller and Auditor General/HC 104 Session 2006–2007, 19 December 2006*. London: The Stationery Office, 2006.

NATIONAL CHILDREN'S BUREAU www.earlychildhood.org.uk

NATIONAL LITERACY TRUST www.literacytrust.org.uk

NEW ZEALAND MINISTRY OF EDUCATION *Te Whariki: Early Childhood Curriculum*. Wellington, NZ: Learning Media, 1996.

NODDINGS, N. *Happiness and Education*. Cambridge: Cambridge University Press, 2003.

NUTBROWN, C. *Threads of Thinking: Young Children Learning and the Role of Early Education*, 2nd edn. London: Paul Chapman Publishing, 1999.

OECD *Starting Strong: Early Childhood Education and Care*. Paris: OECD, 2001.

PALEY, V.G. *In Mrs. Tully's Room: A Childcare Portrait*. Cambridge, MA: Harvard University Press, 2001.

PALEY, V.G. *A Child's Work: The Importance of Fantasy Play*. London: Heinemann, 2004.

PEAL *Parents, Early Years and Learning*. London: National Children's Bureau, 2009.

PEEP *Learning Together*, folders and videos: Oxford: Peers Early Education Partnership, 2000 (www.peep.org.uk).

PRILLELTENSKY, I. & NELSON, G. 'Promoting Child and Family Wellness: Priorities for Psychological and Social Interventions', *Journal of Community and Applied Social Psychology*, 2000: 10.

PUGH, G. 'Policies in the UK to Promote the Well-Being of Children', in J. Scott & H. Ward (eds) *Safeguarding and Promoting the Well-Being of Vulnerable Children*. London: Jessica Kingsley, 2005.

RICH, D., CASANOVA, D., DIXON, A., DRUMMOND, M.J., DURRANT, A. & MYER, C. *First Hand Experience: What Matters to Children*. Clopton: Rich Learning Opportunities, 2005.

RINALDI, C. *In Dialogue with Reggio Emilia: Listening, Researching and Learning*. Hove: Routledge, 2006.

ROBERTS, R. *Self-Esteem and Early Learning: Key People from Birth to School*, 3rd edn. London: Paul Chapman Publishing, 2006.

ROBERTS, R. 'The Development of Resilient Wellbeing From Birth To Three', PhD thesis, University of Worcester in association with Coventry University, 2007, http://eprints.worc.ac.uk/511/1/Rosie_Roberts_complete_thesis.pdf

ROGERS, C. *On Becoming a Person*. London: Constable, 1961.

ROGOFF, B. *Apprenticeship in Thinking: Cognitive Development in Social Context*. Oxford: Oxford University Press, 1990.

RUTTER, M. *Maternal Deprivation Re-assessed*. Harmondsworth: Penguin, 1972.

SCHWEINHART, L. & WEIKART, D.A. 'Summary of Significant Benefits: The High/Scope Perry Pre-School Study Through Age 27', in C. Ball (ed.) *Start Right: The Importance of Early Learning*. London: RSA, 1994.

SHONKOFF, J. & PHILLIPS, D. *From Neurons to Neighborhoods: The Science of Early Childhood Development*. Washington, DC: National Academy Press, 2000.

SMITH, T. *National Evaluation of Neighbourhood Nurseries Initiative: Integrated Report SSU/FR/2007/024*. London: DfES, 2007.

SPENCER, N. *Poverty and Child Health*. Oxford: Radcliffe Medical Press, 2000.

STEIN, A., RAMCHANDANI, P. & MURRAY, L. Impact of Parental Psychiatric Disorder and Physical Illness, in M. Rutter et al. (eds) *Rutter's Child and Adolescent Psychiatry*, 5th edn. Oxford: Blackwell Publishing, 2008.

STERN, D. *The Interpersonal World of the Infant.* New York: Basic Books, 1985.

STEWART-BROWN, S. 'Parenting, Well-Being, Health and Disease', in A. Buchanan & B. Hudson (eds) *Promoting Children's Emotional Well-Being.* Oxford: Oxford University Press, 2000.

SUNDERLAND, M. *The Science of Parenting.* London: Dorling Kindersley, 2006.

SURE START www.surestart.gov.uk

SYLVA, K. *The Effective Provision of Pre-School Education (EPPE) Project: Findings from the Pre-School Period.* London: University of London Institute of Education, 2003.

THE YEARLY MEETING OF THE RELIGIOUS SOCIETY OF FRIENDS *Quaker Faith and Practice.* London: Religious Society of Friends (Quakers), 1994.

TREVARTHEN, C. 'Learning in Companionship', *Education in the North: The Journal of Scottish Education,* New Series 2002, 10.

TREVARTHEN, C. 'Stepping Away from the Mirror: Pride and Shame in Adventures of Companionship: Reflections on the Nature and Emotional Needs of Infant Subjectivity', in C.S. Carter, L. Ahnert, K.E. Grossman, S.B. Hardy, M.E. Lamb, S.W. Porges & N. Sachser (eds) *Attachment and Bonding: A New Synthesis,* Vol. 92, Dahlem Workshop Report. Cambridge, MA: The MIT Press, 2005.

TREVARTHEN, C. & AITKEN, K. 'Infant Intersubjectivity: Research, Theory, and Clinical Applications', *Journal of Child Psychology and Psychiatry,* 2001, 42(1).

TUNSTILL, J., ALDGATE, J. & HUGHES, M. *Improving Children's Services Networks: Lessons from Family Centres.* London: Jessica Kingsley, 2007.

UNDERDOWN, A. *Young Children's Health and Wellbeing.* Maidenhead: Open University Press, 2007.

VYGOTSKY, L.S. *Mind in Society: The Development of Higher Psychological Processes.* Cambridge, MA: Harvard University Press, 1978.

WALDFOGEL, J. *What Children Need.* Cambridge, MA: Harvard University Press, 2006.

WALL, K. *Special Needs and Early Years.* London: SAGE, 2006.

WARIN, J. 'Joined-Up Services for Young Children and their Families: Papering Over the Cracks or Re-Constructing the Foundations?', *Children and Society,* 2007, 21(2): 87–97.

WERNER, E. 'Protective Factors and Individual Resilience', in J. Shonkoff & S. Meisels (eds) *Handbook of Early Childhood Intervention.* Cambridge: Cambridge University Press, 2000.

WHEELER, H. & CONNER, J. *Parents, Early Years and Learning: Parents as Partners in the Early Years Foundation Stage – Principles into Practice.* London: National Children's Bureau, 2009.

WINNICOTT, D.W. *The Child, the Family, and the Outside World.* London: Penguin Books, 1964.

Index

Added to the page number, 'f' denotes a figure and 'g' denotes glossary.